In the Land of the Living

MERCER
UNIVERSITY PRESS

Endowed by

Tom Watson Brown

and

The Watson-Brown Foundation, Inc.

In the Land of the Living

Wartime Letters by Confederates from the Chattahoochee Valley of Alabama and Georgia

Edited by Ray Mathis

with the assistance of Douglas Clare Purcell

MERCER UNIVERSITY PRESS | *Macon, Georgia*

MUP/ H901

Published by Mercer University Press
1400 Coleman Avenue
Macon, Georgia 31207

9 8 7 6 5 4 3 2 1

Books published by Mercer University Press are printed on acid-free paper that meets the requirements of the American National Standard for Information Sciences—Permanence of Paper for Printed Library Materials.

Maps courtesy of The Department of History, United States Military Academy at West Point.

ISBN 978-0-88146-524-2
Cataloging-in-Publication Data is available from the Library of Congress

Contents

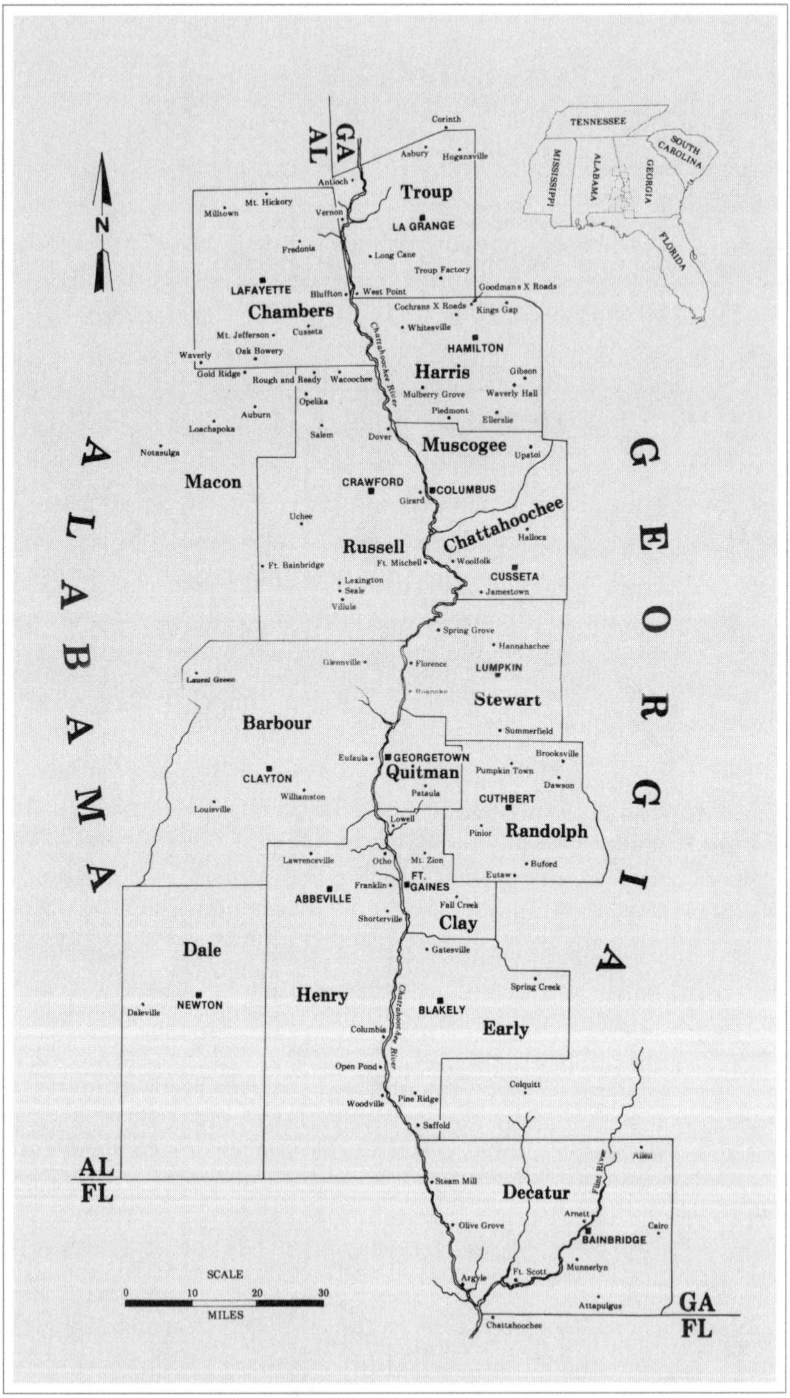

THE LOWER CHATTAHOOCHEE VALLEY IN ALABAMA AND GEORGIA, 1860

Preface to the Second Edition

It is great to see *In the Land of the Living: Wartime Letters by Confederates from the Chattahoochee Valley of Alabama and Georgia* made available in a long-overdue second edition. The book, originally published in a limited edition in 1981 and out of print for many years, is the most comprehensive collection of Civil War letters written by residents of southeastern Alabama and southwestern Georgia in print. Dynamic in nature, poignant in emotion, informative in detail, and broad in scope, the correspondence contained here provides us with a unique opportunity to understand the Civil War and its effect on individuals and families from an intensely personal perspective. The writers, the great majority of them unlettered and expressing themselves in a disarmingly honest manner in their heartfelt missives, collectively paint a compelling portrait of a watershed moment in national history from a regional viewpoint. They make well-known events tangible and lesser-known sidebars illuminating. The book is a solidly researched volume that represents a key piece of the historiographical record of the eighteen-county region served by the Historic Chattahoochee Commission (HCC). It is especially appropriate that it be made available again as our nation contemplates the Civil War and its impact on American history during the sesquicentennial anniversary of its occurrence.

It is a tragedy that its primary author and editor, Dr. Gerald Ray Mathis, passed away before he could see his labor of love in print. He no doubt would have been a major contributor to the growing body of literature on our region's history through many more publications, surely further enriching our understanding of our storied past in many more ways. Thankfully, longtime HCC director Doug Purcell, who played a major role in locating the collections of letters published in the book, continued to work with the HCC for nearly three decades after it first appeared in print. He utilized knowledge gained from this project in numerous others that have helped us better understand this chapter in regional heritage. While a few caches of correspondence similar to that featured in this volume have been discovered in the decades since its printing, the work of Mathis and Purcell still stands as representative of the period.

For this reprint, we have left the great majority of the text as it originally appeared and only made adjustments in page margins to allow the original coffee-table-book-sized volume to be printed in a more standard format. Some slight editing did take place, though all of it designed to facilitate easier reading of the manuscript. This minor editing almost exclusively is associated with the way each letter included in the text is dated. Whereas in the first edition of the book the datelines, or lack thereof, were printed exactly as they appeared if included in the original letter, for this reprint we standardized them so that the location at which the letter was written (if known) appears first, followed by the full month, date, and year (again, if known). We have also standardized the placement of the salutations below the dateline, while keeping all original punctuation and spelling, for easier usage of the material by readers and researchers. The bodies of the letters are unedited.

There are several people I would like to thank for making this second edition of *In the Land of the Living* possible. Historic Chattahoochee Commission graduate-student intern and volunteer Hilary Wehrle helped prepare the bulk of the original text for reformatting by the publisher through a combination of hard work and technological savvy, making both a daunting text-capturing project and intense editing job much easier for all involved. Columbus State University student Heidi Packard prepared portions of chapter 1 and helped get the project rolling. The HCC Publications Committee enthusiastically endorsed the project from its inception and helped guide it through every step in the process to completion. Most of all, I would like to thank Marc Jolley and the entire staff and board of directors of Mercer University Press for recognizing the merit of this important book and facilitating its reprinting. They have been a pleasure to work with on this special project, which we all believe will help preserve stories that interpret a crucial period in regional history.

Mike Bunn
Historic Chattahoochee Commission
February 2014

Preface to the First Edition

With this book, the Historic Chattahoochee Commission adds another volume to its several works preserving local history and resources. For several years, members and friends of the Commission have been collecting and donating letters written by Confederate soldiers to their families who lived in the Chattahoochee Valley. In this book, the valley is defined as the counties of southeastern Alabama and southwestern Georgia, which have a close connection with the river's course, where it serves as a boundary between the two states. The letters were written from numerous camps and fields during the war years, 1861 to 1865.

As one might expect, this Chattahoochee correspondence presents the Confederate soldier in much the same light as he is depicted in Bell Wiley's classic study of the common soldier from the South, *Johnny Reb*. But this edition juxtaposes the writing of commissioned officers alongside those of the private soldier. While the Chattahoochee letters are a small sample, they indicate a correlation between military rank and literary skills. There is, however, a less clear relationship between rank and humane sensibilities. Some of the most compassionate and poignant letters were written by the private soldiers who had the least education or literary ability.

I

To preserve the delightful anarchy of Confederate prose, I have retained the correspondents' phonetic spelling and other eccentricities of style, making minimal use of *sic* (for obvious reasons). I have also limited the book to letters not readily available in published form. Thus, some correspondence that previously appeared in newspapers is republished here, while letters already accessible in book form are not.

Because the dominant theme of the correspondence is Confederate camp life, I have edited the letters to tell that story as it was experienced in specific military theaters. For example, chapter 1 treats Chattahoocheans who were in Pensacola, Florida, and others who were in northern Virginia during 1861. Chapter 2, on Tennessee and Kentucky in 1862, depicts the vicissitudes of

Braxton Bragg's forces during that year. Chattahoocheans in Virginia during 1862 and 1863 and 1864 traces Bragg from Murfreesboro to Dalton and follows James Longstreet from Chickamauga to Knoxville. The fifth chapter, on Georgia in 1864, is the story of the Confederacy's loss of Atlanta. The last part on Virginia and the end recounts the final months of the tragic conflict.

The thematic organization, based on military campaigns, is selective, but it provides continuity and cohesion. This format lends itself to short, introductory paragraphs that precede each letter. These connectors keep the story moving and provide necessary explanation. The focus on camp life serves as a guideline for deletion. A major deletion has been to reduce the repetition of subjects by contributors and at the same time preserve representative statements of universal concerns. A frequent repetition was the correspondent's insistence that he had nothing to write just before he got down to the message at hand. Almost every letter manifests homesickness, anxiety for homefolk, sentimental closings, and endless discussions of clothing. Regardless of length, each deletion is marked with three periods.

II

These correspondents were loyal Confederates. They grumbled, but the complaints were superficial. And they were harsh toward deserters, slackers, and stragglers. A few of these correspondents owned slaves, but they were the exception. Although the non-slaveholder was also acting to protect slavery, these letters manifest no attempts to defend the peculiar institution. In these soldiers' views, they were simply fighting the Yankee aggressor. As one would expect, Chattahoochee Confederates were family men who missed their homefolk and saw separation from loved ones as the major inconvenience of the conflict. While being tough-minded about the fighting, these Confederates could romanticize other experiences, especially home life. Concern for comrades was real. Friends and family tended to stick together in units such as the company and mess, a squad of men who prepared and ate their food together.

Nor was it easy for these correspondents to admit that the Confederacy was losing the war. Apparently civilians had a more objective view of that matter than these soldiers. With death an ever-present companion, religion became more vital as the war wore on and as camp conditions deteriorated to the basic issues of survival. There was heroism. But there was a larger measure of simple determination to do one's duty, no matter what. Once the fighting started in the spring of 1861, the complex issues of former months and years tended to be simplified to the basic choice of defending one's country or shirking. These correspondents sometimes criticized Confederate leaders, but they were loyal to the cause.

Ray Mathis
Troy State University
1980

Acknowledgments

For invaluable help in bringing this project to completion, I am primarily indebted to Douglas Clare Purcell, Florence Foy Strang, and Jean Robinson, all of the Historic Chattahoochee Commission. Douglas Purcell's role in collecting these materials and his research of some correspondents' regiments and companies merit special thanks beyond the credit of the title page. Because those persons who preserved and submitted letters for publication have been prime movers in the endeavor, they are named with their specific contributions in the appendices. Several scholars have been kind enough to give the manuscript a critical reading and make helpful comments, which saved me errors and embarrassment. These readers were Bell I. Wiley, professor emeritus at Emory University; Harriet E. Amos, assistant professor, University of Alabama in Birmingham; and Justin Fuller, professor, University of Montevallo. At Troy State University, the administration and history department have afforded me released time which assisted the project; the research committee provided some funds; the library staff members were always helpful; and the Troy State University Press has seen the book through the publication process. There is no way for me to thank these and others in an adequate manner. But I can absolve them of any shortcomings that I have allowed despite their scrutiny. As always, my wife, Mary, has been an exemplary critic.

R. M.

Gerald Ray Mathis

Gerald Ray Mathis did not live to see this book completed. His death, from a brain tumor, on 25 March 1981, only a week before he would have celebrated his forty-fourth birthday, cut short what promised to be a distinguished career.

Ray was shaped by those things which have been at the heart of virtually every Southerner's existence—the land, the family, the church, and the school. The land was the pine-covered soil of southern Mississippi, the sandy red clay of northeastern Alabama, and the cattle-raising soil of southeastern Alabama. The family was one of farmers turned machinists, turned teachers, turned farmer-scholar-poet. The church was Methodist, which inspired him in his youth and frustrated him in his adulthood. The schools were the public ones open to all and the private ones open to the few who could meet their elitist demands.

Ray will be remembered as a loyal, caring family man by his parents, Paul Monroe and Helen LaVerne Morris Mathis; his sister, Linda Mae Mathis Schaub; his wife, Mary Kathryn Pugh Mathis; and his sons, John Paul and Charles Ray Mathis. He will be remembered by his students as a teacher who demanded much from himself and expected much of them. He will be remembered by his colleagues at Snead Junior College, the University of Georgia, Georgia Southern College, and Troy State University as a thoughtful scholar who researched diligently and wrote carefully. He will be remembered by his readers for his re-presentation of slices of Southern history, first in works about the University of Georgia, *Pilgrimage to Madison*, *College Life in the Reconstruction South*, and *"Uncle Tom" Reed's Memoir of the University*; more recently in a study of an Alabama planter, *John Horry Dent: South Carolina Aristocrat on the Alabama Frontier*; and now in this collection of letters written during the war which shapes all Southerners.

Ray was a contained, complex man of simple tastes and high expectations, a quiet man whose voice has been silenced, but whose written words will live as long as there are people who are interested in the South which made him and which he sought to make live for others.

Ray Mathis was my friend and I cherish the memory of his friendship.

Joseph Mitchell
Troy State University
Troy, Alabama
23 September 1981

1

Florida and Virginia: 1861

Abraham Lincoln was elected President of the United States in November 1860. He won the office under the Republican platform of stopping the extension of slavery into the national territories. Viewing this political pledge as a direct threat to the institution of slavery, several Southern states prepared to leave the Union. South Carolina was a leader of this movement. When she formally quit the nation in December 1860, six other states from the lower South soon followed suit. The remaining four states of the Confederacy, being in the upper South, seceded after the Confederacy's April bombardment of the Federals who held Fort Sumter at the mouth of Charleston harbor.

The motives for secession were both complex and simple. Historical differences between the sections had been constitutional, economic, cultural, social, political, and so on. But all arguments had a way of gravitating to the Federal government's role with respect to slavery in the territories. With the Lincoln government committed to exclude slavery from the territories, many Southerners hoped to protect the institution by separating their section from union with the North. As events transpired, however, the northern part of the Union was willing to fight a war to prevent Southern secession. Then, in September 1862, the goal of the Federal forces was broadened from preserving the Union to include emancipation of those slaves then living within parts of the Confederate States of America still in rebellion. Actually, the average Confederate soldier was not a slaveholder. Nor does this collection of letters mention the protection of slavery as a cause of secession and war. Instead, most Southerners preferred to say they fought for independence and constitutional liberty against the tyrannical Yankee. And to a degree, this was the case. But the social values of the nonslaveholder were basically the same as the master class, which included maintaining the peculiar institution.

Alabama and Georgia were among the early states to secede—Alabama on 11 January 1861, and Georgia eight days later. Soon after secession, thousands of Southern volunteers rushed forward to the military defense of their section against potential Northern threat. Expecting a brief war because they believed the Yankees would not fight them, most Confederates volunteered for short, twelve-month terms and expected to be back home in a matter of weeks. The Northern view of the Southern soldier was not much different. It was a pathetic miscalculation on both sides. But this was neither the first nor the last time Americans (North and South) would make such a mistake.

Actually, this four-year conflict dragged on to be the bloodiest war in United States history. Each side would prove proficient in the devastating art of killing Americans. It did not require much actual combat to sober the early idealization of this war. Thus, in this early phase, Pensacola, Florida, and Centreville, Virginia, became defensive posts of Confederate vigilance. Here, and at other points, the watch was kept by young Southerners who did not yet suspect the full measures that the Yankee foe was willing to take in order to surround and batter the Confederate States of America out of existence. According to Southern secessionists who had studied the American war of independence against Great Britain, the South would once again follow a defensive strategy and hope to be let alone for a peaceful existence. But under President Lincoln, the North launched a tenacious offensive in order to blockade, invade, and strangle the Confederacy to death. This Union strategy was in basic accord with the aging General Winfield Scott's early assessment of the steps that would be necessary for reestablishing the broken nation.

Like most of the South, the Chattahoochee Valley of Alabama and Georgia would send its sons into every major front, where they participated in most of the 5,000 battles of this four-year conflict. "The Song of the Chattahoochee" was poet Sidney Lanier's celebration of this beautiful stream that rises in northern Georgia, passes near bustling Atlanta, and flows southward to mark a long boundary between Alabama and Georgia before joining the Flint River at Bainbridge and moving into Florida, where the waters assume the new name of Apalachicola, also the name of the city at the river's juncture with the Gulf of Mexico. The Chattahoochee, once at the center of lands held by the mighty Creek Indian Nation, is still central to the history of southwestern Georgia and southeastern Alabama. This book provides a cross-sectional view of the concerns of several Chattahoocheans who fought for the Confederacy from 1861 to 1865.

One volunteer from this valley was Stouten Hubert Dent of Eufaula. As a young lawyer and former schoolteacher, Lieutenant Dent's letters were more articulate than the average soldier of this war was capable of producing. Dent, at first an adjutant in the Eufaula Rifles of the First Alabama Infantry Regiment, was among those Confederates assigned to the Pensacola front with the responsibility of observing and containing the Federal force, which was in Fort Pickens on Santa Rosa Island. The

Fort Pickens garrison was the Gulf Coast equivalent of those Union soldiers who for a time held Fort Sumter near Charleston, South Carolina.

In February 1861, no one knew where armed conflict would begin or whether it would last long enough for all patriotic volunteers to experience the heady glory of combat experience. From our perspective (and even the perspective of 1865), most Confederate letters of 1861 seem unreal, the superficial musings of play actors who would never have to face the hot, deadly lead of modern weapons and warfare.

S. H. Dent was only one of thousands who communicated the holiday mood during the opening days of the Confederates' jubilant military experience. His first extant letter after secession was written from Montgomery, Alabama, to his young bride. Anna Beall Young Dent was the daughter of wealthy Eufaula entrepreneur Edward B. Young. She was a fortunate match for one recently arrived in Eufaula. Although descended from an important Maryland family, Hubert Dent was without much financial means until after the sectional conflict. Despite the fact that war interrupted this young man's pecuniary ambitions, he believed that enlistment was necessary for his personal honor and self-respect. And as we shall see, he learned to enjoy the strenuous test of combat.

When Dent wrote from Montgomery, the constitutional convention of the Confederate States of America had been meeting in that city since 4 February 1861 to devise a Constitution and select government officials. The newly elected president, Jefferson Davis, arrived in Montgomery—the first capital of the Confederacy—on 16 February. Adjutant Dent was enthusiastic about the inaugural ceremonies scheduled for the 18th. On the other hand, the youthful lieutenant was anxious to get on to Pensacola lest the Eufaula Rifles and the First Alabama Regiment be unprepared to participate in what he though would have to be a short war. There was no way for him to foresee the monotony of the military "sideshow" that awaited him at Fort Barrancas near Pensacola. Nor could he anticipate the complex chain of events that would keep him in the field of battle until May 1865. For the moment, in February 1861, the twenty-eight-year-old adjutant could perceive only the glory, as he wrote his wife, Anna Beall, whom he affectionately called Nannie.

Camp of the Eufaula Rifles
Near Montgomery
Feb. 14, 1861
My own Sweet Darling,

Here am I in Camp at the fair grounds—all the Commissioned Officers except myself have left and about three fourths of men. I mean they have gone over to Montgomery. The rest of us are here...I preferred remaining here today and sleeping all night so that Tomorrow I will be fresh and walk over to Montgomery and remain all day. Judge [John Gill] Shorter and John T Morgan have visited us—and all the men who came over with us from Eufaula excepting [Captain John W.] Chambers. I forgot to say that we reached here about 12 o'clock. It is now nearly 8. I am writing on the tray of my trunk—up in a Circus wagon—and my bed is up here too...I wrote you from Columbus. It is said that we are to leave here for Pensacola Saturday morning. But the Capt [Alpheus Baker] and privates [James L.] Pugh & [John] Cochran are working with the Gov [A. B. Moore] to keep us here until the inauguration of Jeff Davis. I would like to see the inauguration very much—but I am not satisfied that it would be best for us to remain. It is impossible to have strict discipline while here and drills and the men need both very much. While therefore as a man I would like to remain—as a Soldier I don't wish to remain so long.

I am impatient to get to Pensacola and get settled at least for the time that I have to stay there...The Common opinion here is that we will not have a general war—as to whether we will have any collision at all or not men of information are divided. Judge Shorter thinks we will be releaved in Six Weeks. I would be content with that. Nannie my Darling this is no idle sport that your old Dear has gone into and he knows it. But he has made his mind to bear it all like a soldier without a murmur...But thank God and the Company I [as adjutant] am lifted above the most exposed and arduous duties and I intend to take care of myself. I have stood every thing thus far first rate—never felt better in health...I expect to leave here to-morrow for Pensacola...I think we will be back in two months—our Company excites much Comment and has quite a reputation. The Gov will not consent for us to be the guard of honor to Jeff Davis…

PS. We remain until Tuesday morning—are appointed the Escort of Jeff Davis…

Not everyone was as pleased by events as S. H. Dent. For example, one of his friends had been "in tears" and "could not keep them back" he was so outraged at the "Gov callin us out." Such lack of patriotism was embarrassing, especially to Dent, who advised his wife not to mention the incident. Soon, however, with the inauguration completed, the Eufaula Rifles and First Alabama Regiment departed the Confederate capital as planned, proceeding to the Gulf Coast city of Pensacola in order to confront the Federal troops who refused to surrender Fort Pickens. Later that same month, while stationed in the navy yard at Fort Barrancas (across the bay from Fort Pickens), Lieutenant Dent described his surroundings as a type of tropical paradise.

Barrancas Barracks Florida
Feb. 23, 1861

...I went this morning through the Navy Yard. It is a most delightful place. The officers quarters are very fine—some of the choicest and rarest flowers...I was charmed with the yard and residence of Com[mander] Randolph. I have now before me one of the sweetest scented flowers I ever smelled...So far my experience here is more like visiting a watering place than being on a Military Campaign and if matters go on this way I can't be very much dissatisfied...The tales about mud and bad roads and bad treatment is all stuff. Some men you know are certain to grumble—and I believe would grumble if by some accident they were placed in Paradise...

If Dent was content not to fight, at least momentarily, others were less satisfied with the noncombative situation. With General Braxton Bragg in command of Confederate coastal defense (he arrived at Pensacola on 10 March), the Davis government decided that Fort Pickens was not worth a major contest. Thus Pickens would remain in Union hands, leaving armed conflict to begin officially in South Carolina on 12 April with the Confederate bombardment of Fort Sumter. In this way, Barrancas became an uncertain scene of wait and see. By May, R. A. Wellborn, of Barbour County, Alabama, a private in R. F. Kolb's Light Artillery, was tired of the no-fight policy at Pensacola. It is to Wellborn's credit that he acknowledged a lack of literary grace. McRee was the name of a nearby Confederate fort and a Confederate ship.

Beran cas barrix
May 12, 1861
friends and fellow cts,

I now seate my self to give you a few lines as I Promist to in form you of War matters att this Point I would of writen Sooner but my time Was short the Tinese gwards Was firs here & We have bn emploid all most day & night hard

Work. We have bout 250 guns mounted on Pikens bout 165 Will do exclution and Pikens the Rest are chanel guns 6 days a go in...com 2 boats from Mobile the Keys & lowis. the Brooklin & Saline fired 5 Shots att them one ball went under the bow of the Keys. then Brooklin Run under McRnee...Could of Sunk the Brooklin just as easy as he wanted to We are ankous for the fight to com off. ther is a bout 2 thousand men [Federals] fixing up Pikens evry day it Will bee a hard fight. We ExPect govenor moor [A. B. Moore] here to day. they is bout ten thousand men here of us Ex Cuse my bad hand and bad Spelling...

No sooner had General Bragg arrived at Pensacola than he began the arduous task of shaping raw volunteers into an effective army. For the moment, S. H. Dent was agitated by the monotony and tightening discipline. The latter might deprive him of a furlough home in July when his wife was expecting their first child. At the Confederate government's request, Bragg had recently sent his three best regiments of 2,800 men to the Virginia front. Such drain of manpower must have seemed another reason not to attack Fort Pickens.

Barrancas Florida
June 5, 1861
My own Darling Wife,

...We have moved back to our old quarters where we first were and I am in a tent under the china trees in the yard. [J. M.] Macon is with me. You ought to have seen us to-day fixing up. I hope we will soon be comfortably arranged. We cannot of course be as well fixed up as we were in our house...Dearest I hope I will be able to get a leave of absence in July but I am by no means certain. A great many have applied since the troops left here for Virginia—under the impression that there would be no fighting and that Gen Bragg would be more disposed to grant them. I have been quite attentive to my business since I have been here and they are generally more disposed to favor those that do, and I hope I shall succeed. Col [George H.?] Forney has left us. From what I can learn of Gen [William H. T.] Walker I do not think I shall like him much. He has not yet taken command of the Brigade but will do so I hope to-morrow. I am tired of doing extra work for nothing. I have drawn my pay up to the first of June and am waiting to see about getting a horse—and if I can make the arrangement I expect to make I shall send you some [money]. I want you to try your business qualities...

Soon, however, Dent's infatuation with war revived enough to inspire a romantic (even Byronesque) evaluation of General W. H. T. Walker. Colonel Henry D. Clayton, of Barbour County, Alabama, had been instrumental in organizing the First Alabama Infantry. Dent could even romanticize tent life. His wife had visited him in camp.

Barrancas Florida
June 7, 1861
My own Sweet Darling,

...I am sitting down in my office writing this morning. Macon is making out my morning report. I have been laughing at his mistakes, he takes it all in good part however and works away. When he gets so he understands the business I shall have very little to do and will have a good easy time unless Gen Walker takes some new notion in his head and moves us again or something of that sort. If I have not written before Gen Walker is from Georgia Augusta or near there he was in the old U S Service a Colonel—is full of fight, considered rather rash—has been in several [battles]—manages to stop all the balls that pass near him, has five or six in his body now, but manages to escape some way—he swears like a trooper, is as bad as the army in Flanders, and is rather Communicative, not particular as to the crowd he gets into, but talks away generally interlarding [Treadwell] with many strange oaths. Consequently [he] does not preserve his dignity—or rather the dignity—of his position. Take him all in all I should select him as a suitable man for leading a forlorn hope but not the man to manage and control a great movement or a large body of men. Gen Bragg however is in command as heretofore, and Walker only fills the position that Clayton has occupied...I get a horse after all from Hatch. I received a telegram from him to-day telling me to go to Pensacola to-morrow...I like living in a tent pretty well. I have my office in the house and keep my clothes in there. I only do my sleeping in my tent—and it is glorious. I expect by the time I get home that I will feel like I was smothering in a house. The weather is quite warm here and the dust is intolerable. We have a drill every morning about 5 1/2 or 6 o'clock and even then the dust and heat are very severe. From every thing I can learn there is no prospect of a fight here unless we are attacked, and I do not think that at all likely. It is said that there is a good deal of sickness [among the

Federals] on Santa Rosa and in the fleet. They do not work as hard over at Pickens as they did when you were here...

Increasingly now Dent warmed to the subject of camp life. Perhaps it was less static. General Walker was making changes. Alpheus Baker of Barbour County, Alabama, was captain of the Eufaula Rifles, which included many of Dent's friends. The baby's birth was imminent, camp food was good, but religious services were not yet attractive to unscarred Confederate soldiers.

Barrancas Florida
June 16, 1861
My Sweet Darling,

...Things are going on here quietly. Not quite so many details for fatigue duty as when you were here. Genl Walker has made several changes in the Brigade. He is going to concentrate the 1st Regt west of Ft. Barrancas. I think Baker's company will remain where they are. The 7th Regt will be concentrated North of the Barracks proper. Two of the Independent Miss Companies have been ordered off on Monday and they do not know where they are going. I think from what I can learn that they are going over towards the East pass to build batteries. Three other companies are going with them not from this Brigade. The man that came over from Pickens is still in custody. He is a little more communicative than at first. He is a very determined looking man. I place no reliance in what he says in fact he does not say a great deal. He said there are nine Companies in the Fort some not full [a] good many sick—says they have four Batteris and a great many eight and ten inch Columbiads. Any one can take it for what it is worth. You will recollect the restrictions about what is written from here. Well Darling I hope I shall see you in a month or less time—from what you write I shall apply for leave of absence about the 8th of July. I do hope I shall get it. I do not know what I shall do if I do not. Pretty near go crazy I reckon...We are getting vegetables from Mobile and Montgomery tolerably regularly now and get them fresher than from home—but I do love so much to get such things from home...[The Reverend] Mr McNair is getting along here very well—he does not have large congregations and occasionally has none at all. I hope it will be better when the Regt is concentrated...

As June dragged on toward July, Lieutenant Dent wanted to go home, but he also wanted to be present for the battle he felt would surely happen soon. This internal tension was not easily resolved. Unlike some soldiers, he felt little need to send money home on a regular basis.

Barrancas Florida
June 20, 1861
My Sugar Plum,
...We have been moving all day and are not through yet. We will be a fine mark for Pickens when the fight commences. We are near the Perote Battery, between the Fort and it. I shall be altogether in a tent. I do not think I shall like it very well but will hope to be content. I wrote you Pet about the vegetables...We had to-day beets, potatoes, cabbage, tomattoes & onions and occasionally we have green corn...Darling affairs here now are very different from what they were when you were here. Then a fight was considered imminent, now it is looked upon as quite remote. I have no idea there will be any fight here until after the 4th July next. The trouble with me is that just about the time I wish to go home—these Congresses will be meeting and there is no telling what may happen. It would be most unfortunate if just at the time that I am at home—I should miss the fight. But Dearest I would miss three fights—to see you if I could not see you without. While I might consider it unfortunate but Dearest I should not regret it...I sent you one hundred dollars by John McRae—at least I gave him sixty dollars in gold and a hundred dollar bill and told him to give you the gold and Forty Dollars and bring me back the remainder. I may not be paid off the 1st of July and I don't want to be troubled...

Soon the merciless heat, an enemy worse than Yankees, was taking its toll. Confederates also respected the guns of the Federals under Colonel Harvey Brown at Fort Pickens. And despite Bragg's strict regimen, raw recruits could still raise a ruckus. Nor had Lieutenant Dent forgotten the forthcoming birth.

Camp 'Alabama'
June 23, 1861
My Darling Nannie,
...Dearest you have no idea of how warm how very warm it is here now. I am same sitting with coat off—no vest or collar on, and I am unpleasantly warm.

From early in the morning until ten o'clock is the warmest part of the day—after that time we generally have some breeze. But last night it was very warm—very little if any breeze. I went to the beach and bathed—it cooled me off some and I went to sleep. But this morning it is equally warm and sultry. In regard to going home Darling I hope I will be able to get off. There are more absentees from the 1st Regt now than has been since it came here. I hope most of them will return before I apply. I know if I were to apply now that it would prejudice my application very much, so many being absent...You ought Darling to see our camp. Tents from one hundred and fifty to Two hundred all covered over with brush arbors and various devices to keep out the sun. The men about in groups or engaged in cleaning up their grounds or arranging their tents. Take it all together it is quite a picturesque scene. We are a fine mark for Pickens if it should take a notion to throw some shells amongst us. They have been changing their sand bags since we came here, and I expect they are preparing to move their guns so as to bear upon us. What a scattering there would be if 'Brown' should turn loose on us—half a dozen shells would do the thing completely. Well Darling it is nearly 10 o'clock and I must close and go and hear Bro McNair preach...Well I have found out that there will be no preaching, and therefore I will go ahead and finish my letter...Jim McNab took it into his head last night that he was Field officer of the Day—and after visiting some of the guard himself—sent Tom Brannon to represent him. The result was both were arrested this morning. Brannon in consideration of his ignorance and inexperience has been discharged. McNab is still under arrest. He is nearly dead from drinking. Clark was detailed and being absent McNab without any order undertook and really thought he had to supply his place. Joe Butt and the entire crew have been ordered off...Their places being supplied by Lieut Raney and twelve Marines. Joe hated to go back to his company...

S. H. Dent reported several deaths from the sun and heat at Barrancas. But General Bragg was adamant in his determination to "drill" raw volunteers into soldiers. While achieving this, the wait for battle made everyone edgy. Overreaction to harmless artillery fire from Fort Pickens was to be expected. Thus, events at Pensacola were much less exciting than preparations around Manassas Junction, Virginia, where General Joseph E. Johnston and his Confederates would on 21 July defeat the attacking Union forces of General Irvin McDowell.

Barrancas Florida
June 26, 1861
My Precious Darling,

...This hot sun is telling on our men. There have been five deaths in the Regiment and the first occurred not more than two weeks ago. I am very particular with myself I tell you and go about in the sun as little as possible. We had something like an alarm this morning about 10 or 11 o'clock. Gen Walker has issued an order requiring all Companies to repair to their Batteries immediately upon the firing of any guns at Pickens. This morning a salute was fired and you never saw such running. There has been a salute fired there three days in succession—but the other two were fired on the ships and the order did not apply. Bragg has an idea that the fight is going to come off. It makes very little impression on me because I have heard it so often. So Darling you need not be disappointed if I do not get home between this and the 1st of July or a little later...

By the time of Dent's next letter, his son, Eddie, had been born, and the father had gone home in July to see his wife and baby. Now back in camp, the lieutenant gossiped about daily life and residents of the Chattahoochee Valley. He also was more skeptical about local battle prospects and the supposed glamour of war. Dent had studied law with Edward Courtney Bullock and James L. Pugh. Pugh went to the Confederate Congress and, after the war, to the United States Senate. Both men, along with John Cochran, had been prominent in the Eufaula Regency, a states' rights political organization.

Barrancas Florida
Aug. 14, 1861
My Precious Darling,

...First of all I must tell you about Macon's promotion. He has been appointed a Lieutenant in Capt [James D.] Meadows Company from Tallapoosa. I think he will be a 1st Lieut though that is not settled. I got him the appointment myself. I thought he deserved it and would appreciate such an act from a friend and [w]ent to work for him and got him the position. I could have done if for any other friend as well. I was sorry to lose him as Sergeant Major, but waived all selfish considerations and went to work for him. He dislikes the idea of leaving me himself and I think we will still mess together...About Joe Butt I am surprised that he should permit his own paper to publish such a falsehood as that he was A A A Genl in place of Wood. It is all a no such thing. As Cochran would express it he is in the meat business. He has been detailed on special duty in the Commissary's department and instead of being A A A Genl he is engaged in weighing out pork, flour, and beans &c &c for the different Regiments. I wonder if he will not correct it. Bullock is in Bragg's staff and is Judge Advocate of the army—Braggs legal Military advisor is reference to questions which are constantly arising. It is a good position plenty of work...Things are looking a little like a fight. Companies at Battery are ordered to resume their cannon and Mortar drilling and to fix up their Batteries Magazines &c. &c. Col [S.A.M.] Wood said there were good reasons for all this. That was as difinite as he would express it. We have been deceived so often that I have almost ceased to put any confidence in any thing of that sort...I am very much in hopes the sickness in our regiment will soon get better. A great many men have gone home on sick furlough. Clayton...went yesterday...Some effort is being made here to make Pugh a Brigadier General I do not know how it will succeed...I am in my tent and the fleas are troublesome...

General Bragg continued sending troops to other fronts. Perhaps he realized that one of his real strengths was turning green recruits into disciplined troops. There was also the futile hope that Confederates in Virginia might follow up their victory at first Manassas by capturing the Union capital of Washington, D.C. Meanwhile, in Florida, the Federals had begun small raids from Fort Pickens, which culminated in a shaky retaliatory act by Bragg's force on 9 October. S. H. Dent was too proud to request another furlough at this time.

Barrancas Florida
Sept. 9, 1861
My Dear Darling,

...I wrote you of the burning of the dry dock on the 3rd...The telegraph I suppose carried the news you heard. Things are moving on here pretty much as usual. Gen [Daniel] Ruggles has assumed command in ordinance to an order—from Genl Bragg. I suppose [Gen. Richard H.] Anderson has done the same though as we have nothing to do with him I have not seen the order. I learn that an artillery Company, the Continentals, stationed at Pensacola also a Louisiana Company [&] Capt St. Paul have been ordered to Virginia. I do not know how

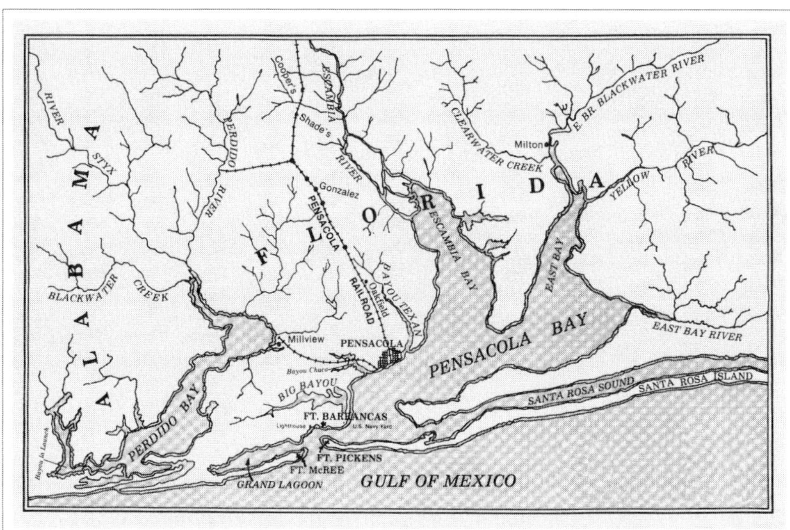

PENSACOLA BAY AND SURROUNDING AREA, 1861

true it may be, but think it likely it is so. Nine of our Marines have deserted last night and went to Pickens at least it is generally believed they went there. It is supposed they went under the idea that they would be better paid over there. We have had some flying telegraph rumors [from Virginia] about an attack on and the capture of arlington heights. It turns out to be untrue although it is stated that our forces are advancing and have driven the enemy from Shooter's hill in the vicinity of Alexandria. I look for some stirring news from there soon...Sickness is no better in camp—out of forty officers in the Regiment only about Eighteen are fit for duty of all sorts—some can attend to some little matters but are unable to go on Guard particularly when the weather is bad...Any such man can get a furlough. Well ones have more trouble and in many cases are refused. In the present condition of the Regiment I do not think it would be right for me to ask a leave of absence—and if I were to ask it I have no idea I could get it and I do not wish to be mortified by a refusal...

The long-awaited "fight" finally occurred on 9 October. It was a limited skirmish on Santa Rosa Island near Fort Pickens. Making no effort to take the fort, General Bragg intended that the exercise be a retaliatory one, which gave some green Confederates a taste of combat. Though not a grand encounter, S. H. Dent missed the skirmish and subsequently resigned as adjutant in hopes of a more active in field command. He explained all this to his beloved Nannie, as well as the disadvantages of her visiting him when Bragg's limitations on mobility were so strict. Dent's initial enlistment would expire in February 1862.

Barrancas Fla
Oct. 18, 1861
My Dearest Nannie,

...I wrote you particularly about the fight and what Companies were in it. If John McRae was in it—he went with some other Company not the Rifles. As I wrote you in my last I have resigned my position as Adjutant and as soon as I can move will rejoin my Company...I have been Adjutant long enough to learn everything that can be learned in the office, and I want to drill and have a Company Command. Baker will not be well enough to take charge in some time and I will be in Command and if there is any warm work to be done will try and have a hand in it. There is not the slightest chance for our Regiment to be moved from here and the position of Adjutant here [will] not [be] as good if a fight [bombardment] takes place as to have Command of a battery. The next thing is I was prejudiced somewhat in the Company by taking the [adjutant] position and I want [to] try and reinstate myself [so] that I may keep some position if I want to go next year—and besides I want to be familiar with a Command so that if I got one I would not be awkward about it. These are selfish reasons all, but then these are selfish times. I sold my horse to Capt [George W.] Dawson [of Pike County, Alabama] I have just been talking with him and bragging on my boy...There is no Communication between Pensacola and the navy yard [Barrancas] now except to bring over freight. No passengers are allowed. To get to Pensacola, Every one must go by land and As there are a few horses here walking or staying in camp is the order of the day. To stay away from Camp at night Genl Bragg's permission must be obtained which it is not very easy to do. So you see Darling that your visit to Pensacola would not be pleasant to either of us. Besides no one can leave Pensacola without obtaining a permit from the officer in command over there—and the rail road agent has to furnish the Army with the names of those who come down on the train. These precautions are taken because of the flight of some persons from Florida to Santa Rosa [Island] some time since. I expect you saw an account of it. At least I suppose that is the reason and it is only a suggestion...My Love I think you may as [well] give up all idea of [seeing] me until next February...

General Bragg's strict discipline included the harsh measure of execution. Lieutenant Dent disliked having to witness such events, but otherwise thrived on camp life and the exciting news of the times. Although Confederate ports were under blockade by the Union Navy, Mobile Bay was free of Federal warships until August 1864.

Barrancas Florida
Nov. 17, 1861
My Own Sweet Darling,

...To-day or rather this morning we heard heavy firing about Mobile which lasted for several hours and everyone I saw thought Lincoln's fleet was there making an attack on the place—about two O'clock the large Steamer that was here the Colorado got under way and went off in the direction of Mobile and that made us think stronger than ever that the fight was going on. Well this evening I learn that Genl Bragg had received a dispatch saying that the firing was only one of the blockade vessels firing at a target. Excitement died out suddenly at that news and no more conjectures were heard. Two men are to be shot tomorrow one from the 10th Mississippi Regiment for killing his 1st Sergeant and the other from the Louisiana Infantry for striking his Captain and other acts of very great subordination. Our Regiment is ordered to be under arms at 9 1/2 O'clock and I am very much afraid we will be marched off to witness the execution. I do not wish to see it. Men grow callous enough at best in the army and I do not wish to witness any more of such sights than are absolutely necessary: There is a very great difference between shooting down men [enemies] [at least to one's feelings] when the blood is warm and we are excited to the highest pitch & witnessing the shooting of one of our men. Reub Kolb has furlough for twenty days and will leave tomorrow. Billy Cargile goes with him as he is too weak to travel alone. His Dr thinks he has symptoms of typhoid fever—our Company escaped pretty well through the summer but we are suffering now. My own health is as robust as usual, and everybody says I am fattening up. What do you think of that. I however do not see any difference in myself. The weather is very pleasant now...Oh! The tale I had heard about enlisting the four Companies for the war and discharging the others was all humbug. Genl Bragg had never given any such intimation. Well I hear the drum and must go to roll call. Well roll call is over and the day's duties are done. There is much speculation as to what the steamer that was here went toward Mobile for. Some think that the fleet is about rendezvousing there to attack the place. You will however have learned if such is the case before this letter reaches you...

Beginning on 22 November, Fort Pickens's batteries and two Union war ships shelled Confederate positions at Fort McRee and Barrancas for two days. Receiving 5,000 rounds to their 1,000 rounds fired, the Confederates sustained the more damage and casualties (forty Confederates, fifteen Federals) than their enemies. Barrancas stood the attack in good form, even as Dent reported it. Amid enthusiasm for that excitement, he finally admitted what he had been hinting, that he would probably reenlist when his year's term of service expired.

Barrancas Florida

Nov. 23, 1861

My Dear Darling,

...Capt Baker Judge Cochran Mr. Wellborn and Jim McNab reached here about day light this morning. Baker has not yet taken command he is leaving every thing to me. I wrote you last night that the enemy were firing at the Navy Yard. Well they kept it up until about 4 O'clock this morning so the sentinals informed me. They then ceased and have not fired a gun to-day. I presume they will open in the morning. The last shot fired from our side was about 12 last night and we have not fired a gun since. There was no fight at deer point as I wrote. Genl Bragg visited our battery this morning and told me there was no fight there. None of our men were killed in the Navy Yard. Not much damage done in there so far. A few mules were killed. We lost six men at McRee. Five of them were smothered by the bursting in of a rat hole. They were in there to protect themselves from the shot. A shell struck it and it caved in. One man was Killed by the cannon there. He is the only man killed in that way—seven are wounded. Genl Bragg is in the finest humor imaginable and compliments the 1st Regt highly. They occupy the post of danger and of honor and Bragg says they have sustained themselves well. I do not feel the slightest apprehension about danger personally and I believe we have the best of the fight. I have seen several holes in the walls of Pickens and I believe we can batter them down...Well Darling we have waited and worked a long time for this fight and it has come at last. The first day the enemy fired very rapidly. The rest not so fast. We have been shooting very slowly all the time. I think the enemy must be satisfied that it is no easy matter to silence our batteries. We drove the ships from [Fort] McRee yesterday and our men say one of them is badly damaged. There are now five here in all, I think two of them however are only transports. We confidently look for the fight to commence early in the morning. [Colonel Harvey] Brown has been busy all day piling up sand bags that we have knocked down—and I suppose repairing damages generally I am glad the fight has opened. I did not want to go home and say that I had not fired a gun at the enemy. I think now that I will have plenty to talk of when I go home—and that is the best part of it I expect to go home. Every one tells me I am looking so well. I feel in fine health and it would be a great shame for one of Brown's shells to knock up such a healthy hardy man. I attribute a great deal to my temperance not only in drinking but in eating. I have seen a circular from Genl Bragg [which would have been made public but for the fight] appealing in the strongest manner to the 1st Regt to reenlist. I have not determined exactly what I shall do. I have been spoken to by a prominent man in the Regt who expects to reenlist who desired me for Major of the Regt. I would like such a position very much—would prefer it to a Captaincy or a higher position. In fact if I could get that position in a good regiment for the war I would be perfectly satisfied. But I must have some time to go and stay at home. I can't go in right away without some privilege of that sort...

Despite Dent's hopes, the Confederates did not take Fort Pickens; they simply repaired Forts Barrancas and McRee. All disclaimers to the contrary, army life suited him quite well. He loved it, patriotically and otherwise, and had no intention of settling down in Eufaula until the war was over. John W. Clarke and J. W. Mabry were captains in the First Alabama; they were from Barbour County. Hubert's father, Dr. S. W. Dent, was an outspoken Confederate sympathizer in Federal-held Maryland.

Barrancas Florida
Dec. 7, 1861
My Dear Nannie,

...Every thing is quiet and excepting the destruction of property it looks here very little like a fight had taken place. Genl Bragg is building new batteries about McRee and otherwise preparing for a renewal of the fight. He sent over a flag of truce a few days after the fight but it was not received—and there is some suspicion that old Brown was killed. It is all however mere suspicion. I wish I could see in the future for a few months. I am troubled a good deal about what I may be able to do another year. As a matter of calculation if I can get any position I had better reenlist and I shall try. It would be much more pleasant for me to be at home, but what could I do there. I am afraid nothing at all, and I can't bear the idea of being a hanger on doing nothing. My poverty presses on me heavily at times, not for myself Darling, but because I am able to do so little for you and the boy. I hope some day to be able to do better, but it looks very little like it now. The condition of my family in Md also troubles me. I know I can do them no good but still I can't [help] feeling badly...This war has made a great change in my calculations and expectations. If peace had continued I was in hopes that I would be able to get an humble home and settle down quietly to my [law] profession. But when that can be done no one can tell. Soldiering does not suit my tastes or inclinations. But unfortunately for me at present it is that or nothing. If I could have you with me even it would be much better. And I think if I succeed in getting any position here that I will arrange that you can be with me. That is my wish and my intention...I suppose you have seen Genl Bragg's circular to the army. I am afraid he will not succeed very well in securing recruits. There seems to be great difficulty in getting men to reenlist. The freshness and first excitement of the war has worn off and men, many of them at least, are tired of the service. It is I think an alarming symptom. Many troops will be entitled to their discharges in the next six months and it will not be easy to supply their places...Clark & Mabry will go home 17 Jan. We will be discharged a day sooner. I see Soph is going in for 12 mos. I never expect to go in that way again. I do not want to be turned loose in the middle of the war in this way again...[J. D.?] Smith is very anxious to go home, but has great doubt being able to get a 'leave,' Baker protests that he does not wish to go, but that is all in my eyes. Bullock is quite sick, and quite alarmed. He fears for his lungs. The Company generally is quite healthy...

Premature rumors of Yankee destruction in the Deep South moved Lieutenant Dent to advocate the dark principle of invading the Union and wreaking vengeance in kind against the aggressor. Amid the Confederacy's great need for seasoned troops, he could see no recourse but reenlistment. Alpheus Baker had been elected colonel of a regiment stationed at Fort Pillow on the Mississippi River above Memphis.

Barrancas Florida
Dec.13, 1861
My Dear Nannie,

...Baker left yesterday on a Twenty-days leave of absence to go to Memphis to see after his regiment. If it is accepted he resigns the Captaincy [here] and takes it, otherwise he returns. He went direct to Eufaula and you will hear all about it before this reaches you. He was escorted out of the lines by three companies the Pioneers Clayton Guards and Rifles. I do not expect he will return. Somehow I feel very much oppressed and dont feel like myself. I am very anxious for my time to be out here. I want to get home. I hear to-day [erroneously] that Charleston has been burned and that Montgomery and Selma have both been set on fire—oh the horrors of this war. It is enough to make the blood run cold to think of any civilized and Christian people conducting a war on such principles. I believe I am in favor of raising the black flag and neither giving or taking quarter. I hope the government will see the necessity of invading the north and making them feel some of the evil effects that they have visited on us. Well enough of that. I can't do justice to the subject. Henry Shorter has resigned his position to take effect the 22nd Dec. He wants to be at home during Christmas and retire from the service. There will be a great many changes during the next two months. I believe Watts' regiment will take the place of the 1st Ala. Burnett's company will take our battery. They send over a squad of men every morning to drill on our mortars so as to be efficient when the 9th Feb comes...Baker has offered me the position of Adjutant in his regiment with the rank & pay of Captain. If he gets it for me I am going there. I would sooner do that than run the chances of doing nothing or getting no position—at the end of that time something may turn up. I will see a part of the country that is new to me and would be more apt to see active service. I expect about the time my service is out here that the thing will be fixed up. If that fails why I will try something else. I am in the war and expect to remain in it. I see congress has offered bounty &c to men who reenlist. I think it was a very judicious move. Thousands of 12 mos men will be discharged in the next six months and it would be very hard to supply their places and the truth is something of the kind ought to have been done...

Dent reenlisted, this time in the artillery, and now he wanted his wife's approval of the act. He overestimated the negative effect of the Trent *affair on the Union's war effort: Great Britain was protesting the Federal's questionable removal of two Confederate diplomats, James Mason and John Slidell, from the British steamer. The issue would be resolved peacefully. Dent also regretted that his former law mentor, E. C. Bullock, was dying.*

Barrancas Florida
Dec. 19, 1861
My Dear Darling

...I have just returned from seeing some men in reference to enlisting for "the war" [the duration]. What do you think Darling of my going in. Well I am in. The temptation of going in with [Captain Felix H.] Robertson with his light artillery was so great that I have concluded to go in with him. I am busy trying to raise the Company or assisting to do it. I do not know yet whether many of the Rifles will go in or not. Cochran says he had rather have my position than be Lt Col of regiment. I do not feel exactly that way about it but I would prefer it to the Captaincy of an infantry Company. Robertson offered me the position of his own accord, and being the kind of service I preferred above all others I went in. I concluded to go in. I have this advantage over enlisted men I can resign. I hope my Love that you will not feel that I have done wrong in going in. I think it will be a month or more before the battery is equipped and ready for service. In the mean time I want to get as long a leave of absence as I can and stay with you as much as I can. And another thing my Love I want you to be with or near me during the time I stay here...My pay is $100 per month. The same I have had this year with better chances for promotion and distinction. I feel that it is a grave responsibility and I have tried to think of it as I ought and I sincerely hope it will receive the approbation of my friend[s]. If the news we have heard in reference to England's demand of the surrender of Mason & Slidell be true and it seems to be confirmed I do not think the war can last over a year longer. It looks very much like Lincoln was trying to get up some decent pretext to end the war. Well enough of war & politics. We are all getting along here about as well as usual. [Bill] McTyer is well and has been entertaining us as usual with snatches of song &c; Reub [Kolb] is well. Henry Shorter leaves for home on Sunday next. I expect to send a letter by him. We have not much to do. Drilling is light and every one is looking forward to the time when he will be at home. Christmas is nearly here. I wish it was so I could be with you all...Cochran left us to-night. I miss him a good deal. Too Bullock is not expected to live. I received yesterday a letter from Governor [John Gill] Shorter saying that his case was considered hopeless. He will be a great loss to his family and his country. In many respects he is a wonderful man—and I doubt very much whether I shall ever look upon his like again—what a brilliant career was opened before him...

As Dent well knew, his Nannie could hardly disapprove of anything her darling Hubert did, including his reenlistment. Now he expected a thirty-day furlough, was in fine health, and took pride in his own honorable course, which would bring him back to camp promptly, not straggling like some of the "disgraceful" sort he mentioned.

Barrancas Florida
Dec. 30, 1861
My Love,

...I expect to-morrow to see Genl Bragg and then get a leave and go home...I do not know yet how long a leave I shall get not less I think than thrity days and will take the other thirty some other time. It looks like a short time to be at home after twelve months absence. But my Love I think that the best. Then when I get you and the boy down here—how well pleased I expect to be...[J. D.] Smith is busy making out muster and pay rolls for to-morrow. I have done nothing to-day since 9 O'clock this morning. It is rather tiresome...I expect Baker will return to Eufaula and may be here before he takes Command of his Regiment. Bill McTyer is in as fine a humor as ever and very well. I am as hearty as ever. No more dyspepsia since I quit smoking and syrup. Our Company is in good health. We have only two men sick and they are not much sick. The men generally are very anxious to get home. I have heard not a very good account of some who have gone home...[In coming home] I will stop a day in Montgomery I think as I want to attend to some business there...

Early in 1862, Dent would leave Fort Barrancas for northern Mississippi and Tennessee. General Bragg and some of his coastal force were transferred there to help General Albert Sidney Johnston's Confederate army try to stop the advance of Union forces under General Ulysses S. Grant. This campaign is the subject of chapter 2.

Meanwhile in 1861, Chattahoocheans of lesser rank, such as Green C. Barron and Thomas Jefferson Barron, were involved at the Virginia front. Since Pensacola was a holding operation and the Confederate capital had been moved in May from Montgomery to Richmond, Virginia became a more important theater of war than the Gulf Coast. The first battle of Manassas (Bull Run), Virginia, on 21 July—not a fair test of either side—ended in a rout of General Irvin McDowell's Federal troops and underscored the growing belief that the war would be won or lost in that state. Throughout the fall and winter following the first Manassas, the Confederacy expected another Union attack in Virginia. This, however, did not come until the next spring, owing to Union General George B. McClellan's overly cautious response to McDowell's experience at Manassas the previous July. Still, Southern recruits were rushed toward Virginia to swell the army of General Joseph E. Johnston for the necessary defense of Richmond.

Green C. Barron and Thomas Jefferson Barron, a father and son, both joined Company D of the Fourteenth Alabama Infantry. Organized at Auburn, Alabama, on 1 August, the regiment would be in Yorktown by November. Recently arrived in camp at Auburn, G. C. Barron wrote his wife, Martha, who was at their home in Milltown, Chambers County, Alabama. His letter is a good example of how low literacy and proud determination to communicate could combine to produce a near classic piece of folk art. His "box lead" was probably ammunition.

Camp Johnson
Macon Co. Ala.
Aug. 31, 1861
Der Wife,

I tak my pen an ink an box lead to drop yu a fue Lins to Let you know that we ar well this mornen hopen thes fau Lins will find you all well I resev yours Letters Last night at 8 o clock an I wous glad to her frum you all ouy Mess is all well this mornen Same Barron is well and Thomas Tomson is well Martha, you rought that we must com home iff we coud I wil com if i can. Cor T J Judy seas that 2 men [from each] company Can hav a fur[lough] at one time Soe it mae be [some] tim befor it [comes my] tim. I woud be very glad to Sea [you all]. Martha I send 2 stripes of news paper for [you to read] that Solders letter is a good letter an I wount you to tack cer of hi I [nor] Thomas [his son] hafter Stand Gard today we will Com of to morer at 7 o Clock we wouck ouy pouste 8 hours in 24 Soe tell the Chrelden houd for med an all mie inquiren frenze Soe I must Com to a Clous you must excust my bad righten for I ame Seten one a pine Log with my box lead in my lap. Soe nuthn more present but remany yu Loven Husben un tul Death...

Three weeks after Green Barron's letter, his nephew, Thomas Josephus Moore, wrote his "Dere Ant" Martha Barron from western Tennessee. Although a resident of Fredonia in Chambers County, Alabama, Moore was a private in the Thirty-Eighth Regiment of Tennessee Volunteers. While geographically incongruous, Moore's note nevertheless illustrates the power of family commitment to transcend the war's barriers of distance and time. Far from home and somewhat bewildered, Moore's hope for meaning was rooted in letters from relatives.

Rossvill postofis
Lafaett County tenesee
Sept. 20, 1861
Dere Ant,

i take mi pen in hand in inform you that iam Well at present time and hoping thes few lines reaChis you thay find [you] in join the Same besing. Ant i am along wase from home i am a bout Sevn hondred miels from home about thurty miels from Memphis at abimton Camps i want you to rite to me if you plese and rite When you have hern from unkle grene and tom i have binleft home four weeks to morrow and i herd from them last Week and thay was all Well and Wood like to here from them no tel gorgean mary i want to See [them] i have nothing of importance to rite i send my respect to you All Ant i Want you to rite to mee you must excuse my bad ritein for i had not time to rite nothing more...

While Moore was in Tennessee and the Barrons on their way to Virginia, James Cantey, a planter from Russell County, Alabama, and colonel of the Fifteenth Alabama Infantry Regiment, began writing illuminating letters from the Virginia front. A month after the first Manassas, Cantey wrote his wife from Richmond describing his troops' impatience to see active service. Although the Union Army was in disarray following Irvin McDowell's embarrassing retreat in July, the Confederate force under Joseph Johnston would not make the attack on Washington that many Southerners desired.

Richmond
Aug. 21, 1861
My Dearest Wife,

...We leave tomorrow for Manassas, and the men are noisy with delight at the prospect of getting into active service, they are much improved in looks and drill, and present now a very fine appearance. They are the most orderly, quiet and tractable men I ever knew, and have won a good name for their good deportment.

The public officials keep very quiet as to the movement of the army and nothing is known, so far as known everything is quiet, and there is no telling anything about the matter. We are all organized and all the officers go to work...

There is so much noise in camp tonight that I can't write. I will write from Manassas...

...Sam and Winter [slaves] are complaining. Tell the Col and Aleck to send me all the recruits that they can get and set all my friends to do the same. I want 300 men more to fill the companies to 100 men and to organize the remainder into an artillery company, which the President [Davis] says I can do.

The "colonel" back home in Russell County was Samuel C. Benton, Cantey's father-in-law. Camp diseases, not the Yankees, were the immediate problem. Cantey was interested in gaining new recruits, equipment, and uniforms from his supporters back home.

Pageland, Near Manassas

Aug. 26, 1861

My Dear Col.,

We have been upon the move ever since we left Richmond, last night we reached this place and probably we may be stationary for several days. We're under the command of Genl. [Joseph] Johnston in whom to my surprise I have the pleasure of meeting an old friend and comrade in the Mexican War. Our encampment Pageland, is 8 miles from Manassas on the extreme left and the most advanced post in that direction. I am near and with the 11th North Carolina Regt. under Col. Kirkland. His Regt. has and is now suffering immensely from sickness. They have Measles, Mumps, Typhoid fever and Diarhoea, it is a terrible sight to see the poor fellow, out of 1100 men the Col. Tells me [he] has not 300 fit for duty. I fear that a terrible ordeal is ahead of us, for we've already 2 cases of measles and of course it will go through the entire Regt. Otherwise we have been very fortunate so far, little or no sickness. Sam has been quite sick all the time, and still unfit for service and I fear that I will have trouble with im, and perhaps have to leave him. Winter has got well, but had the misfortune to loose his trunk on the way. Our encampment here is a pleasant place, and apparently healthy country, the days are warm, but the nights very cool. As to future plans of operation I can say nothing, for nothing is known, our troops are advancing slowly towards the Potomac, and the enemy preparing to defend the Capitol. A thousand rumors of fights and skirmishes come in daily but reliance can't be placed in them. Our Camp is in view and only 1 mile distant from the [first Manassas] Battlefield, which is said to be the next no one knows...

You must all try to get up another uniform for the Cantey Rifles by the end of Oct., also shoes and blankets, and I should like to have all the recruits you can get. I am anxious to kep the Company 100 strong, and also to form another Company of Artillery to be attached to the Regt. and they must be 150 strong—Send word to John Burch and all other friends of the Company & Regt. and I should like the people of Russell to uniform all the men that comes from that County, and Croft will forward them. Good-bye to you and Heaven bless you...

By November, Cantey was experiencing wintertime in northern Virginia. Picket duty on the advanced lines was very taxing, especially when one's slaves were ill and could not be taken to do the hardest labor. Cantey had hoped he would be sent to join the defenders of the Gulf Coast. The "Leesburg affair" (the Battle of Ball's Bluff) was a Federal reconnaissance that crossed the Potomac in force on 21 October only to be beaten back across the river into Maryland.

Centreville
Nov. 5, 1861
My Dear Wife,

...I am ordered off again tomorrow on the advanced lines to be gone 3 days. I regret it very much for I am not feeling well at all, and Winter and Sam both sick and unable to go, and we are not allowed to carry any wagons, tents, or anything except 3 days cooked rations, a blanket, and forty rounds of ammunition, and if the weather should be bad as it is ure to be, it is pretty hard work, in fact it is a tiresome and fatiguing service, no chance to sleep, and no fires allowed.

I wrote you a few nights ago, that I was writing while the rain was falling and the wind blowing a gale, it lasted 30 hours and was certainly the most trying and terrible night and day I ever saw. The wind blew a perfect hurricane, and blew down nearly all the tents and the poor men sick and well had to stand in the rain all night. Tom Woolfolk and Winter were both sick in my tent, and I spent the whole time in driving the pins and tightening the cords and propping the poles to keep it from falling upon them, as it was they got wet and everything in the tent, for the wind was so severe that it blew the rain in, and I got wet and stayed so for the whole time, consequently it gave me a bad cold and pain in the back, it also produced a good deal of sickness among the men. I therefore, feel very little like going on picket duty at this time. Military orders are peremptory and must be obeyed and there is not getting around it. The anxiety and excitement which all have felt here for the past ten days in anticipation of a great fight, is gradually subsiding and everything is assuming a sullen quietude, as there is no report of the enemies advancing upon [us] yet in any direction since the Leesburg affair.

The Army is still busy building forts, fortifications, and redoubts, till now the whole country around here is completely encased in a vast line of fortifications, and I begin to fear that some of us will be kept here to defend this place through the winter, and my luck is so bad I feel certain I shall be one. We have a great many rumors here of the enemy's intended attack upon the Southern coast, and I was greatly in hopes that we might be ordered South to defend the Coast, but that is too good luck, I fear to be true, still I should like it very much. What disposition will be made of us this winter I have not the most remote idea. Nothing can be found out, from the Headquarters of the Generals...

Centreville was just north of Manassas, only a few miles form Washington, D.C. Although the Confederates had expected another Yankee attack, General George B. McClellan, who replaced McDowell over the Potomac Army, was too busy securing the Union capital and drilling troops to make an advance before spring 1862. Cantey described the strong Confederate defenses that awaited possible attack. Such constant tension was enough to upset one's digestive tract and more.

Centreville
Nov. 15, 1861
My Dear Wife,

...I also received the box safely containing the comfort, shirts, and neck comforter, for which I thank you very much and send you a kiss for pay. The comfort is just the thing, and is very comfortable indeed. I have had all my shirts packed and will send them back. The collars are much abused by bad washing and the body will probably bear another collar, and they are too cold for winter.

We are still here in a daily expectation of an advance of the enemy. The head generals are very confident that we will be attacked at this point, and are very particular in keeping everything in fighting order and readiness at a moments notice. All the fortifications around this place are completed and fully armed and manned. These fortifications extend a distance of nearly six miles and are certainly very formidable looking things. These are built and located so as to connect with the works at Manassas, and should we be repulsed here we then fall back upon Manassas. In spite of the firm and repeated opinions of the Generals, that we are bound to fight here, no approach of the enemy is yet announced by our vidett[e]s, still that is no reason why they should not move at any time. The whole army is encamped in line of battle, every Brigade is in its place and every Regiment in the place that it will occupy in line behind the breast works and it is a very grand and imposing sight. Great alarm is felt here for the Southern coast, and for Kentucky and Tennessee, for those are the points to which the war will be renewed to, in my opinion.

I have been a little unwell with my bowels, but am well again. Winter has been very sick and just now able to sit up. Woolfolk has been quite sick also. He is up today. I had them at a house a little distance from camp. Woolfolk speaks of going home as soon as he is able to travel, and I intend to send Winter with him. He can't stand the winter here, and will be useless to me. I will write Jack to send me Francis or Sam...

I am very busy getting the sick all sent to Richmond this morning...

In his next letter Cantey described a picket position that was more comfortable than ordinary ones, which allowed only rations and a blanket. The colonel's dependence on slaves' assistance is interesting, but it was not typical of the average Confederate's slaveless condition.

Chantilly
Nov. 19, 1861
My Dear Wife,

I am seated tonight in a nice little school house with a comfortable stove, and everything so comfortable that I can't help writing you, rather than go to bed, for it is much more pleasant sitting around the fire in a house than to sleep upon the hard floor with only two pair of blankets. Chantilly is one of the ouposts of the pickets 4 miles in advance of Centreville. It is a most beautiful old Virginia County seat of the Stuart family. They are very wealthy, and have spent a great deal in beautifying and adorning the premises, a very much more beautiful and interesting country around here to any other part of the state that I have seen yet, in fact ll the residences and farms are more stylish and elegant and looks more like the homes of FFV's [First Families of Virginia].

This picket duty comes around pretty often no and although this is a more pleasant place than where we are encamped, still we are not allowed to take any tents or baggage or anything except 3 days rations and blanket. The men build bush arbours to protect themselves, and only the reserve of the pickets are permitted to have fires. It is terrible hard and trying upon the soldiers to stand all night on watch without any fires these cold windy and rainy nights.

I wrote you a few days ago that I had been suffering from a fit of indigestion, since that time I have got all right again and now feel as well as ever. The weather has been very disagreeable...

I will send Winter back...his lungs I fear is affected and the exposure here this winter will ill him. He seems very reluctant to leave me, but feels convinced that he could not live through the winter, the struggle between the two is pretty hard with him. I got Neddy to telegraph Jack to send me a boy, and Sam has gotten pretty well again so I think I can get on pretty well...

I must send you another kiss for the nice leggings you sent me, they are very nice and just the thing...

Near the end of November, heavy snows had reduced the possibility of winter campaigns in northern Virginia. Tents were no more than temporary shelter in this harsh climate, which would soon require more permanent housing. James Cantey was still concerned for the security of the Gulf Coast and the West. He evidently owned a plantation near Memphis.

Centreville
Nov. 24, 1861
My Dear Wife,

...It is [a] cold and cheerless night, and the snow is falling quite fast. Fortunately for me I have Neddy located quite near me, and he had a very good mechanic in his company who built me a very snug chimney with rock to my tent, and you can't imagine how comfortable and warm it makes the tent, and unless the snow shall be heavy enough to burst the tents we shall be pretty comfortable.

This will most certainly dispel all chances of an attack by the enemy, for the roads will now be impassable to the passage of artillery and baggage wagons. Winter seems to have set in here, and we can expect nothing in future but cold, rain, sleet and snow, and with it much suffering and sickness among the soldiers, in fact there is now a great deal of pneumonia among the troops. Nor order has yet been received to build huts and the men still use the tents. I feel afraid, however, that we will soon have to make better provision for the winter, for it is impossible for the men can't stand the winter in tents in their present exposed position.

Everything here is quiet as possible. Great excitement and interest is now felt for the fate of the coast. News has just reached here of the commencement of the attack by the Federals at Pensacola [shelling on 22 November]. The officials here have the wires under guard and will not let a word of news from that place go out of the office, so we are kept in great suspense as to the progress and result. I have great apprehension for our people have not improved the opportunity afforded them through the summer to put the whole coast in a perfect state of defense. We boast too much and act too little, and worst of all we have not a sufficiency of arms to place in the hands of the people. If, however, we can only successfully repulse them at Pensacola it will be a fatal disaster to them. I was greatly in hopes that after it was ascertained here, that no attack would be made that a portion of these troops would be ordered South, but now I don't think that they will allow a man to leave this line, so the people left at home will have to defend the coast. I feel considerable uneasiness at the state of things in the West, if the Federals should be successful at Columbus, Kentucky, they will take Memphis and that is getting very close to my little concern. The Col. [S. C. Benton] will have to go out and run the Negroes off when they get to Memphis...

As Cantey correctly foresaw, the Federals would drive into Kentucky and Tennessee early in 1862. Meanwhile, before that transpired, his next letter dealt with the Virginia front and described Confederates' more "permanent" winter quarters in the less forward position at Manassas. It was two days before Christmas. Despite harsh weather, there had been a recent skirmish with the Yankees near Leesburg.

Manassas
Dec. 23, 1861
My Dear Wife,

...We have been very busy moving from Centreville to within a mile of Manassas to winter, and are now in the midst of building log huts. Such a din and clatter you never heard. Some cutting poles, others putting up logs, some daubing, some building chimneys, some cutting out stumps, and all singing and hallowing enough to run a nervous man into fits. I am glad that we have been allowed to build huts, the weather has been very cold and has again set in to rain and sleet and I have no doubt that the hard winter has fairly set in, and I am only sorry that our houses are not all done so that we might have spent Christmas in them, but we will not have them done.

Lt. Malone with about 20 men are very busy in putting up a very snug cabin for me, the men would not allow my servants to do it, declared that I should have a good house. The logs are hewed nicely and it is a most comfortable looking affair, and when completed I shall enjoy it much...

I think that Gen'l [Joseph] Johnston has given up all idea of an attack upon Centreville by the Yankees and all the disposable force [except enough to guard the works]...have [been] sent back to Manassas to go into Winter quarters. Everything has been quiet until last Friday we sent out 300 wagons for forage under the escort of 2000 Infantry, a squadron of Cavalry and 4 pieces of artillery, they met about 12 miles in the direction of Leesburg 8000 Yankees and had a short skirmish with them, in which we were pretty badly worsted. Our casualty was some 30 killed and 60 wounded. The Colonel of the 10th Ala. Regt. lost an arm, and the Lt. Col. Was killed in the field, that was the only Ala. Regt. engaged. We sent the next day a larger force out, but the enemy was gone. We unfortunately have a lot of shallow pated Generals that are constantly trying to do something big, in the hope that they will be promoted, and the poor soldier has to pay for their ignorance and carelessness.

I often think of home as Christmas approaches and wish I could be with you...Tell Winter to be sure and have my pants altered and sent back to Woolfolk.

I was very much gratified to hear that the members of the Alabama Legislature had unanimously recommended me for a Brigadier-General to the President and tho' I know that the President will not appoint me, I still feel much gratified by the action of the Legislature none of whom I know. It is gratifying to know that my state is satisfied with me, but Mr. Davis will appoint none but West Pointers...

I want you to send me that pair of high quartered shoes with thick soles I got in New Orleans, if they are not broken and are worth sending, for shoes and boots are scarce here...

Despite his pessimism about promotion, Cantey would become a general before the war was over. But on 5 January 1862, the colonel discussed his dyspepsia, the winter cabins, the Yankees' rumored plan of attack (which he was correct to doubt), and the futile hope among Southerners that the Mason and Slidell affair would bring Britain into the war on the Confederate side, even though the Federals had released the Confederate diplomats.

Manassas
Jan. 5, 1862
My Dear Wife,

...I have been suffering very much since Christmas day with dyspepsia or indigestion. I have been compelled to quit the use of tobacco. I feel a good deal better for the past day or two, but have a good deal of sourness in my chest and bowels yet. I live on milk and mush, sometimes rice and toast with tea. I mean to use every precaution to prevent a recurrence by living very light and not using Tobacco any more.

I have gotten into my cabin which is very comfortable indeed, and the men have nearly completed their huts. The bodies [frames] are up but find great difficulty in getting boards or plank to cover them. I am in hopes that they will in a few days be all finished and the men comfortably housed, but how long we are to remain I have no idea.

Rumor is again very rife that the Yankees are to make an early advance upon us, the spies and couriers from Maryland and Potomac say that the blockade of the river at Evansport, and the destruction of the locks above Washington, have reduced them to the necessity of fighting or evacuating Washington, and that the people are pressing upon Gen'l McClellan to fight rather than abandon Washington City. A good deal of credence is given to these rumors by the Confederate Generals and much preparation is being made to be ready for them at the 3 points which it is said are to be attacked, namely, Leesburg above here, Evansport below, and if we should be compelled to send any reinforcements to both of these points so as to weaken the Centre, then McClellan is to move with 200,000 men on Centreville and carry that place, thence to Richmond will be easy enough. I am inclined to think it is only big talk to divert attention from their pusillanimous backing down in the Mason and Slidell affair. What a humiliation in the eye of all the civilized world. I hope still that the English people will force the blockade and then it will be easy with us.

The weather is becoming very cold here and disagreeable...

Thus, for these correspondents from the Chattahoochee Valley, the first year of war ended. From a military point of view, very little had been decided, except that the struggle would be longer and more costly than either side had anticipated. Soon now the rapid Federal advance under General U. S. Grant into Kentucky and Tennessee would make that western front the next crisis area of war. Chattahoocheans in the western theater also penned impressions of that situation.

2

Tennessee and Kentucky: 1862

The war would be a long one, a fact that became more obvious as the months of 1862 slipped past. While the Confederates held their own against McClellan in Virginia, it was the year of "see-saw" in the west. Here, the Federals first penetrated the Upper South states of Kentucky and Tennessee and then the Lower South states of Alabama and Mississippi, only to have the Confederates counterattack from Chattanooga with a rapid march across Tennessee that took the war back to Kentucky. Having returned to Kentucky with force, the Confederate leadership would nevertheless mismanage affairs before, during, and after the battle of Perryville (8 October). This military engagement was no defeat for either side, but the Confederate army in Kentucky under Braxton Bragg precipitately withdrew back into middle Tennessee for a lengthy stalemate with Union forces in the vicinity of Murfreesboro. This chapter presents a few Chattahoocheans' firsthand views of these and related troop movements.

So much for an overview. Before hearing from the correspondents, however, a more detailed introduction is necessary.

In Kentucky and Tennessee, events had been moving toward a showdown since late 1861 when both Confederates and Federals violated Kentucky's precarious neutrality by occupying Columbus and Paducah, respectively. As the Federals organized in Kentucky under generals Henry W. Halleck, Don Carlos Buell, George H. Thomas, and U. S. Grant, the Confederates concentrated Albert Sidney Johnston's force at Bowling Green, Kentucky, and sent P. G. T. Beauregard (the hero of Fort Sumter) from Virginia to aid in the defense of the western Confederacy. During February and March 1862, the Federal thrust into Kentucky was strong enough to force General Johnston's Confederates to fall back from Bowling Green to Nashville and eventually to Corinth, Mississippi. With Grant continuing up the Tennessee toward Alabama (the river runs north), the Confederate government also transferred Braxton Bragg and a sizeable army from the Gulf Coast area with instructions to join the retreating Johnston at the important rail center of Corinth in northern Mississippi. Still trying to stop Grant's southward move, the Confederates would on 6–7 April attack his army at Shiloh Church near Pittsburg Landing on the Tennessee River. This first large battle of the war merely slowed down the Federal advance.

Meanwhile, S. H. Dent, now a first lieutenant in Captain Felix Robertson's artillery, served with A. S. Johnston's army in northern Mississippi. In describing the Confederates' confusion at Corinth in March (two weeks before Shiloh), Dent blamed General Daniel Ruggles for contradictory orders. Actually, however, the confusion was also the result of Bragg's indecisiveness. Because General Beauregard was ill, Bragg was acting commander at Corinth until A. S. Johnston arrived from Nashville on 23 March, the day after Dent's letter was written.

Camp near Corinth Miss
March 22, 1862
My own Dear Darling,

...Troops are still concentrating here. And field works are being made between this place and [the Tennessee] river and the Yankees will have pretty hard work to get here whenever they think proper to try it. Genl [Leonidas K.] Polk is here and Genl Beauregard is expected so you may judge from that what sort of an army we are collecting here and with what determination this place will be defended. Genl Polk commands the 1st Grand Division of the army of the Mississippi Valley, Genl Bragg the second and I do not know who may command the third. Genl Beauregard is not yet well and being at Jackson Tenn is coming down here for greater safety as in case he should get unable to travel. The Yankees might take him there alive. Beauregard would be a prize of great value in their eyes. Since Genl Bragg came here we have no more ration orders—before that Genl Ruggles sent us every day or two orders to cook sometimes five and sometimes three days rations—and occasionally ordering us to harness up and be ready to move or report to him as soon as we were ready. As I was saying however we have not has one such order since Genl Bragg landed here and every thing is going on much more quietly. Our scouts run against the Yankee pickets ever once and awhile some times having a small skirmish with them. The last news I have of their whereabouts is that they are encamped about one & a half miles from the river under the cover of their gun boats. I heard today that the 1st Ala Regt had a fight with some gun boats of the enemy at Island No 10 above Memphis and that they sunk one gun boat and crippled two others driving the enemy off. The Regt is highly complimented. I do not know what other troops are there. We are drilling and fixing up and if we only had fifty more men as good as some we have I would not be afraid of any battery that could be sent against us...I hope our Generals will soon be able to act on the offensive and go and look for the enemy...It is surprising how little one know here of what is going on right around him...

Island No. 10 was a Confederate stronghold on the Mississippi River at the Tennessee-Kentucky line. When it fell to the Federals on 7 April 1862, 6,000 Confederate troops were taken prisoner, and the river was opened to Union traffic down to Memphis. One of the Confederate prisoners, Furney Clarke (probably of the First Alabama), had grown up in the Chattahoochee Valley. In an undated letter, Clarke wrote his parents about the surrender and his subsequent imprisonment and good treatment by the Yankees.

Camp Chase, Columbus, Ohio

Dear Father and Mother,

I retire to my seat to inform you that I am in fine health with the exception of a cold.

You have no doubt heard of the surrender of the Force at Island 10. Our company was among the number. A good many of them made their escape. Lieut. O'Neill is supposed to have made his escape. The privates were sent to Chicago, Illinois. I am getting along much better than I expected I would. We are treated very well. I am without money and clothes both, though I will get some clothes in a few days now. The people here have been kind in furnishing the prisoners clothes. Mother and Father, I don't want you to give yourselves any uneasiness about my welfare. It is true that I am placed in a rather unhappy condition, but I am in hopes that I will not be here long...

There were prisoners on both sides. Following the battle of Shiloh (6–7 April), a stream of Federal captives passed from Corinth into the Deep South. J. Cook Lewis, a Confederate officer from the Chattahoochee Valley, wrote his wife about some of these unfortunate Federals.

Montgomery, Ala.
April 15, 1862
My dear Lila,

...I must tell you of the Yankee prisoners, from Corinth, brought here on the boat today. I went down and saw them bought out. There were three hundred on the St Charles & to night we expect several hundred more, among whom is Genl [Benjamin M.] Prentiss, the Federal Gen'l. They look badly and woe-begone. Among them were several little fellows, & when I looked at them I thought of poor P [Pierce Lewis, the writer's younger brother who, ironically, was later captured by the Federals.]...

J. C. Lewis found it impossible to ignore the intelligence and dedication of the Union prisoners. Two weeks after the Montgomery letter, he was in Auburn, Alabama, describing the rapid organization of new Confederate regiments as well as the persistent idealism of the Northern foe.

"Camp Johnson"
Auburn
May 4, 1862
My dear Lila,

We reached this point yesterday, having bid adieu to Greenville several days ago. We are pleasantly situated here, decidedly the nicest place that I have seen since I left home...Three Regiments are organizing here. A thousand Yankees passed here yesterday for Macon. We had a good look at them & talked to them for some time. The two trains which carried them stopped for the down train to pass. I had quite a discussion with a very intelligent man—a prisoner. He said he hoped that after the war was over that we would meet & have a long talk. I told him that I expected to fight him for a long time & "get him" if I could. He said he would do the same by me. He was from Iowa...I am with some of the nicest men here in Alabama. I spent the night at Captain [William F.] Slaton's house. He is a candidate for Major. He deserves it, and will very likely get it...

Everybody must now enter the service. If you had heard those Yankees talk yesterday, when they said they had no other idea but that they would subdue us. I told them, when we are subdued, no one of us would be here to know it—for all would be dead! I reminded him of their outrages upon our fair women, who had always been, and are still ready to dress their wounds when we take them prisoners. They said they ought to have been killed...that they did not uphold any such acts...

J. Cook Lewis, "Cookie" to his wife, was soon sent to northern Mississippi near Columbus, where in a matter of weeks he died of the camp fevers whose pestilence was rightly dreaded by both armies. Meantime, the hard fought battle at Shiloh was not soon forgotten. A full year after the event, on 5 April 1863, Lieutenant Dent recalled: "Twelve months ago I was with the battery in line of battle near the enemy's camp at Shiloh—little thinking that I was going through the bloody scenes of the next two days."

It was bloody. Shiloh would be known as the testing ground that turned cocky civilian volunteers into sobered veterans. The armies of both sides were green when they went into this fight. Thus the Confederate troops of Johnston and Beauregard made an awkward approach and still managed to surprise Grant at Shiloh. But the Federals' luck was to hold out until they could be reinforced by D. C. Buell and thereby press Beauregard back to Corinth—but only after heavy casualties on both sides. On the first day of battle, General A. S. Johnston died after a bullet severed an artery. On paper, then, the battle was a draw. But over the long term, it hurt the Confederates more than the Union forces.

S. H. Dent had his baptism of fire at Shiloh. Soon after the battle he wrote Nannie of his minor wound and its ready healing. He also noted that the Confederate withdrawal from Shiloh allowed the Federals to advance to Huntsville in northern Alabama.

Camp Near Corinth Miss
April 23, 1862
My own Dearest Wife,

Your letter of the 8th just reached me to-day...Your letter has been so long coming that I am afraid you have suffered some interruption of the mails. Perhaps the Yankees got some of my letters when they took Huntsville...Yes Darling the battle is over and I am safe thank Heaven...Dearest while sick at the hospital I thought over many things and I felt I had great reason to be thankful...We have had transferred to our Company forty men from an artillery Company that was broken up for inefficiency of its officers...What do [you] think I did to-day. I took two men and started in the Country to find something to eat. I rode for several miles—but could not find anybody willing to sell me a

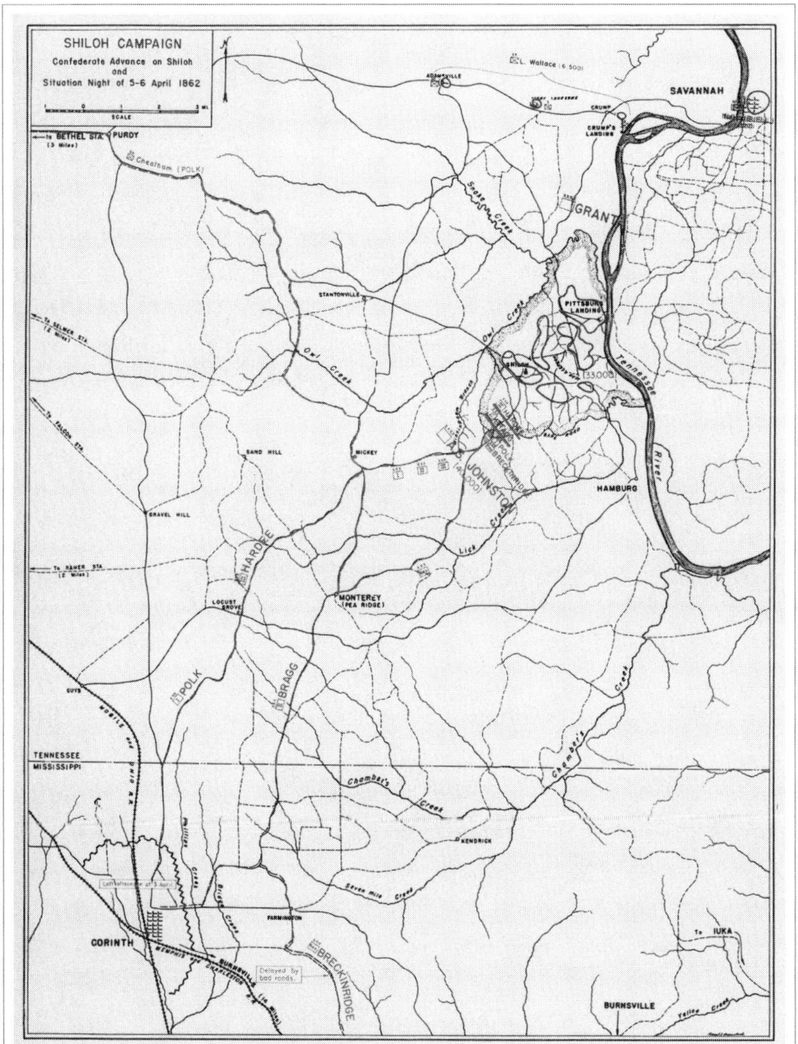

SHILOH CAMPAIGN, 1862

chicken or anything at all. At last I met a wagon which had only eggs. I had despaired of finding anything. I bought from the wagon forty-three dozen eggs—and would have taken them all the man had over a hundred dozen—but had no way to take them into camp. I paid 33 1/3 cts a dozen for them. I have eaten nearly a dozen to-day—of course I divided with the company as well as I could—but I kept about fifteen dozen for my own uses. If I could only have found some butter I would have lived like a lord for a few days. I have a great appetite since I got well...I believe still the [war] will last a long time—through the whole of Lincolns term perhaps—three years longer...Many of our officers are resigning since the fight. I do not like the indication. Many a man has found out that he could not stand the service on account of health since the fight who to all appearances at least were perfectly healthy before the fight. I tell you my Love they have had enough battles. I know very little of what is going on here. I believe part of [Earl] Von Dorn's & [Sterling] Price's army is here but I know nothing except by mere rumor. Beauregard rode past our battery this evening—the first time I have seen him since the fight. He is very gray...

With A. S. Johnston dead, Beauregard was in command of Confederates in the west until President Davis replaced him with Braxton Bragg in June 1862. Meanwhile, after withdrawing from Shiloh, the Confederates defended Corinth, waiting for reinforcements, which came, but not in as large numbers as the Federals believed. Advancing slowly, owing to caution bred by the surprise at Shiloh, the Union army under General Henry W. Halleck edged up to Corinth. But Beauregard, greatly outnumbered, chose a secret evacuation of the city on the night of 29 May, leaving it for easy Federal occupation the following day.

Just three days before the evacuation, A. J. Burton, a native of Chambers County Alabama, was ready to fight and make Corinth the Armageddon of the Confederacy.

Corinth
May 26, 1862
Dear Father & Mother,

It affords me great pleasure indeed to communicate [to] you the intelligence of my good health an inestimable blessing which is so essential to the soldiers and to the success of our good men and glorious cause. It is true we have had a great deal of sickness and deaths in our army, the same is true of the Yankee army more die from sickness than is killed in battle. The two armies of

Corinth have now got in gunshot of each other and you may not be surprised to hear of a great battle at any day. Very heavy skirmishing is going on every day between the pickets I believe our pickets have been victorious in every engagement and I believe furthermore that the whole Confederate force and whole Yankee force will meet here in this valley of Miss and the great contest will be settled though this is a mere believe of mine it is founded upon the fact that there are already now more men concentrated here than any place in the Confederacy and still they come. I hope and trust the contest will soon be ended and that we all will return to our homes to enjoy a calm and quiet life in a land where all is peace.

Brother Jacob is gone 8 or 10 miles from Corinth to tend on Thomas Brooks who is very low...Tell Bro William to come in Camps as soon as he can for Maj Beall has requested the Capt to publish all that is abscent as deserters...Capt Wright says for him to come in as soon as he can but not until his health improves and for him to bring in all he can with him and that there will be an election in which they will cast Maj Beall overboard. I don't think he can get many votes in this Battalion. We are stationed for the present at Chewalla a bout 10 miles from Cornith...

Although Corinth was evacuated without a fight, the Confederacy was preparing to stop the Yankees elsewhere. Vicksburg was a major point of resistance on the Mississippi River. Similarly, Chattanooga would become the logical place for Confederates to launch a countermove into Tennessee and Kentucky. J. H. Lewis of Stewart County, Georgia, a private in Company E of the Third Georgia Cavalry, was a part of the Confederate force assembling at Chattanooga. As an unhappy recruit, Lewis might have been a recent conscript. His regiment was still unorganized when he wrote his wife from Columbus, Georgia.

Columbus
May 20, 1862
Mattie,

...I cannot be examined until after the Regiment is formed, Capt Thorton says it will avail me nothing...I cant say that I like camp life much so much noise & fuss that one is not being accustomed to it is frustrated very much. Mattie you cannot tell how bad I want to see you & the little ones I hope it will not be long before I go home. It is getting late and I must close.

May 23rd I have the opportunity this morn of writing more I am not feeling so well this morning—sick stomach and diarear I am in hopes it will not last long. I intend on coming home as soon as I can. I think the organization will come off Saturday. My Dear Mattie I would give the world to be with you and the little ones once more in peace for there is nothing half so sweet as your face...and presence, but [I] must close. Your husband—Goodbye. Kiss all the children.

For these rural, family-centered people, the physical separation caused by war was wrenching, requiring major adjustment. But the Confederate soldier was as resilient as he was homesick. After a month of service, with his regiment still unorganized and unarmed, J. H. Lewis wrote more sanguinely from northern Georgia.

Randolph Camp Calhoun
Gordon County, Ga
June 22, 1862
My dear Mattie,

...I am well...The rest of the mess is all well. Some of the Company are sick with bad colds, two cases of measles; William Worth and Jones. We left Camp McDonald on Thursday last and reached here Friday 19th. All our things came through railroad safe. We have missed nothing as yet. Camp Calhoun, Randolph, is a very broken rough place. A part of it nearly covered in white flat rock and not a stick amiss on it. Water pretty plentiful tinctured plentifully with limestone. We are more than two hundred miles from Columbus and about twenty four or thirty more from the Yankees. They are said to be at and around Chattanooga trying to cross the Tennessee River to cut us off from Dalton. I do not like to be so near them without arms or protection. It is roumered that in two weeks we will go to Atlanta to guard the city. That arrangement would suit me very much. The Regmt is not organized yet...I cant say that I like camp life as much though as well as I expected. We have plenty to eat as of yet. Our horses has not fared very well up here forage scare as yet. My horse keeps about the same...Mattie...when I think of being from you three years or during the war, I cannot bear the idea. Remember that you have a large share in my love, my sympathies and my prayers. By day and by night [you] air I my thoughts and often the unbidden tear flows down my cheek when I think of your sufferings and dangers. I hope if we never meet on earth, we will meet where wars and roumers of wars can never disturb us, but where love peace & joy forever reign...

When the Federals occupied Corinth on 30 May, Beauregard's army retreated south to Tupelo and Okolona, Mississippi. During this withdrawal, S. H. Dent and his battery had an interesting clash with a Union force at the Tuscumbia River in Mississippi, a few miles south of Corinth. Dent wrote his wife about the encounter and enclosed a captured Yankee letter that confirmed the Alabamian's account.

June 22, 1862

Dear Love,

I believe I have sent you nearly every thing I could in the way of a Yankee relic except a letter well here is one. Dr Terry brought this over to me this morning—because it contained the Yankee account of our skirmish at Tuscumbia [Mississippi]. I send it to you to let you see what my section did there. I know this was my section because we were fighting dismounted Cavalry. One of our Cavalry Companies went up to the Memphis and Charleston railroad a day or so ago and burned a bridge—also three thousand bales of cotton collected by the Yankees and Captured a mail train—and this is one of the letters. Some of the letters captured give terrible accounts of this country—and it seems to be pretty certain that Buell with his army has gone to East Tenn. Terry told us that we would have orders to march in a few days perhaps today—but where we are going no one knows except Bragg—who is now in Command of this Department. Beauregard has gone to Bladen [sic] Springs [Alabama]. I am glad Bragg is in Command. I therefore look for stirring times soon. If it would serve the interests of the Country as well I would like to remain here a week longer—our men and horses improving...

Beauregard's leaving the army for his health's sake had given President Davis the welcomed opportunity to replace him with Bragg. The enclosed Union letter (with an illegible signature) described the skirmish with Dent's battery in northern Mississippi, giving full credit to the fighting ability of the retreating Confederates.

Camp East Side Tennessee River
Near Tuscumbia Alabama
June 18, 1862
My Dear Wife,

After the evacuation of Corinth our Six Companies being joined, Colonel Oakes Commanding. We proceeded in pursuit of Beauregards Army, General Pope taking one road, and about 1500 Cavalry another. Of course our Six Companies being in the advance. Four or five miles from Corinth we came on the rear of the rebel Army. They had burned a bridge, and we had to dismount and fight on foot. We did not make much of this work, for the enemy opened on us with a masked battery in the woods Killing 5 and wounding 9 of the 3rd Kentucky Cavalry. Our 6 Companies were mounted to Charge if an opening offered. Captain Crittenden was along and very Sick, So Sick that he had to be carried away in an Ambulance.

Next morning our Commanders were not Satisfied. So we went down again. This time Our fellow took on foot, and Some Sharp Skirmishing went on for about half an hour, when Colonel Oakes Seen the enemy was Surrounding us ordered a retreat, which was very well executed "D" Company covering the others till they all got mounted.

When we broke for our horses and left one man of "G" Company was killed and one man of "K" Company wounded. We are attached to General Buells Command and dont know where we are going to. Some of the mess Say Tennessee, and Some Virginia. This Country is very rich large fields of corn and potatoes very little of anything else is planted. I have only seen one field of cotton...N B I forgot to Say that we escaped very lucky in the Skirmish. We found out afterwards there was 6000 rebels waiting for us...

The Confederate cavalry raid on the Memphis and Charleston Railroad, which ran from Corinth to Chattanooga, shows the Federals' difficulty in maintaining a railway line deep in rebel territory. Yet Buell's Union army would try to cross northern Alabama to eastern Tennessee, the goal being to occupy Chattanooga before the Confederates could reinforce it. Buell, however, was detained by railroad repairs and further Confederate raids in middle Tennessee directed by N. B. Forrest and others.

Bragg, in the meantime, was beginning to execute one of his most successful moves against the enemy. Taking advantage of Buell's delay and using rail connections from Tupelo to Mobile, Montgomery, and Atlanta, northward, Bragg would move his army to Chattanooga in record time, beat Buell there, and prepare an offensive march across Tennessee into Kentucky. Transporting some troops in June in order to test the circuitous route to Chattanooga, Bragg sped the move after 22 July. Still, the transfer required time, and some of his troops were in northern Mississippi for several weeks.

It was in this context that T. Q. Stanford, the crusty captain of G Company, Thirty-Ninth Alabama Infantry, would write home. He addressed his wife, Eliza, from Saltillo, Mississippi, ten miles north of Tupelo. The Stanford's home was in the Bush community on the Barbour County-Henry County line of Alabama. Here, he described camp life in Bragg's army, where many still awaited transportation to eastern Tennessee. The times were not all unpleasant, especially for commissioned officers who had the luxury of slaves as body servants.

Saltillo Miss
July 22, 1862
My Dear Wife,

...Since we left Tupelo, there is Still a great deal of Sickness in camps and the men are Scattered from Quitman Miss to this place. I have 13 men Sick here...they are in the Brigade hospitle which is Several acres of land cleared up and Tents & arranged and nurses cooks & Stewards put there for them...Eliza I am Sory you put your Self to So much troubble about getting those shirts for me. I hope you have not got them as I bought two from Tom which will do me till cold weather then I will need thick ones if I can get them dont cut up your dress it would make good ones for Summer, but the Summer is too near...gone. Now Casemere or Something that you could weave at home A wool and A Cotton would make good ones for winter if you have the material. I would like to have enough grey or mixed jeans to make me a pair of pants and a sound Coat for winter...I long to See cool weather & hope we will have less Sickness...and I would like very much to visit you this fall or at any time but I fear it will be out of the question the orders for men or officers getting leave of absence is now allmo[s]t out of the Question. No one can leave unless it is recommended by the Surgeon of the Brigade as being beneficial for his health & neither can an office[r] resign unless he is unfit for duty by reason of disability. I have not asked a leave of abesnce yet for any thing ferther than my Col could grant but I intend to try to get off this winter and go home if it is but a Short time I would like very much to be at home now during the fruit Season I want to see my children very bad. I hope they are good children you must be good to them and teach them to be good and obedient...

Stanford's next letter (16 August) would be from Chattanooga. In the meantime, S. H. Dent wrote from Tynersville, Tennessee, on 6 August; he was ten miles northeast of Chattanooga on the railroad toward Knoxville. Dent's rail trip from Mississippi had required only eight days, but he arrived before his horses. In this removal, some artillery was sent over land rather than by rail. Lieutenant Dent was all business and very impatient for promotion.

Camp near Tinersville Tenn
August 6, 1862
My own Sweet Jewel,

I am in Camp once more after a rather long and fatigueing trip of eight days. I am on the Knoxville railroad and about ten miles from Chattanooga, right in the woods with plenty of good water and a country that does seem to afford a few things more than that portion of Miss in which we have been encamped. There are not a great many troops here yet...I have been quite busy since my arrival and indeed have not got [straight] yet—a Camp to clear up and my guns to get in Camp—you see I have no horses—and every thing of that kind to do with only half the Company...Clayton is in Command of the Brigade. He is the only Colonel here and [Franklin] Gardner has not arrived. I wish I had known that I was coming up in this country in time to have let you know it so you could have come along...I hope the letter I mailed you in Montgomery reached you safely...I saw Capt [Reuben] Kolb and a good many Eufaula men at Dalton Ga on my way up here. Jim Hunter told me he had seen you and the [boy] recently and that all were well. They were waiting there for transportation to Louden Tenn. They seemed very glad to see me. I do not think we will remain idle long. I have just seen an Extra published in Chattanooga in which there is a good deal of stirring news and I think old Bragg will keep the thing in motion. This is as you know a rough mountainous Country and it will be pretty hard on artillery horses—but I hope I will be able to get hold of some new ones soon. I am out of boots and am very anxious to get into another Yankee Camp and get hold of a pair or pull a good pair off a dead Yankee either will suit me very well. I will save at least $25 by it as that is what boots are selling for all up in this Country. I do not expect however to have another such a chance as I had at Shiloh...I believe I have [lost] all hope of promotion and think it is fated for me to go through this war as a 1st Lieut. There is no doubt that Fortune is blind...It will take me three days to get every thing to running smooth. You see our fixing up camp is just like a family moving. Every thing gets into Confusion and it takes some time to get things in good fix again. I expect I was the dirtiest fellow when I reached here you ever saw travelling in a box car or on platform cars—all the dust and cinders from the engine had full play on me...

By 16 August, Captain T. Q. Stanford was also camped near Chattanooga. The captain's relaxed demeanor is an interesting contrast with the compulsive Lieutenant Dent. Stanford described the scattered disposition of troops from Mississippi across four states. He wrote of his attachment to the men and concern for their well-being. His long letters bespoke of much free time. The "helpful" Jim was an obliging slave who was adroit at the enterprise later Americans would call "scrounging."

Camp Gladden
near Chattanooga Tenn
Aug. 16, 1862
My Dear Wife,

...[T]he most of my men come in this week excpt 5 who were at Quitman & 5 at Montgomery 2 from [?] and 1 at Atlanta those who came from Montgomery are Sick yet there was 38 came to the Reg from there & 30 of them put on the Sick list next morning, it is a great mistake in men leaveing a hospittle before they are fit for duty, I have 3 men yet at Okolona [Mississippi] So they are scattered badly & [I] fear we will never all get to geather a gain, the most of them here are now in good health & better Spirits than they ever have been tho Some will play baby in Spite of all that Can be done but I have many excelent men & good Lts and I am very much attached to them and dont think they woul be willing to Swap me for any one else and I try to do the best I can for each one wheather I do wright every time or not. I don't have So much to do now as I did for a long time my lieuts take much off of my hands I go to bed at nyht as Soon as I please & get up the Same, they attend all the roll calls & I have two good Sergeants who take a great deal of my hands tho I am never Idle long at a time for there is allways plenty to do in Camp we have a beautifull Camp on a level plain good Shade and all the Streets Cleaned up good and a large parade ground Cleaned up and we have kept it well trampled Since we came here we have been drilling like we Should have commenced at the first of the book and then recite a leson each day at 10 Oclock So we have done more drilling & harder Studying than ever before in the Same time and the officers and men are very much improved by it, Well, this [is] Saturday and we have just had a long battalion drill and come in So no more drill till 6 Oclock P.M. then dress parade when evry one has to do his best with Clean Cloths & So the men have most all gone to the Creek to wash and tomorrow morning Sundays we in variably have Regimental inspection of every thing in Camp and if each man does his duty today in Cleaning up there is no drills on Sundays except dress parade in the evening which is a Short and very pretty drill.

Jim has gone to wash and generally has late dinner on Saturdays as he takes in washing but he is So lazy he dont take much he has improved a great deal in cooking and is just as good as he Knows how to be but I Cant keep him from being lazy the men all like him and he trades with them and loves to make money the best I ever Saw but he dont take care of it he does all my trading Keeps the Accounts him self and Settle with him his acquaintance here is more extensive than mine he hardly ever Says anything about home only to ask how all is & I dont think he ever has any thing the matter with him he bought me Some of the best Cider this week I ever drunk he goes out as far as the pickets and meets wagons comeing in with Such things to Sell, but So ma[n]y troops have moved in between us and the Section where we Could get any thing that it is almost imposable to get anything of the Kind, but that dont make any difference now for we are looking momentarily for marching orders the adjutant Capt [J. M.] Macon told me just now that the Quarter master of the Division was ordered to furnish transportation to move this Brigade a cross the Tennesee river today, but it cant be done now So we may move to morrow So we are makeing ready our wagons have not come yet. I dont know how we will get along...

Soon now, Bragg's army would begin a fast march across east central Tennessee into Kentucky. Buell's inability to stop Bragg would eventually cost him his command. Placing the Union army back on the defensive in these two states was perhaps Bragg's greatest military achievement. In the meantime, before the offensive move began, time weighed heavily on soldiers, especially those like the impatient T. Q. Stanford. This captain was particularly discomfited by Bragg's stripping the army (including officers) of all extra baggage for greater mobility.

Camp Gladden near Chattanooga Tenn
Sunday 3 Oclock P.M.
Aug. 17, 1862
My Dear Wife,

...[L]ast evening our Regt recd orders to Cook Two days rations and be ready at a moments notice to march So everything else was disspenced with and each one preparing for the trip or to remain at a time when we get Such orders all the Sick are exspected to Stay and then the lazy and cowardly next try to Stay and Some effect the trip. So all has been bustle & Confusion Since getting ready and there is no little to do to get a Company ready for Such after they have been Stationed a while Change guns accoutriments & but we have completed all that and are now ready and anxcious to leave or do anything for we [are] not in a good humor by any means for I am as mad as ever the devel was when he was disappointed in Some great undertaking we had two orders reducing bagage & we have now 6 flies [shelters] for every one hundred men I have 5 for my Co. the others in porportion we are not allowed any boxes of any kind So it is a bad chance about carrying our provision, but I have mine packed in a barrell So I have them this time according to order. I Shall try to carry my matress two blankets and a Quilt but I dont know wheather I Suceed or not. I have packed my Camp Chest box with various articles of Clothing for myself & Co. I have a carpet bag in it and one blanket and Some large Knives and a pr of Scales I have a good Casemere Coat the Same Kind of pants & a pr of Shoes for myself & Will and in a black Carpet bag of Espy s there is a pr of boots of your Brother the others are all labilled with the owners names pined on each. I am going to try to Send it home by express to the Care of A. Stow Eufaula So you may enquire for it there you will have to pay the freight before you get it Send for the box if it gets there Send each bundle home or let the owners Know as Soon as you can or Send down To Lawrenceville to Some one for distribution if you get the box let me Know What the freight was and I divide it with the Co and if you dont get it it will be a cleare loss to all, but who cares for that I want my box to go any how Keep it for me and remember that I have eat a many good meal Set on the top of that Camp box. Well...our armes are all Stacked just in rear of where our tents Stood yesterday with all the accoutrements all hung and ready

Knap Sacks packed Some men Setting in Small groups talking Some lyining in the Shade a Sleep Some are Sewing up there cloths and they are engaged at various Sports and amusements the Sick the lame and the lazy cowards have all been moved out of each Co. to where our hospittal tents did Stand and thev are lying under the harbours [brush arbors] and my own Camp and Company head Quarters look...badly my hickery pole bed is Still Standing and Espys by the Side of mine and we Slept on them last as Sound and Comfortable as when I had a tent & fly and I guess we Will Sleep on the Same beds a gain to night as I dont think now that we will leave till morning our wagons have not come yet but we are to be furnished with others my Company and Capt [Lemuel] Hargroves will have one wagon for the two Cos and if we get a good team it will Carry all we have with ease it takes just half my valiece to hold the books and papers of the Co. So I have a Knap Sack that I will Start with then I will put it in the wagon. My Clothing now consist of my over coat one oil coat and a Short Coat, like the men have and my brown pants and those blue Casemere pants I bought 3 years ago at Lawrencevill 3 shirts White & 3 over Shirts 3 draws So I have plenty Clothing it is perfect foolishness to have too many Cloths in the Army. We will cross the Tenn river in 4 or 5 miles from here Some Say will remain there Some time but there is [no] telling. Only we will move northward Soon I am Sorry our Chaplain Saw fit to leave us this morning for I was liking him much hopeing he would induce me to believe in an endless hell of fire and brim Stone for if I could believe there was one I would be a great deal better Satisfied...

Bragg's army was moving by 19 August, but not all at once. While waiting for his unit to move, Quince Stanford wrote his brother, probably William, discouraging his entry into the Confederate army, but at the same time recognizing the difficulty of staying out. Quince's brother Monroe was already a member of the captain's Company G of the Thirty-Ninth Alabama. And William apparently joined them at a later date.

Camp Gladden Near Chattanooga Tenn.
Tuesday
Aug. 19, 1862
Dear Brother,

...I hope Monroe will get well a gain Soon as I doubt very much his getting a Substitute and if gets one it will have to look well and look like the best Soldier or it will not be excepted So there would be a loss on him. I dont think there will be a difficulty in his going home and remaining till he is well if he dont stay too long...I dont want him to return till he is well...Tell him to try at every place where there is Quarter Master to get transportation or he will be troubbled to get to the Regt I am very Sorry you cant remain at home in peace for a few months but I know you cant av it in any degree of Satisfaction unless you could content your Self in the hills & hollers but I exspect they are filled provid the best you can for our folks before you [leave] them. I know of no opening that would Suit you, in fact I know nothing but what is in our own Reft we have been under marching orders for three days with rations cooked & every thing ready to go I guess we will march tomorrow I have Seen Seven Regts Start today we leave a great many Sick in a Brigade hospittle over 100 from this Regt...I am tired down & my back troubbls me Some today. I have been on active service part of yesterday til 12 oclock today puting tents in the Brigade hospittle. I had 100 men 83 tents and it broke me down to keep them at work our men are all learning to Solder more the longer we remain in Service it almost frightens me to think how changed I am myself to what my nature once was but it is So & it becomes a man to be content with his lot but that is out of the question. I know that I was fortunate in getting the position that I did & will try to do my duty...we have a great deal of Sickness contajeous diseases I leave 14 men in the hospittle here none very sick but Joe Bracewell the ballance all able to able to cook & eat. We have had plenty of chickens duck geese apples peaches & much fruit & Jim got to the wagon yesterday &...stole a watermellon & he concealed it & brought me half all that I have had since I have been here the members of the Regt enquir after you frequently hopeing to hear from you Soon I will close & write when I Stop agn—we move northward...

Still waiting to move out, Stanford showed much interest in clothes, perhaps more than any other correspondent represented in this collection. He also commented negatively on Bragg's reorganization of the army. Despite Stanford's bias, however, administrative organization was one of Bragg's strongest points. In fact, the recasting of his 30,000 troops into two corps of two divisions each was so effective it was eventually copied by Federal as well as other Confederate commanders.

Harrison Landding Tenn.

Sunday evening

Aug. 24, 1862

My Dear Eliza,

[Y]ou will learn from this that we are Still on the banks of the river wanting to leave very bad and we leave in the morning part of our Brigade left today they have gone out three miles from here where I learn there is good water and a good place to camp and as camp is home I am all ways anxcious to know about what Sort of place we get for a Camp but usially every one gets tired of it and wants to move no matter how good a place we have it is natural for Soldiers to be restless and more especially when they are Idle and we have not been on drill or done any thing but Some little fatigue duty which Soldiers dont like to do. Well Eliza...you must not dispair or think the yankees have me if you dont hear from me So often in future for I am certain you will not...I must thank you for those fine marina Shirts you Sent me they are Quite the Iota[?] and just fills a Solders eye. I went to the river this morning took a wash put on a change of clothes and one of my green Shirts and dim the bank to my flie when I had many enquiries as to where I got them and if I would Sell any of them & now I might Sell them but it would take a good purse to get them...I want a pair of heavy jeans pants for winter with the legs Small I dont Care what Collar you can put a Stripe down the Seams Send them if you have an opportunity I believe that is all I think off to ask you for now. I hope Monroe will bring my uniform from Columbus tho I dont Care much about it I need it Sometimes...

So you will please get your ambrotype taken and Sent it to me and I will wear it with me and prize if for the Sake of the original whom I prise higher than all else on earth...I was a long time getting mine and it was the chance I had in Montgomery that I got it at all it was not a good picture the best could be done in a hurry the Sash I had on would indicate me on duty as officer of the day which was my duty from there to our camp.

...I have worn a cap during this month and the Sun has burned me dark but that is So much the better for the winter is comeing when I shall need a thick Skin to Stand the Cold winter winds of this Climate. Eliza this [is] Monday morning and our men are packing up without orders we want to move...[Now] if a Captain dies or is discharged the first Senior Lieut [the one who has the oldest Commission] in the Regt takes the place of the Captain and if a first Lieuts place is made vacant the Senior Second Lieut in the Regt takes his place, and if a Second Lieuts place is vacant the Senior third takes his place, and the...place of the third is filled by an election. This is a law of Gen Braggs and our Regt protests against it but I know it is no use...I think I wrote you that Dock Espy was my orderly Serft and he is now the best in the Reft with out any exception He does more for me than both my lieut and he can call the roll in the dark as well as in the light he stays with me...Well Eliza this evening the Sun is low and I am Sitting on a hill...distant from our new camp. We moved about 10 oclock 2 miles up the river and about a mile from it So and have a very pretty place in the woods and a large Spring of the best water I ever drank I think we will all get. well now I did not come up When the Regt did. I with some others who are complaining came on behind and when I came up Jim Had us a warm dinner and I eat with him & Espy and then I left them to the ballance So I lay off in the Shade till I concluded to finish this letter. So they put up my flie and was building a pole bed when I left them So I will have a pole bed again and it will be a treat to Sleep on poles again for I had a mean place on the bank of the river it was very rocky to Sleep on...I would rather have a jug full of Bailies best than two blankets I think it would go well with the cold water Send me a bottle of brandy when you have a chance...Some of our men flinched from there Knapsacks this morning they had burned their backs Sore in the river the first I knew of it Saw one of my men hideing his in a barrell and covering it up and Sent a Sergt to put it out and he told me his bach was Sore made him try to hide it in the Barrell...we get a mail to night there was a wagon went to Chattanooga yesterday to return to tight...I begin to think we will have no fighting to do unlese it is only to get possession of this State nd Kentucky and I think the yankees will give them up & the union men become Southern as fast as our army [confronts] them...

Believing that Tennessee and Kentucky could be easily "liberated" from federal troops, Stanford underestimated the resistance. In a similar vein, Lieutenant S. H. Dent expressed hope in an undated letter from the Chattanooga area that Bragg's army would soon march against General Buell, who occupied Nashville. Bragg's line of march, however, would be east of Nashville in order to flank Buell and hurry into Kentucky.

Near Chattanooga

Fall 1862

We had a report here a day or two ago that [E. Kirby] Smith had captured [George W.] Morgan [Federal] at the [Cumberland] Gap—but it turned out untrue. I saw Genl [Simon B.] Buckner at Chattanooga the other night. He looked rather thin but very much like he might be a General. He is a medium sized man—hair looked at night rather light—rather a thin beard he wore moustaches—had a fine grey eye. He will take command of a Division...I expect from what Pugh said that Congress will raise the conscript act so as [to] embrace men up to 45 yrs. Substitutes will then be higher than ever...I hope [to get to] Nashville and that I will stop [there long] enough to have you come and see [me]...You may soon begin to look out for us either marching or fighting somewhere between here and Nashville...

Finally, Dent's artillery joined the strenuous march. And it was a demanding one, rubbing flesh and bone across the grain of mountain ridges like clothes on a rub board. Dent described the painful progress, even as he clung to hopes of tarrying in Nashville. It was a very poor country.

Camp in Sequatchie Valley Tenn

Sept. 2, 1862

Well I am on my way towards Nashville and have travelled this far. The Division crossed Walden's ridge yesterday and [a] pretty severe crossing it was. We went up up up until it looked as if we were on our way to the moon and then after travelling five or six miles over such roads as we ordnarily find we commenced going down down down until it looked like we were on our way to the [lower] regions. We reached our present Camp about half an hour before sunset yesterday and will remain here to-day from present indications. I received orders about 12 O'clock at night on Wednesday to leave at once for Harrison's landing. I however put it off until day light and then left for the Tenn river, camped over that day and Camped about two miles from the river from there I sent back a letter which I hope you received. Well I will give you a short account of our trip. We left our camp on this side [of] the river on Saturday—travelled every day since—on Sunday we reached the foot of the Mountain. [Walden's Ridge]—and commenced going up. There were so many wagons on the road that [only one section went up that morning] and only half way that evening...very late when finding there was no chance to get up—I laid down and went to sleep on my saddle blanket & over-coat—no supper—next morning no breakfast except a ear of corn—and no dinner. Supper last night went first rate—rained a little yesterday. I think the road we travelled much worse than the road up look-out [Mountain]—a great many more rocks—and very large flat rocks—and the horses would slip down on them. In one place the hill was so steep that the [wagons] would slide down very rapidly although locked. The horses would fall down but fortunately no accident. The people [along] the road stared at us in silent wonder. In only one place did I see a handkerchief wave. I think however that handkerchiefs are rather scarce articles among most of these people. They seem to be poor and ignorant. We are now camped in a very pretty valley [Sequatchie] Walden's ridge on one side and the Cumberland Mts on the other. We are right on a creek bank under some very large and fine shade trees. I expect we will Commence crossing the Cumberland this evening or to-morrow. Twenty-two miles across—The Yankees are said to be holding one of the passes through which Genl [S. B.] Buckner [will have] to pass—and some say they are occupying McMinneville and others that they have abandoned it. Genl [B. F.] Cheathim's Division is crossing the Mts today. There is very little for man or horses in this country so far. The Yankees have foraged it pretty thoroughly. I hope we will get some where after a while where we can find something—our horses are suffering...I am now very well—much better than while I was in camp at Tynersville...

As stated above, the Confederates went directly into Kentucky. Once there, Bragg's plan was initially successful, forcing Buell onto the defensive and providing a means for Kentuckians to support the Confederate cause. But Southerners overestimated Kentuckians' enthusiasm for secession. And as volunteers for the rebel army were few, Confederates soon became disheartened. Also Bragg and his subordinates began to bungle the campaign, so that even the loyal S. H. Dent had doubts about the strategy. Dent's letter from Kentucky was written shortly before the setback at Perryville (8 October), which would cause the Confederates to retreat from the state. He could not resist teasing his wife about the "ladies."

Camp near Bardstown Ky
Sept. 27, 1862
My own Dear Wife,

...I went in the country to-day the first time since I reached this camp I found more people favorable to our cause than I thought this country contained. I made some purchases for our mess—prices more reasonable than I ever found them before. A Young Lady gave me a secession flag. Don't you feel jealous—especially as she singled me out of three Gentlemen the other two being single ones. But that is not all—she knew I was married—another promised to come and see me at our Camp. But I have just learned that we are to move camp to-morrow so I think it doubtful whether she will find us or not. It seems to me that we are going to hunt a good camp and remain here for the winter—that seems to me rather strange. I thought we would certainly take Louisville—but I suppose Genl Bragg knows best...I think however that we are going to hold the principal portion of Ky and give the people a chance to do something for themselves and if we increase our army by Kentuckians joining us that we will try and get possession of the entire state...a good many of our men are sick I mean in our army. They suffered a good deal on our march. I still preserve my usual health...

Bragg was a controversial general. This had been the case from the beginning of the war, even at Pensacola. A good organizer and trainer of troops, he was not an effective field commander. Abandoning his offensive plan at Perryville when he still had a chance to win, Bragg accelerated the officers' and troops' disillusionment with him. T. Stanford, who had been separated from his company, was particularly embittered by retreat out of Kentucky. Stanford was surer of where the army had been than he was of where he would be going.

Tennessee
Fall, 1862
Eliza,

...I have already told you of the hardships & trials of our men which will cause you to pitty & grieve for them but they all Seem to rejoyce & talk as tho they gained a victory at getting this far back they never felt Safe till Since they passed the [Cumberland] Gap the Yanks followed them close up & pushed them hard and they are So much pleased at getting through that they are willing for the march through Kentucky to be blotted out of the page of history that Shall mark there course and be remembered as Braggs great retreat every man that I have conversed with regrets being connected with it to have an army

Suffer So much and at Such Cost and accomplish So little is too bad is outrageous, but I am not the one to write about this affair, as I did not participate in it I wrote you this morning that our destination was Murphysbourrough but I have heard Since that we would be ordered to Mobile or Some where on the Coast which I am inclined to think is most likely to be the case as Gen [Jones M.] Withers & Gen [Franklin] Gardener are bothe from Mobile and I am in hopes we will go there I had rather Know to day that our Regt would go to the Coast this winter than to have a Forty days furlough if I go to the coast any where in Ala or Floridy you can come to See [me] when ever you please for I dont exspect to go home any more during the war if I keep my health & Company altho I May want to See you ever So bad...But I hope the war will close this winter. I cant See how it can continue long I think their are many men will appreciate the freedom and pleasures of a pleasant home who never did before if this thing would close out but many good farms will have vacant Seats round their fire Sides whose places never can be filled. So much for this righteous war...I know I troubble you a great deal but I allways troubble those I like best...and while I am in the Service I intend to have what I want if I can get it. Tell Mary Collins I have worn my blue Pants She wove for me everyday Since I left home and remember her Kindness greatfully & also Mrs Ryan for the Blanket She was So Kind & considerate to give I wish them long & happy lives. Well Eliza it is now getting late in the day and every axe is busy cutting wood we have just put on Some big logs & have a good fire that will burn all night the Snow is most all gone & I think we have fine weather now. Capt [Lee H.] Jennings found my muster & pay rolls and took care of them for my valiece was robed before he got to it...

Others might be sent to Mobile and Mississippi, but T. Q. Stanford was in Jones M. Withers's division and would remain in eastern Tennessee where he would continue trying to rejoin his company. For the moment, there was time to rest and write, because Buell was not pressing Bragg's army. For mismanagement and excessive caution, Buell would be replaced on 30 October by the seemingly more ready fighter, General Williams S. Rosecrans. Once in command, however, Rosecrans required several weeks to secure his lines before he began a march southward from Nashville. During the lull, Stanford told his wife, Eliza, how fortunate she was to be safely away from the western front, where civilians suffered considerably more than she did, he was sure.

Noxville Tenn
Oct. 21, 1862
My Dear wife,

I returned to this citty today at 12 oclock am after marching 16 miles as Soon as we could get a camp ground which 1 1/2 miles south of the citty...This was the greatest of all wars on the records of history ancient or modern there are not many fire sides but has a vacant Seat and many never to be filled a gain on earth...there are a great many troops camped a round this citty and Braggs army is comeing in [J. Patton] Anderson's Division is to be here to night. I cant hear of Withers Division and I dont Know where I go from here [John C.] Brecenridges men are leaveing for Nashville or going in that direction via of Chattanooga I guess we will be crowded here in a day or two I hope I can transfer my Co to there proper [command] or Some one else. I am...ancious to get to my own

Wednesday morning Sun up...I have Seen many the last few days who were in troubble they are Southerns from Ky. fleeing from the enemy they have left all except a few horses or a negroe or two. I have Seen many Caragees & old Stages filled with Southern ladies who have to leave every thing to Save them Selves now just think of their case & compare with those of Ala or Ga. If you recolect I told you that our people Knew nothing of this war and I Stick to it you ought not to grieve & take it to hart So bad I hope you will become more reconciled to your lot...I am here now waiting orders Subject to move at a moments warning and Know not where I may go towards Nashville or to Corrinth or Mobile or perhaps back to Ky, but thank God I am Well and can go any where that any other Soldier goes...Well we have just eat breakfast and had coffee & Sugar fried bacon & I got no coffee but a few time on the [grounds] an Irish man gave me they are the best folks in the world allways ready to obey I will rite to Will Soon I want to See him very bad but he is a legal exempt & he had best remain at home...the Major has gone to the citty & left me in command today...

Stanford's long, rambling letters are revealing of peaceable camp life, and especially the foot soldier's ready disillusionment with what seemed to be meaningless marching. In fact, this captain was almost ripe for the guerrilla cavalry. He also appreciated the recent reunion with his slave Jim, the trusty scrounger.

Camp 1 1/2 Miles North of Knoxville Tenn
Wednesday
Oct. 22, 1862
Dear Brother,

...[O]ur Army under command of Gen [Samuel B.] Maxey about 6000 Strong left here on Saturday the 11th and We marched 150 miles in ten days which was to the gap and back I did intend to give you a full detailed account of my march but when we had to turn back it threw Such a damper on the whole army that it also frustrated my plans as regards writing but to be Short I will Say...[we] went up by way of Clinton on the Clinch river, and Jacksboro also a County Site we marched 5 day along side of the Cumberland Mts the Scenery was beautifull. We came back by way of Taswell a Shorter rout we left the gap on Saturday & reach here yesterday 12 Oclock a. m. 16 miles from camp we came back apart of the way on the Waldens ridge...but the road runs the Valleys which are generally narrow. I Saw Some good farms well improved but the most people I Saw are of the 2nd or 3rd rate order I was very anxcious to visit the gap but Could not do So A corier met us 5 miles South of it on friday at 12 oclock we then camped for further orders I thought I woul go & See it then but Lt Col Presley issued an order to make out a transfer for the men as we learned that the army was comeing So I had to do it next morning we were about going up when this bugle Sounded for marching we went up within one mile I could See where the Yankees had cleared up and planted there batteries it is not doubt an interesting place but we had to turn our backs on it and return to Noxville the men came along in moody Silence Save now and then a cutting remark at Bragg or Some one else but that Soon wore off the men all want to join their commands very bad and So do I I dont like Such an organisiation there is not restrictions enough and our Major is an old Parson and did not Curse much So he was too Soft and easy to get his rights all the time but he is a good old fellow. I have no Idea how long we remain here [J. Patton] Andersons Division was to be here last night but [I] dont know whether it came or not. I went down to the Citty yesterday evening after we came and learned that Greenwood had come & brought Jim I did not See either of them as Green was on guard in town & Jim gone foraging I left my location for him and at daylight Jim came to my tent and was very glad to See him I miss him on the march tho Lt Grubbs had a good and faithfull cook but he never tried to get anything. Tom Culver was head of our mess and procured what he Could besides our rations allowed 11 days cost each $9.40 I did not leave the head of my Co but one day to forage I went before got milk & bread & alday at night I Saw a house away off under the edge of Mt I and Tom went to & got Supper So I fared well that day and next day I was Sick had Cholreamorbas but got Wms old filly rode 3 or 4 miles it wore off and Since then I have been as well as I could ask we bought Some mutton Some few chickens & Some geese on the way which was very good but all cost high as there has been an army here all the time I Saw a long train of wagons and wounded Soldiers comeing South and many Kentuckians both men & women negroes & horses fleeing from the Yanks I have [seen] Some of the best horses I ever Saw in my life coming from Ky but they could not be bought Well I am anxcious for a month or two to pass off I want to See what will take place in that time if this war continues longer I want to try guerrilla warfare and if was not for my men I would resign my Commission and be a private in a cavalry co. rather than hold a position in the infantry but I cant leave my men where they are...I find that I can march with any man I have found but I take care of my feet wash them every night & Keep my Shoes in good order. I hope you have been suckessful in Salt making...I want to go to town this evening if the Major gets back I am in Command today...

Some correspondents emphasized the gore of battle while others avoided it. G. D. Bush's description of Perryville (8 October) was particularly stark. The Bush letter is part of the Thomas T. Bigbie collection, which is introduced in chapter 4. Apparently Bush, like the Bigbies, was in Company G, Thirty-Third Alabama Infantry Regiment.

Knoxvill Tenesee
Oct. 22, 1862
Dear Father and Familey,

...[T]he Boys is sow badley scattered that i cant hardley tell you a thing a bout them...our Regment was in a battle at pareys vill Cantuckey but the Bush Boys was not thare our Companey went in with 14 men and thare was 6 wounded and 1 kiled D. A. Thomas was kiled Dead on the Field A. J. Nobling was wounde verey Bad L. W. Bigbie was shot in the sholder withe one ball and in the neck with another but the wounds was not Dangerus J. M. P. Talley Shot in the leg Henrey McCulough shot in the knee and broke his knee all to smash

Jas. M. Ellis slitley threw the belley W. G. Waren struck with a peace of a bum on the sholder Thomas Branon was wounded but Dont know how Bad Capt [W. E.] Cooper was in the Battle and come out safe he come on to the Cumberlin Gap and Then he got with us thare and come with us to this place this is all i know a bout the Battle Wm. J. Spears is Deade W. D. Bush is Dead R. H. Adams is Dead Now i will tell you who of the officers of the Regment aot wounded Colonel [Samuel] Adams shot in the foot Capt [M. C.] Kinney shot threw the Bowels verey Dangerous Capt [W. E.] Doddson threw the leg Lieu Jos Pellum shot threw thigh and thigh broke verey Bad and that all that i know but thare is lots of the rest of the officers that is wounde the Regment went in to the Battle with 380 and thare was 167 kiled and wounde sow farther i can say to yo that [General] brag has left Cantuckey he was on his way to this place the last i new of him...

In contrast to Bush's graphic account, S. H. Dent consciously avoided such explicit detail about Confederate suffering and death at Perryville. He chose instead to write about horses and clothes but finally slipped at the end of the letter into the "horror" of executing Yankee bushwhackers. He understood the necessary dehumanization of war. Dent had not been home since he reenlisted at Pensacola in January 1862. Despite his joking, he had no intention of risking court-martial, being too honorable and ambitious for that. But the horrors of war were catching up with him. E. B. Young of Eufaula was Dent's father-in-law.

Camp Eight Miles from Knoxville Tenn
Oct. 25, 1862
My own Dear Wife,

...I have some idea that our...destination for the winter is Corinth or that vicinity...I do not know how long we will remain here—but several days I expect. Men and horses are very much fatigued and worn down. The men are actually emaciated from long marching and hard living—for four days my men had for bread—corn. The officers among the number. A supper of parched corn and pork does not go so badly after all. Our Division is really reduced in numbers since we entered Ky and I think the men will not be fit for duty under an month's recruiting. About the only thing I have to show for my Ky Campaign is a good looking bay horse which I got up there and which I want to send as a present to Mr Young when I get near Eufaula...I was offered $250 for him yesterday—but I refused to sell...He would be worth a good deal more than $250 in Eufaula. Horse stealing is quite Common in the army—and I had my horse stolen from me one night—but found him next morning. I saw Pat Powers yesterday going to Knoxville hunting his horse which some one had stolen from him at the Gap. He was well and said his Company would be at the Gap this winter. I heard that the whole of Hillard's legion would be there. I went into Ky thinking I would get every thing I needed but I came out not a single bit better than I went in. My shirts are wearing out—my boots in the same fix and hat utterly gone. Unless I get some clothes soon I do not know what I will do. If I had got into a fight as I expected I would have supplied myself abundantly. Well Darling it has been now nearly nine months since I was home. It seems to me it has been at the least two years. It seems hard that the best part of my life should be spent in the army...The weather is warm and pleasant for October—much more so than one would expect...If I can't get a regular leave—and we go to Chattanooga and all around Corinth I am going home by getting off the cars...And run the risk of being Courtmartialed. What do you say to that? I hope I will get a regular leave however and be saved all that trouble...Darling if you can send my coat [overcoat] to me I wish you would but I hope to get home and then I can get it myself. I am so tired so very tired of this horrible war. What think you Darling of sixteen men being hung in one pile. Well sixteen Yankee bushwhackers were hung on the Cumberland river on our retreat. They were taken by our cavalry and it is said they had been following up the army on this whole march. This is certainly the most horrible war the world has ever seen. What a horrible condition society will be left in when it closes...

Having tried for some time to locate his regiment, Captain Stanford finally rejoined his men near Knoxville. In this grieving letter, he wrote his wife of the deaths and suffering of their mutual friends during the hard retreat out of Kentucky. The troops had been hungry and ill clothed, but things were now looking up. The camaraderie with his company was warm, although the Thirty-Ninth as a whole included some thieves who in Stanford's absence had appropriated his "things."

Near Knoxville

Fall, 1862

M y Dear Eliza,

...[O]n Friday last Col Clayton came to my camp at Knoxville i learned from him something of...our Regt also with much regret that Corporal Owens of my Co was killed by a Shell bursting and a piece passed through him killing him instantly...no better nor braver Soldier died than Corp S. B. Owens on yesterday morning I took the men of our Brigade of Hospittle Rangers who belong to the 39th & we marched through the Storm to our Regt...the Snow melting is a nasty time to any on the march...[Several were] left not far behind I think they will Soon come up the men have had a hungry time tho most of them look well tho they had a long time on very Short rations they lived on parched corn and acorns for a Short time tho & the most of them need clothes very few have more than they had and a great many are very near barefooted it is hard to See them in the Snow without Shoes but they complain but little I am truly grieved at their condition When I cant help them...last night a[t] 9 oclock we got two good tents to each Co & [pitched] them and got Some Wheat Straw and made a good bed So we have fared well So far but Some men have no blankets all my things was thrown out I lost every thing but my Shirt and wash pan all my Co books and papers & all the officers in our Brigade [it is said] suffered the Same way but I believe the most of my things are here in the Regt for I Saw my vest just now. I will lookout for them and have what I can find that is worth having...we have the best beef I ever eat & good flour & the men Say When they get enough to eat they can Stand anything & I believe it I hope I can remain with them here after they are a good Sett of Men and gave me a hearty acception hopeing I never would leave them again I will not while I can Serve them...I learn that we remain here for the day then go to Murphysburrough but all uncertain...

T. Q. Stanford's next letter was from Tullahoma. Now he was closer to Murfreesboro, where the Federal General Rosecrans would meet Bragg in a major battle at year's end. Under pressure from Washington to invade eastern Tennessee because of Unionists and rail connections there, Rosecrans nevertheless concentrated at Nashville and made further preparations before moving. Thus, Stanford had time for a long letter to his physician brother (apparently Will), in which the captain advised the other to stay at home out of the army and attend to their business or else join the guerrillas if he had to fight. Stanford was enjoying the relative improvement in living conditions for his company. Although preoccupied with personal comforts, the captain sensed that military activity around Nashville was quickening.

Tullahoma Tenn.
Wednesday evening
Nov. 19, 1862
My Dear Brother,

...I wish I could be with you I think [I] would enjoy it for a while especially the fishing & hunting and more So the eating part...you will make any alterations in our [live] Stock & that you See proper...

[November] 20th...I would have been very glad to had you come with me but it goads me to think you could not remain as you were but that is past and we must look to the future I am pretty Sure you Could (get! the Same position here but would you have it Sometimes I want you to have lit) then I think it would be makeing too great a Sacrafice of feelings to do So I am anxious for you to do Something in the Service Knowing what you Can do had justice been awarded to merit. Dr. Thomas has resigned and left us Very mueh to the Satisfaction of the men of the Regt Dr Dickinson died whose death was much regretted by the Whol Regt Dr Crimes is absent Sick & no one Sory nor many out side Co B would not Shed tears if he died or left the Regt Dr. Jones has been acting for Some time A young man Dr. Fletcher has been assigned here I know nothing about him I want you to See those guerrilla Cos & Satisfy yourself with them their may [be] a good opening there but at the Same time I want you to remain with our families tho I Know it will not Satisfy you but you are cleare by two Chances Claim your [medical] practice will cleare you or take charge of our business either will do and we have a great deal at Stake and no one to look after it now if you don't asi[s]t our Mother and our families Who need protection as much so as any other families in the Confederate States and we are tolerable well represented in the [army] and can Say without any compunction of concious that we have done as much for the Southern cause as our means would allow and no one has made greater Sacrifices than yourself So if you Can (after weighing tho carefully) remain with our folks it will meet my hearty approbation...but I will not advise as I am not able to follow my owne...but I would Say this to you if you ever...go in to it go mounted either in infantry or Cavalry and if I never come home again and my boys grow up in your reach Say to them to go to war at the first Call & go mounted if posoble I will not Say how many advantages they have but enough to Convince me I will here State one little circumstance the Pickets round here does not halt a mounted man neither Soldier or citizen When a foot man cant go any where without a pass...there are So many men absent Some off in hospittles that never intends to come not one of my me[n] at Tyners Station have come in yet they are Stewards details & & Some are too cowardly to come...I would be glad [if] all my men that is worth having could keep well I have lost Several good men that I dont Know what has become of them...I have only 31 men present...What men I have here (except Taylor) are good effective men and I am very much attached to them they are good Soldiers give me but little trouble they endeaver to please me in evey particular and we are all getting to be tolerable well drilled we have two Co. drills before 12 of one hour each one battalion drill in the after noon which Keeps us busy from daylight til dark and a lesson to recite in each Volum of [William J.] Hardees T. Ts [textbook on tactics] I am getting along much better than I use to but my Ranger Co rubed the rust off before I got to the Regt and I went to the discharge of my duties with an intention of coming fully up to the medium if I cant come up best. My health is good never better I am heavier than at any time in my life and I enjoy the life as well as anyone here tho I Stay close about my Qrs there is not much intercourse between the officers here I have almost none out side Co B...Col Clayton has been more Social with me than he use to be and fact has done me Some favours which I apreciate tho [I] like him very much & for gives his petish ways and so far as can guage up to ate he is good to his men, but pretty hard on Some officers. Some deserve it too...we are not So destetute as I onced feared we were for we can now get plenty of Clothing & Shoes all Complete for a soldier except hats yesterday we drew good Shoes at 4.50 pr Pair I drew Shoes for all but one man who wore large nos we did not draw much lothing...you would laugh to See Some men hanging cloths they was off & burn their old cloths put on their new ones and feel much better nd they are all in good Spirts now a good Camp round plenty wood & water good rations of bacon beef & flour new cloths & plenty money yesterday we Paid off the Companies up to the 31st of August nd I am now at work on Pay rolls to pay up to the 30th Oct Which I think we will get the money on as soon as we are ready to receipt for it I regret their not getting it in time to Send home as their is where he most of it ought to be for they Spend it freely here. Soldiers now live on the principle of (to day we [li]ve to morrow we die) and they let tomorrow provide for its Self. I hope you will get me a good pr Boots or Shoes I had mine Spoiled by the 1/2 Sole hat was put on in cleyton [Alabama] which is raw hide. I drew a Splended pr of Pants made of Blue cloth for $9.50 which would cost me at Clothing house $35 the Clothing was made at Opelika Singular incident for it to come to their beloved 39th Ala most all the officers present took a pair & lef plenty I will Send you & Monroe a pr each I can get express Transpotation their was Some good over shirts but I did not get any of them they were Scerse & the first that got them took all So now on dress parade the 39th is a Spotted or Striped Set or a variety of uniforms out Some in new Suits from fine English Sock up to a fine Cloth Cap down to Slick raggs and tied up Shoes & hats...I think the intention was to reinforce our Troops who were in a Skirmish Near Nashville at that time the Indications now are to remain here Some time perhaps a month...

By the end of November, Stanford was at Murfreesboro where he described the Confederates' weak line of supply from Bridgeport, Alabama. The troops were now clothed, but some still raggedly. And the Federals had begun to sally out of Nashville down to La Vergne. Confederate uncertainty as to Yankee intentions probably explains the cheap, temporary quarters for winter that Stanford mentioned. Preaching and prayer were obviously more meaningful in these uncertain times. Reminders of death were always present, even for those like Stanford, who had every intention of living. Yet he would be killed in the battle of Murfreesboro (31 December–2 January). The following is his last extant letter.

Murfreesboro Tenn
Sunday evening
Nov. 30, 1862
My Sister Rock,

...[W]e move about So much that it is a bad chance to get letter I have not had but two letters from home since I left Knoxville a month ago...The chance from Chattanooga to this place is very difficult to get mail matter or any thing else the bridges being burnt at Bridge Port [Alabama] So there are but few cars on this Side the Tenn river and the engines are So light they cant pull a long train and it takes all they can do to transport the government Stores a few troops & Tho the bridges are nearly completed So I hope for better times in that respect Soon. I heard last night that Some of our detailed men were there not able to get there boxes on for want of transportation among [them] is Sergt W. C. Espy who I hope will Come in Soon for we are needing him very bad or the Clothing that he went for, every Sunday morning and this morning on inspection my company passed (good) in Point of arms and accoutrements but did not pass well in regard to neatness of dress and the reason is this Some time ago the Regt was all a like about Clothing but Some of the men who were Sent home for Clothing have come in and Some Companies are well clad while those Who Sent home for their Cloths and not received did not draw any either looks tolerable ragged by the Side of those who have the new Suits...it is much best to get clothing here as the government furnishes Such things much cheaper than any one at home can

We are camped on a Small river where there is plenty of timber which we need for fire as we have cold weather here...

Last Thursday morning I heard the commencing of a Sharp Skirmish which took place at L[a]vergene 15 miles above here between our Cavalry forces and the enemy we lost 5 killed and some wounded the enemy advanced three miles and drew back burning houses and destroying property of cittizens as they went we...were put in readiness for the action but did not move tho we may not be Idle long. Tomorrow we commence building winter Quarters on a cheap plan by Setting up rails and poles round a pole on forks then cover with leaves & trash and dirt then build a chimney to one side and then we have a house we are learning to live here more eaquinomical than we use to think of at home we had preaching today in our regt. I heard a good Sermon and an excelent Prayer which I fully endorse in every particular God grant it may be So...

S. H. Dent was also near Murfreesboro at this time and, like other Confederates, was not quite expecting the coming battle. Thus, he was more concerned about the Mississippi situation (which was not yet so bleak as he intimated) and about his desire for a furlough. He enjoyed boxes from home and was embarrassed to think how unkempt he would appear to his beloved Nannie. The forthcoming furlough would remove Dent from the battle of Murfreesboro. President Davis was about to make Joseph Johnston coordinator of the western armies in Tennessee and Mississippi. Pemberton, Van Dorn, and Price were on the defensive in Mississippi after losing the battle of Corinth on 3 and 4 October.

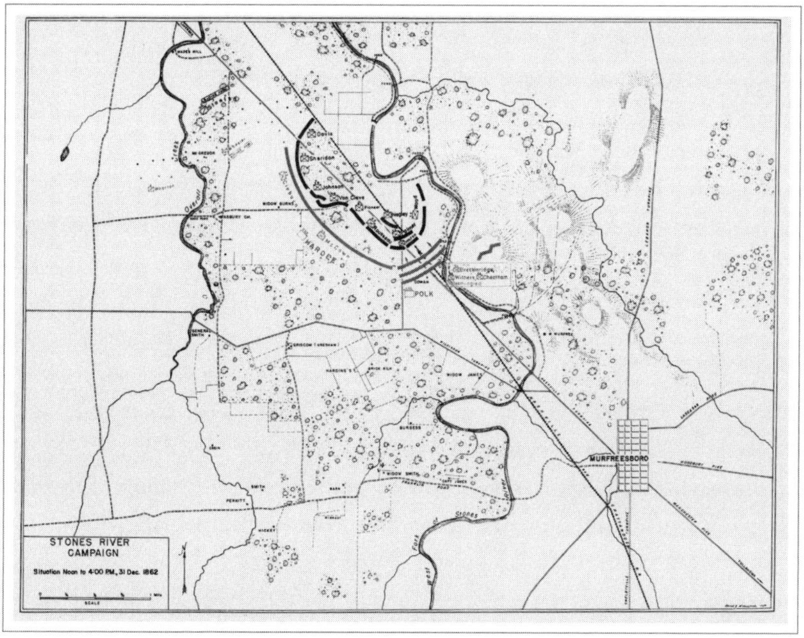

STONES RIVER CAMPAIGN, 1862

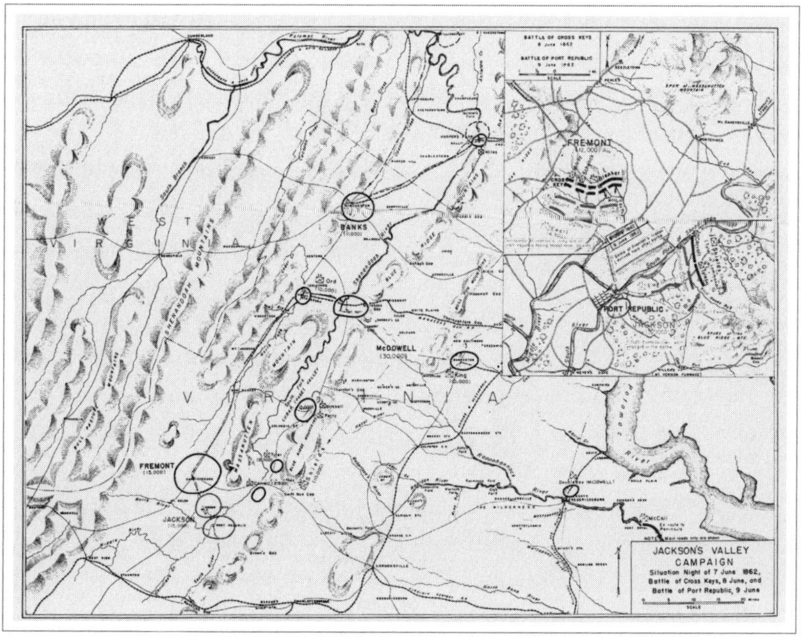

JACKSON'S VALLEY CAMPAIGN, BATTLE OF CROSS KEYS,
AND BATTLE OF PORT REPUBLIC, 1862

Camp near Murfreesboro Tenn

Dec. 11, 1862

My own Darling Nannie,

...[John H.] Morgan's affair at Hartsville [Tennessee] was brilliant. He took more prisoners than he had men. Twenty-one hundred and ten [nearer 1,700]. The Yankee prisoners were in Murfreesboro Tenn yesterday being paroled. They were a dirty rough looking set of men. I thought some of our soldiers looked hard and rough—but these prisoners looked as rough as I ever saw any of our men look. They were better clothed than most of our men. This is very fine weather—as fine as one could wish. The Company is very healthy...Well Darling I shall make out my application to-day for a leave of thirty days whether I get it or not and I am going to give a Chapter of reasons as long as my arm. I am going also to see Col Garner, Bragg's Adgt. Genl. Genl Joe Johnston I hear left this morning for Miss. I hear it rumored that we are going there—but I cant say any thing about it. From what I hear it looks as if some one ought to go there and stop the headway of the Yankees. They will soon have all the State. Bruton has just received a box and I have got molasses candy all over this side of the paper—none of their boxes come up to mine. The rice and potatoes are heartily enjoyed, by all hands...The rail road between here and Bridgport is in a horrible fix. The cars are full of lice and no seats...I am sorry Darling that I have no nice uniform coat and pants and vest to wear home. I think I shall order a suit in Augusta it will cost me one hundred and thirty dollars—rather heavy and I hardly know whether I can stand it or not. I expect you will have the same opinion of my appearance that Bill McTyer had when you see me. I am rough looking and hard looking and I am not certain that my friends will know me when I get home—my hands are black and rough looking and inclined to be chapped. My beard is haggard and rough—and my clothes are about on a par with the rest. I have set around a log fire and been smoked so much that I am in a fine state of preservation however and look as if I would keep for a long time...Every thing has quieted down here about a fight and the general impression now is that we will not fight. Cheathim made a reconnoisance some days ago—but found the enemy too well posted and too strong to effect any thing and therefore fell back to his original position...

I heard to-day that President Davis was in Chattanooga and that he had dispatched for General Johnston—but I hear so much that turns out to be untrue that I don't know whether to believe it or not. The department of the west is certainly in a very bad fix. Pemberton's army seems not to be worth any thing—or rather the army of Van Dorn and Price. The fight at Corinth turns out to be a very serious disaster. I see foreign intervention is again talked of. If it is coming I wish it would hasten I should be delighted to be able to spend the winter at home—at least the balance of it...If I have good luck I will be at home about eight or ten dats after you receive this...

On the day after Christmas 1862, Rosecrans's army left Nashville, moving southeast to find and fight Bragg. It was a cold and rainy time for it. But the two armies soon confronted each other near Murfreesboro at Stones River, with Bragg striking first and with strength at dawn on 31 December. That day's fighting ended with the Confederates in position to defeat Rosecrans's army. But Bragg again manifested his indecisiveness and unwisely waited for two days before he resumed the attack. When the Confederates' tardy advance stalled on 2 January, the temporary setback persuaded Bragg to retreat, thereby giving the Union forces a victory they were genuinely surprised to receive. Now Murfreesboro was Rosecrans's, and Bragg moved to Tullahoma and other points south. His only satisfaction was that the Confederates had so mangled the Union army they would require several months to recuperate before moving against Chattanooga (June 1863). Despite the growing distrust of Bragg's combat ability, he would remain in command of the Army of Tennessee until after Chattanooga had fallen to the enemy.

3

Virginia: 1862–1863

In 1862, while General Braxton Bragg saw his promising Kentucky campaign disintegrate, Confederate forces in Virginia successfully contained the Union's several offensive moves against Richmond. The defense of Richmond during 1862 and 1863 is the broad concern of this chapter. As previously noted, Colonel James Cantey spent an uneasy winter at Centerville, Virginia, late in 1861. There was, however, little danger of a Federal attack then because General George B. McClellan was reluctant to use his well-trained troops until he could be sure of landing a death blow to the Confederacy in one mighty campaign.

Such certainty, of course, is seldom possible, especially in war, and particularly when up against opponents such as Joseph E. Johnston, Thomas J. "Stonewall" Jackson, and Robert E. Lee. Denied the certainty he desired, McClellan continued to drill his troops and enlarge his army until it doubled the size of the Confederate force in northern Virginia. Unaware of his numerical superiority, McClellan waited until the Lincoln government virtually forced him to attack. But when the Union army finally moved, McClellan's undue caution played the hands of Confederate defenders. Perhaps this Federal commander had overlearned the lesson of Irvin McDowell's humiliation in July 1861, when his undertrained volunteers appeared to break under fire before they ran back to Washington away from the battlefield of the first Manassas.

Whatever the full story, McClellan's trepidations in 1862 led him to plan a less direct advance on Richmond, this time by way of the peninsula between the York and James rivers. To accomplish this, Federal troops had to be moved southward by water to the peninsula during the months of March and April. Meanwhile, other Union commanders with smaller forces were supposed to occupy northern Virginia, particularly the Shenandoah Valley, from which place they would later reinforce McClellan's main army, which would be pushing up the peninsula toward Richmond. The idea was to put the Confederate capital in a vise that would destroy it, thereby killing the nation and ending the war in one mighty sweep.

This, however, was not to be for three more years. In the meantime, Joseph Johnston, commander of the outnumbered Confederate army, moved into position against McClellan's advance up the peninsula. And though Johnston would have to retreat back toward Richmond, T. J. Jackson in the Shenandoah Valley proceeded to show that a "Stonewall" could move very rapidly. The nickname came from the first Manassas battle. But what had stood solid at Manassas was now like lightning, as Jackson's corps delivered rapid blows against the Federals who were advancing in the valley. Jackson's numerous strikes in northern Virginia and his feints toward Washington (from 23 March to 9 June) kept a large number of Federal troops near their capital and therefore away from McClellan, whose peninsular campaign was beginning to bog down before the defending Confederates. Then, at the Battle of Seven Pines (Fair Oaks) near Richmond in May, General Joe Johnston was wounded. This development meant that the resourceful Lee would now command the Army of Northern Virginia. McClellan's difficulties on the peninsula and Jackson's success in the valley enabled the latter to neutralize Federal troops near Washington and still have time to join Lee for the successful repulse of McClellan in the Seven Days' Battles around Richmond (26 June–1 July).

It was in this context that an ecstatic William Pouncey wrote his parents in Daleville, Alabama, about the excitement of being with General Jackson in the valley campaign. Jackson, a staid Presbyterian, hardly seemed the type to inspire such romantic loyalty. But this was the case, nevertheless. Pouncey was nineteen years old and a private in Company E of Colonel James Cantey's Fifteenth Alabama Infantry. He wrote home in the interval between the valley campaign and the Seven Days' Battles.

Valley Va.
June 11–15, 1862
Dear parents,

...I have some news to write you this time; we have Joined "Jacksons Army" & went up to frontier and got after "old Banks" [Nathaniel P.] & ran him on the other Side of the potomac into Maryland—it caused A great deal of excitement in Washington City! Old Linckon called out all of his malishigs, but the funnyest part of it was, when we were up at "Harpers Fery" the Yankies sourrounded us and we had to fight our way back! Our regiment has not been engaged but once. W. B. Mills Lt. was killed; he Is the only one that was killed in our Company. Bert Lanier was wouded in the foot; the ball never entered into his foot, it struck him on the Shoe heel, brused it and burnt a blister—I the loss in our iment was: Nine killed and thirty Six wouded. We were in the fight on the 8th of June [at Cross Keys, where John C. Fremont was immobilized] that is the day that lieutenant Mills was killed he was shot through the head. It was A great loss to this Company. Nearly every Man in the company loved him like A brother. In going to Harper's ferry and back—Jackson had Seven [or five] fights and give them A whiping every time & captured five and Six thousand prisoners, two are three thousand dollars worth of medicine and A good many Wagons and several batterries; we never got very many men killed; until the fight on the 9th of June [at Port public], we had A good many killed & wounded, I heard that Johns[t]on had given them A good whipping at Richmond [Seven Pines]; ran them back to their gun boats! I recond I have said enough About fights, when I come out of the fight I came out hout any clothes; but what I had on; we were out picket duty and they came too large A force for regiment and we had to retreat back to our es and we were so near...rundown; we cut loose knapsacks and left them; and that left us all without Clothes, only what we had on—& I lost that Shirt that Albert brought me. When you get the chance send me another one like it; and I will put it on if the Yankies get it—they will get me with it!

McClellan's peninsular campaign met immediate Confederate resistance at Yorktown, Williamsburg, and other points. G. C. and T. J. Barron of the Fourteenth Alabama Infantry (whose letters appear in chapter 1) were among the army there. No sooner did their regiment reach Virginia in November 1861, than it proceeded to Yorktown, where it was brigaded under General Roger Pryor of Virginia in James Longstreet's corps. Falling back with Johnston's army before General McClellan's advance, the Barron's Fourteenth Regiment fought at Williamsburg, Seven Pines, Mechanicsville, and so on through the Seven Days' Battles. At some point in this fighting, the son, Thomas Barron, wrote home about strenuous troop movements, berry picking, and the blisters on his hands from building breastworks of log walls that protected the defending Confederates from lethal Federal firepower.

Priors Brigade Camp At [?]

Dear Mother & Sisters,

...We move yesterday from the camp that we were at when Mr Brisky was here we have move a bout three Miles today was a very hot day [for] a soilder to move for he [has] to toat all he has Mar [when] I got here an put up [my tent] I went out in one wouds [and picked] some hucles berries there [are] heaps of

Them. I eat [some] for you all It made me imagine Some of our berry huntings Mar we have got [to] throw up brestworks my hands are blistered I done it last week a throwing up brestworks I have not work more before Since I left yorktown Mar Par [is] as well I am as well as [I] ever was in all of my life...

Sometime earlier than Barron's letter, while Confederates were still at Yorktown, William W. Andrews of Milltown, Chambers County, Alabama, wrote his widowed sister, Elmira Crowder, of his willingness to look after her oldest son, James, "if he wantes to go to war." This is the introduction to James P. Crowder and his several letters, which play a central role in this chapter. Yet Andrews's message has several points of interest in itself. As a member of the Thirteenth Alabama, which had been in Virginia since July 1861, he exemplified relatives' looking out for one another in the military, the uncertainty of adequate food, and a soldier's carelessness in managing money. Finally, he was near the Merrimac, *which was the Confederate ironclad that at Hampton Roads on 8 March 1862 momentarily terrified the Federals until they, on the following day, sent the Monitor, another ironclad, to neutralize the threat.*

Yorke Towne Va
1862
Dear Sister,

I have the opertunity to in forme you that I am well & I hope theas lines wil finde you & all the reste in good health I am stationed in Yorke Towne I have heard from you several times but not from you by leter, this is the first that I have writen to you I wal like to receive a leter from you very much we have colde wet wether know prospect of a fight we have got out of our cloth tents, in our cabins we know fare sum beter I wante James to come hear if he wantes to go to war Sende him to me I get plentey to eat tell Nancey McKnight to write to me for I wante to hear from her very much I have had the misfortune to loos twentey five dollars & fifty cts I drew 35 dollors, Jesse Robertson & John Daniel has been hear to see us tell all the children howdey for me I wante to see them all & all the reste of my friends or hear from you often we have 50 or 60 canons on Xd round our linest work & a cros the river we have as many more I was in the notion of going on boarde Mary Mc a war St[eamer] I have give out the notion I close by Sidecircling by self you afectionate brother until death fare wel...

James P. Crowder did not join his Uncle William Andrews in the Thirteenth Alabama. Yet he did leave his widowed mother and eight younger siblings at home and proceeded to the Virginia front as a member of I Company, Forty-Seventh Alabama Infantry. Enlisting for a three-year term, Crowder was at Loachapoka, Alabama, in May 1862 when the regiment was organized. Already in Virginia by late June, his outfit was assigned to General Jackson's corps and soon saw the ordeal of battle at Cedar Mountain on 9 August 1862. Before that date, however, there were numerous skirmishes as the Union army organized for another offensive in northern Virginia. From Gordonsville on 1 August, Crowder described preliminary conflict. The time was about midway between the Seven Days' and second Manassas battles. Crowder's concern for relatives in Virginia was indicative of the sense of "place" or rootedness that characterized many Southerners.

With the Federals threatening Richmond, his description of rapid troop movements illustrates the continued mobility of General Jackson's army.

Camps near gordans Vill Va

Aug. 1, 1862

Dear Mother sister and brothers,

...I can here the cannons every day or to I herd very hevy cannon action last night to wards Richmon tho I dont no where it was our reagtment and several others was march out las Satur in to the battle field for a fight 'ho the yankes did not stay to sea us come up when we got there tha was all gone and then we went back to the camps that we left that morning witch was abou 5 miles from the place where we went to attack the yankes on Tuesday night after wards we had orders to cook up too days rashins by 3 o clock that night and to bea read to start by day light now we all thoght that tha was a going to hav a fight tho we march about 10 miles and struck up camp and there is no yankes a ner here...yo wanted to no whether I got my bedclose or not I got them all and I hav got me a good pare of shoes and as for wooling close I think that I can get them here as cheap as yo can so dont bother abou them yet a whyle Mother yo said somthing abou Uncle Wiliam Anders I have not herd a breth of him yet I hav herd of Cosen henry Crowder since I hav bin up here he was in the fight at richmon [Seven Days] and got slitley woonded tho he is well now I hav not never herd of Gus nor Seaton Weaver since I hav bin up here it is said that the 13th Ala redgment is about one mile from our camps and if I can get a pas tomorow I will go and

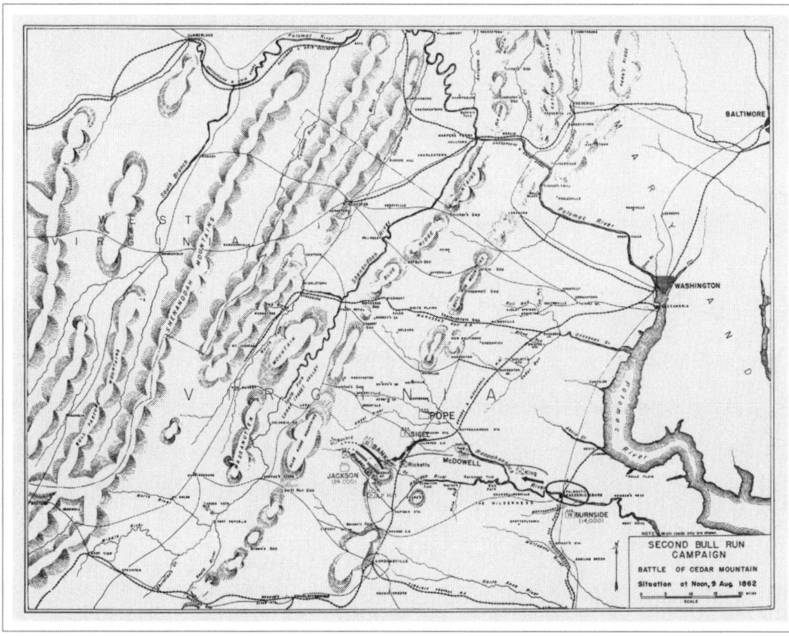

SECOND BULL RUN CAMPAIGN, BATTLE OF CEDAR MOUNTAIN, 1862

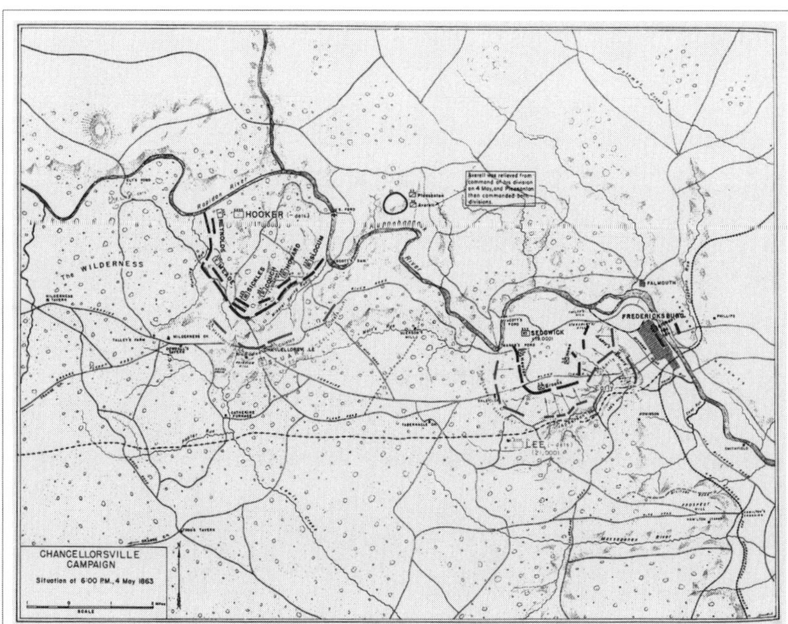

CHANCELLORSVILLE CAMPAIGN, 1863

sea if I can here any thing of Uncle Wiliam yo must excuse my short leter as paper is hard to get and as for stamps we cannot get them that is the reason why I do not right to the girles I cannot get stamps to put on the letter. So I must come to a close...

Early in August, as the discredited George McClellan was withdrawing from the peninsula south of Richmond, Union General John Pope was already preparing another offensive in northern Virginia. Once again, Thomas J. Jackson interrupted Federal plans by attacking the Union advance under Nathaniel P. Banks at Cedar Mountain on 9 August. While Cedar Mountain was a Confederate victory, the whole of Pope's army was too large for Jackson to challenge alone. Thus he waited until R. E. Lee (freed by McClellan's withdrawal) could march northward, where they united their armies against Pope's force in the second battle of Manassas (29–30 August). It was the victory over Banks at Cedar Mountain that Crowder described below. He was mistaken about numerical inferiority in this preliminary contest. The casualties were 2,400 Federals and 1,300 Confederates.

Camps near gordons Vill
Aug. 13, 1862
Dear Mother,

...I ricken yo will here of the fight before yo get this letter and I know that yo will want to here from me tho I can say for my self tha I went through safe Mother on last fryday evning abou one our by sun we lef our camps and marched abou six mils and stop and staid there all night and the nex morning we started again and march ten miles and pitch in to a fight we had abou ten thous and tha had about twenty thousian the fight commenst about too ours by sone and continued untill after dark a whyle tho we gaind a complete victrey over them takened a good many prisners and run them clear off our redgment was in the fight and suffered grat lose we went in to the fight with a little over three hondered men and got a 11 kiled or woonded out of the redgment our Company went in to the fight with about 40 men and got 1 kiled and 13 woonded tho I did escape unhurt tho the bulets past me as thick as hale I shot 30 times at the enemy tho whether I kiled ary one or not I shal not say tho I can tell yo that I slep all a monkst the ded yankes that night we slep on the yankes battle ground I recken yo want to no how many that we lost in all tho I can not tell yo for we do not no yet tho hit is said that we loste eight hundered in kiled and woonded and the yankes lost ten thousan in kiled and woonded and takned prisners tho I dond no how true it is I will not be sure un till I do no hit tho tha say hit was the hardist fight tho that has ever bin yet for the length of hit tho we run the yankes back and got thousans of there arms and camp equipege tho I never pick up nothing but a inder ruifier haver sack and a canteen Mother if I cold sea yo I cold tell yo more nuse than I cold right in a weak tho as I hav bin a marching for the last sex or eight dais without much rest I will come to a close...

Eleven days before second Manassas, while Jackson's corps waited before marching against Pope's supply line, Crowder penned a description of his mild-mannered and puritanical commander. This strict Presbyterian of benign appearance was actually an avenger of the Southern cause. The troops' devotion to the Cromwellian Jackson is obvious. Images of the recent battle were still so strong in Crowder's mind that he relived Cedar Mountain (9 August) as though he had not previously communicated it. This young Alabamian had been near his army's left wing, which Jackson had momentarily mismanaged and allowed to be flanked, causing the heavy casualties Crowder described.

Camps near Gordans Ville Va
Aug. 18, 1862
Dear Mother Sister and brothers,

...[Y]o said that yo wanted me to send yo my amber type b u t ...there is no chance...we are abou one hundred miles from Richmon and I no noother place that I can get hit takened Mother yo all do regret that we are under Stonewall Jakson tho I had rather bea under him than any other General that I ever red of for he is the most mildes man that I ever saw for every time he passes by his men tha hollar so yo cannot here your ear for the nois he will rase his cap from his head and then his men will shought. he past by just as I was a reading the letter that I got from yo and I had to stop and hollar all the time he was passing b y his men is just as glad to se him pas by as tha wod to sea any of there folks...

Mother on last Saturday the 9th I was in a fight tho I did escape without a scratch but hit was a naow one for hit was a terible sight to sea the men foling all around some kild and others woonded we lost the most when the yankes flank our redgment yo ought to have sean the yankey cavaldrey trying to make a charge on our men tha came in to the field where the fight was agoing on and thare was not but fore of five that did escape the men fell from there saddels like rain...the fight was terrifick...last eavening...[?] had his gun in his han and hit was loded and he put his gunstick in hit and hit went off and shot off too of his fingers and his thum he is in my mes...

Mother I must com to a close for we have just now got ordors to cook up too days rashins and put it in our haversack and bea read to start on onfe minutes warning so I think that we will have a fight before many days again so I will come to a close and right again soon...

From the middle of August until Crowder's next letter in October 1862, the Army of Northern Virginia fought two major battles—second Manassas (29 August–1 September) and Sharpsburg (17 September). Second Manassas was a Confederate victory for Lee and Jackson over General John Pope. Sharpsburg or Antietam in Maryland was more of a draw between Lee and McClellan, though the Union claimed a victory there to use as a backdrop for President Lincoln's Emancipation Proclamation. Crowder's Forty-Seventh Alabama was engaged in both campaigns. And while the scope of the war was actually broadening, Crowder dared to hope the fight would soon be ended. His regiment's casualties at Sharpsburg were so large that he might purposely have avoided the subject of battle. He was a dutiful son who tried to comfort his mother and the children. It is possible he was at Burr Hill near Fredericksburg when he wrote the following.

Camps near bunkers Hill
Oct. 5, 1862
Dear Mother,

...[W]e are a doing well up here now we get a plenty to eat...tho we hav to drill very hard hit is the opinion of some that there will not bea any more big fiting till peace will bea made and I hope hit ma bea so is my prares.

Mother sicknes is a raging in camp since we hav stoped...I want yo to send mea one suit of close by the Right boys...If yo send me more than one suit I will hav them to through a way...I hav not got no close only wha I hav got on my back. I threw a way one suit of my close fin battle over one month ago tho I hav got a good blanket tho that is more than some of them has got ther is a heap of them that tha has not got any coat not blanket and no close only what tha hav got on there back there is no men that did take that long march [into Maryland and back] that has more than one suit of close and ther is a right smart of them bare footted we hav drew no money yet tho the oficers has fioet [fiat] to draw too or three times tho we hav not got any money yet the oficer has made out requicition for close for us tho we hav not never got any yet and I dont think that we will ever get any. that is the reason why we think that peace will bea made thay are not a fixing for winter Mother I hav got ten dolars and if I knew that yo was a neading hit I wood send hit to yo tho I will send too of hit to yo in this letter and risk hit by male Mother yo nead not bea a fraid of mea a lerning to play cards nor gambling for I hav not handle a deck of cards since I left home the last time we hav some thing to do in this contry besides playing card so I recken yo are a getting tired of reading so I will come to a close right to me as soon as yo get this letter...

Following the costly battle at Sharpsburg on 17 September, McClellan was again removed from command, this time for reluctance to pursue Lee's weakened and retreating army. Lee was soon safe in Virginia behind the Blue Ridge Mountains, and Ambrose E. Burnside replaced McClellan. By 13 December 1862, when Burnside was ready to cross the Rappahannock River at Fredericksburg, Lee had had time to assume a strong defensive position in the heights on the southern side of the river. There, in mid-December 1862, the Confederates repeatedly repulsed Burnside's several stubborn and foolhardy frontal attacks, inflicting heavy losses on the Union army before it withdrew into winter quarters north of Fredericksburg. Two weeks after this event, James Crowder wrote from Port Royal, which was near Fredericksburg. Here, the entrenched Confederates were once again watching the enemy across the Rappahannock. Despite the Yankee presence, there was plenty of time to think about winter clothing, religious services, and candy. Family lore argues that Crowder never received a furlough to visit home.

Camp near Port Royal
Dec. 28, 1862
Dear Mother sisters and brothers,

...[W]e are camped on the raperhanok about fiftey miles from Richmond and we are fortifing on this side of the river here very strong we can go to the river and sea the yankes on the other sid of the river as thick as thay can bea and thay have bin commuading all day up the river Mother yo sed that yo wanted me to get a furlow and come home tho ther is no chance for me to get off to come home for thay are a frade to let a man go home for fere that thay will take the small poks home Mother I have drewed 16 dolars and we are a going to drou a gain...the last of this month and I will try to send yo 25 dolars if I can by any one and if yo nead any more send me word and I will send yo all tha I can for I spend more here than I oght candey is seling here at 4 dolars a pound and me an J. Th. Walls boght 15 dolars worth of candey this morning and yo ought to sean us a eating candey appels is a seling at 8 to the dolar and every thing els according to that Mother I want yo to send me that poket Book that folds up severl times it is the one that paw uste to toate so much this one that I hav got is nerley wore out and I no yo hav not got any use for hit so I want yo to send hit to me when Thomas Right comes to the regtment and send me too pare of coton socks I dont want wool socks for thay scall my feat every time that I have to march Mother yo sed that yo wanted to hyer George out tho if yo can makout with the money that I send to yo dond hyer brother George out for we are bad a nuf scatterd now tho if yo think best to hyer him do so tho I want yo to send woord every time that yo nead money tho thay have quit giving any competition money and makes us pay for the clothing out of our monthley wages so that takes the biges potion of them to cloth us.

I have got from the government one pare of shoes 6 dolars one pare of pants 6 dolars twelve and a half cents one fine pare of drors 3 dolars so hit all a mount to 15 dolars and this morning I gave 5 dolars and a half for a good wool hat so I have got a good hat Mother there is [religious] meating this eavening so I will clos and go to meating.

Mother tell all the children howdey for me and all my friends Mother all I crave in this worlld is to sea yo all one more time on this earth So I will close by saying I remain your affectionate son untill death...

In January 1863 (shortly after the final Emancipation Proclamation and shortly before General Burnside crossed the Rappahannock again for an ill-advised "Mud March" against Lee), James Crowder wrote of his keen concern for the family at home. Some of these "worries" were repeated regularly throughout his correspondence. He addressed his brother, Thomas S. Crowder.

Campe Near hamtons Crose
Jan. 9, 1863
Dear Brother,

...I was very much pleased at your letter to think that yo was a trying to learn to right if yo will ceape a practing yo will sone bea so Mother neadent get no bodey to right for her yo can right for her your self I can read your riting very well after looking over hit I have no nuse of any importance to right more than I am in hering of the Yankes every day and sea there [observation] balloon.

Brother I was sorry to here that the small poks had got so closte to our house tho I hope yo all will try and stay at home and not get them amungste yo Brother I want yo all to bea vacktionated untill hit takes good an yo all and I wante yo to bea cearful and not get the smallpoks if yo can help hit It wood run me nearley distracted it I was to here that yo all had the smallpoks so bea cearful about them Brother I want yo all to bea good boys and worke hard and try to make something to live on for I wante to try to pay for the land for yo all to live on for if I was to die and the land not pade for yo all cold not pay for hit so I wante yo all to worke hard and les pay for the land this year there has bin a very large snow up here hit has bin nee deepe up here so I must close...

Finally, in winter quarters at Port Royal, Crowder reported that the clothes sent from home had been lost. He still needed them but was resigned to the bad luck that "will happen some times." He also gave an interesting description of the variety of "housing" in a Confederate winter camp.

Campe near Porte Royl Va
Jan. 13, 1863
Dear Mother sisters and Brothers,

...Mr. Peaters got to the Regt laste eavening he loste all the close that he had and also all the letters that was sente by Him I wod a have bin very glad to a have got my letters and gladder to a got my close for I have got on all the close that I have got the bad luck will hapen some times Mother we have got our house done and move in hit and we are a living well tho I wood like to come home and stay a whyle tho hit is a bad chance I think Mother we have to drill three times a day and that very harde Mother we have got all of our things from Richmond that we lefte there when we first went there

Mother I wish yo cold sea our winter quarters some of the men has got little loge caben dobd up with mud and some of them has got holes dug in the ground and covered over with dirt and some of them has got tents with chimleys to them and others has got flys to stay in the house that my men bilt is ten feate wide and twelve feate long we have got hit covered over with board and a good chimbley bilt to hit and we have got all the craks of the house dob up with mud so hit is a warm place tho I dont no how sone we may have to leave hit Mother I have not sean Uncle William [Andrews] in some time tho I here of him moste every weake he is camped about three miles from here so as the drum is a beating for drill I muste come to a close...

Once Burnside's "Mud March" had failed, he was replaced by Union General Joseph Hooker ,who began reorganizing the army of the Potomac. Hooker restored the troops' deflated morale and shaped them into an effective fighting machine. (It was this same army that would go on to win the war under the leadership of U. S. Grant in 1864–1865.) Meanwhile, as Hooker prepared for the spring offensive that would become Chancellorsville (1–5 May 1863), Crowder's letter from Richmond suggests the monotony of daily life for these Confederates in their defensive positions.

Camp Near Richmond, Va.
March 3, 1863
Dear Mother,

...We are Camped in 4 miles of Richmond tho I dont no how longe we will stay here...yo sed that yo was a going to sende me some clothing tho I donte neade them bad Mother we will draw money in a fiew days and tell the boys if thay will bea smarte I will sende them som money as swon as I draw if we donte move till I get my money I wante to go to Richmond and have my Ambertipe takned if there is any chance...

...[T]hay have stoped giving furlows for a whyle...I wood give all the money that I have made to sea yo all and stay with yo all awhyle

Mother I wante yo to plante a heape of corn and other stuf to live on for by nex fall what yo donte have yo cannot get for love nor money Mother as I was on garde duty...laste night I will close...

By mid-March, James Crowder was well advised to expect another Union attack toward Richmond, where Confederates were constructing special defenses. Meanwhile, his regiment's morale was good, although Crowder's love life was a shambles. He had finally received some new clothes and was obviously the cook for his mess.

March 15, 1863

Dear Mother sesters and brother,

...I have drew...[money] and I have bin to Richmond a time or too and I have spente som of hit and I have sente up a pass to go to Richmond to morow and I will get my ambertipe takened...Mother I think that there will bea a nother bige Richmond fite this spring fo thay are a bilding up the briste woacks every day thay are a fixing up to on the south side of Richmond this spring I think that juste as soon as the wether dos brake off so the yankes can travel that we will have the biges fite that has ever bin in Va. thay are a cuting down all the timber all a round Richmond and leavening them on the grounde. Mother we are a faring very well we get plenty to eate such as hit is We get [flour] and bacon and sugar and the army is all well cloth and shoes the army is in the beste condition that I ever saw hit for a fite the men is all well rested and in hy spirits and can get a plentey to eate and to drink...Mother I wante yo to send me som sowing thred in the nexte letter that yo do send...Mother I received a letter from R. A. hammond this morning tho hit was not a much of a one I think that she has found some one that she likes better than she does me so I donte intend to rite to her no more...I wante yo to rite to me ho is a going to sea her bea sure too to rite I wood like to sea her and talk with her a little I think that I cold change her notions to some degree.

...Mother donte yo sinde me no close without yo get a responsable man to bring them I have got close a plentey to do me some time till the spring of the year dos come and then I donte wante many close to toate for we will have to march as soon as hit gets warm Mother as hit is nearly diner I muste come to a close and get diner I will have rice and sugar for diner and fride Eggs and bisket with soder in them the Eggs coste 2.00 dolars a dosen and the soder 4.00 dolars a pound so I must come to a close...

Although the Federals were already launching raids, a late snowstorm delayed serious campaigning. In this situation, according to Crowder, a soldier might as well have a snow fight.

Camp Near Richmond Va
March 22, 1863
Dear Brother,

...[T]he Regt was orderd to go back to fedricks Burg the Yankes croste at fedricks Burg laste weeak and thay had a good smarte fite tho old Stward [E. B. Stuart] run them back [our] Regt lefte here laste wendsday morning with out geting there brekfast to go to fedricks burge thay march 24 miles and stop for the nite and that nite there came orders for the men to bea tuck back to there old camps at Richmond tho nex morning the men had march so hard the day before thay stade at camp all day Thursday and a thursday eavening hit comenste snowing and hit snowd all nite and a friday morning the snow was about nee deepe and then the Regt started back to old campes near Richmond and when thay got back friday eavening to there old camps the snow was nee deepe to them all the tents all was hald to Richmond except too C Company that had not bin hold off tho as good luck hapened I never wente with them I was detald and left to help hall bagage to Richmond so I got out of all worste of the wether and out of the marching tho I had a bad time at beste the snow is a melting off and hit is mitey wete and slopey Brother we had a bige snow fite to day the 47 Ala Regt whiped out the 4, 15 and 48 tho we had a harde fite the 15 Ala Regt took our flag away from us tho we got hit back agane Brother I sente my ambertype by Capt Burton that is furgaso [J. Fargerson's] old company commander he lives som where down above lafayett my ambertype coste me 6 dolars I had on my jeans coat that mother sente me laste fall hit had on bras butons as soon as I got the coat I cut off the tin butons and sode on brass butons that I cut off ave a dead yankes coate thay are nise butons I hat on a gray pare of pantes that I drew...

Fasting, prayer, and preaching probably prepared some Confederates for battle better than it did others, who apparently preferred fishing. Rumors of Crowder's regiment, the Forty-Seventh Alabama, joining the western army (in Tennessee or Mississippi) were persistent but unconfirmed until the following fall.

Campe Near Richmond Va

March 27, 1863

Dear Mother sisters and Brothers,

...[T]o day is a day of fasting and prar we have had meating in the Regt this morning I heard a good sermon preach and prar made by several good men...the boys is all gone a fishing sence preaching we donte have to drill to day Mother I received the Boots uncle James Emrey sente to me...my olde shoes was begining to ware oute tho if thay a bin one day later I wood a had a new pare of shoes...

All is quiet around Richmond...the Regt boys is generaly well thay are all in hy spirits and ready to march at a minets warning Mother there is som talk of us going to the western army tho I donte no how true hit is tho we all hope hit is so I have not heard from Uncle William [Andrews] in some time tho we are som distance aparte...

With Lee watching Hooker from the Confederates' near-impregnable trenches at Fredericksburg, General James Longstreet and his corps were detached southward to forage and protect against Federal attacks in the Petersburg-Suffolk area. (The rail connections at Petersburg made that place of central importance in the defense of Richmond.) Thus, James Crowder, whose regiment was recently transferred to Longstreet's corps, wrote from Petersburg in early April concerning rumors of their destination.

Camps Near Peters Burg Va.

April 7, 1863

Dear Mother Sisters and Brothers,

...[W]e are camped in three miles of Peters Brug we are closter to home now than we have bin since we got to Richmond laste Spring we drew five days Rashings laste eavening we have got orders to march in the morning at daylight we have got to cook up our rashings to day some ses that we are a going to north carliner Som ses to tenese tho I donte no where we will go...so as I have to cook rashing I muste come to a close...

By mid-April (shortly before Hooker's army began moving toward Chancellorsville), James P. Crowder was hospitalized with typhoid fever at Petersburg. An unnamed chaplain explained the situation to Crowder's mother. She must have appreciated the kindness that motivated this fragment, which bears no signature.

Poplar Lawn Hospital
Ward N 98
Petersburg, Va.
April, 1863

...I write at the request of your son, J. P. Crowder, who is now sick in the hospital at this place. He came to this city from Genl. Longstreets Company, which was then and is now in the eastern part of this State near Suffolk, on the 16th instant, having been sick only two days before he left his regiment. He is now improving, and he desires me to state to you that he is doing as well in all points of comfort as can be expected under the circumstances. The hospital in which he is placed, has kind nurses and skillful physicans to attend upon him, and I think, therefore, under the kind providence of God you may soon expect to hear from him as again being in good health and better prepared for the duties that await him in life.

As a minister and Army [Chaplain] I visited his bed this morning and in religious conversation with him found that he was very much in doubt as to the genuineness of his early profession of religion. He fears he has been deceived as to the true condition of his heart, and that he is not really a christian. I conversed with him freely and read to him al little tract entitled "Christian Invitation."...

As James Crowder recuperated at Petersburg, Thomas Barron and his father, Green, were with Lee at Fredericksburg, where young Barron, mindful of coming battle, thought to write his sister a sentimental aside on his pride that the army had made a man of him. Now he regretted his former sloth and remembered to say that Pa was well.

Camp Neer Fredericksburg VA
April 19, 1863

...Sister I am proud of my [self] I am glad The [army has taught me] to work Sister [I shall] never want more [?] happaness [for I am now] a man not a little Boy as when you last saw me Sister I am feared That you would [not know me as I have] changed so mouch my cheeks are not thin an pale [but] are full an red I will not discribe my Self to for you will Know me When [I come] home if I ever do Sister I often Think of you [?] I see you in dreams I Think of the blissful hours we have [enjoyed] together...in childhood but Those innocent pleasures have pass But I hope only for a short period...I want you to teach Mary all you [can] for...I...was a fool while [I was in] school I spent my time [in] idlness But the time [has] gone and I lament at it...Par's well...

On 6 May, two days after the battle of Chancellorsville (near Fredericksburg), James Crowder could report from a Petersburg hospital that he was "a mending." Being in southern Virginia, generals James Longstreet and John B. Hood had missed the battle of Chancellorsville in northern Virginia. Although a Confederate victory, it was a Pyrrhic one owing to 12,000 casualties in Lee's army and Stonewall Jackson's wound, which would soon kill him. It apparently never occurred to young Crowder that the legendary general might die.

Poplar lawn hospitle firste warde
Peters burge Va
May 6, 1863
Dear Mother,

...I am a mending I am able to go to the spring an get me a canteen of water and site there under the shad trees on the benches that is fix for the soldiers the treas is juste begining to bud out tho there is a good cool spring near the hospitle tho hit is a very steape place to go down and up Mother I have a clean nice bed to ly on and can get my close wash when I wante them wash I fare a grate deal bete than I expeced to fare at the hospital I get a plentey to eate and that is very [good] it is lofe bread and dride fruite and chicken and chicken soope...I was glad to here that yo had got my Ambetype tho the close that yo sente me by Dr. Barton I have not got them...so I will lose my cake for hit will spill before the boxes ever gets here if I donte lose my close hit will bea a wonder to me it is reported that [John B.] Hood's division is in this place today and if hit is my regt is in this place today thay started for fedricks burg tho old lee has whiped the yankes back on there on side of the river and ther is no use of hoods division going up there thay had a very hard fite up there with old [Joseph] hooker tho the papers say this morning that thay have all gon back to there side of the river olde Stone Wall Jackson got badley woonded the papers say this morning that he has his lefte arm takened off between his elbow and sholder tho thay sayde that he was a getting along very well and as generl A. P. Hill is slightley woonded our Generals seam to have bad luck in the laste fite thay have got too bea too brave thay go to close to where the little buillets fires too thick there has not any of them got hert for a long time so thay ware too brave...I have had the tifoid fever tho Dr. Burton broke hit up before hit got a good holte on me or I wood a had a worser time of hit than I have had So as I am tired I will come to a close for the presante...

Stonewall Jackson died on 10 May 1863 from complications of bullet wounds inflicted accidentally by Confederate pickets, who in the dark at Chancellorsville mistook him for the enemy. James Crowder, like the entire Confederacy, was stunned by this tragedy. Nor did Crowder overestimate the services of the mighty Stonewall when he hoped for "another Jackson to leade our men in battle." But as General R. E. Lee too painfully knew, there would be no replacement for Jackson. And as though this death sensitized Crowder to his own mortality, the young soldier from the Chattahoochee Valley now pondered anew his rejoining the regiment, responsibility to family, and the need to live a Christian life.

Poplarlawn hospitle warde No.1
Petersburg Va
May 17, 1863
Dear Mother Sisters and Brothers,

...I will bea able to go to my Regt in a shorte time...I got 22 dolars and I will sende yo som of hit the firste chance I get...the laste time I drew money I never sente yo any money for we was close to Richmond and I soon spente hit all...

Mother I have heard a good sermant preach this morning by a good preacher I think or he look so at leaste I have heard severl sermans preach since I have bin at the hospitle Mother I have bin taking the papers ever cence I have bin at the hospitle the paper onley coste 25 cents a weeak tho there is no nuse in it worth mutch it is trew that Stone Wall Jackson is dead tho I do expect yo will here of hit long befor yo get this letter tho yo will dout hit he was wooneded by his one men tho hit was not his woond that kiled him his death was cas by the atacks of numonia his death is regreted a grate deal in this state and I recin hit is regreted all over the confederacy tho we hope for a nother Jakson to leade our men in battle Mother I donte wante yo to sende me no more close to bea loste and I never get them at all...

James Crowder was unrealistically optimistic about prospects for rejoining his regiment. Even as he was writing home in mid-May, Confederate leaders were deciding for Lee's army to invade Maryland. By early June, Crowder's regiment was with Longstreet's corps on its way to the place of destiny at Gettysburg, Pennsylvania. Meanwhile, the recuperating Crowder, evidently knowing nothing of the march, grew more impatient to rejoin his fellows. Amid so much dying at the hospital in Petersburg, the young soldier understandably took the time to consider the ways of Providence.

Poplarlawn hospital first ward
Petersburg Va
June 1, 1863
Dear Mother,

...I sente yo 5 dolars in the last letter that I rote to yo I wood like to here from hit soon whether yo ever got hit or not Mother I have sente the boys too papers and to day I will sente them too more theas is religeos papers and that is the sorte of papers for people to read theas days I wante the boys to read them and pay good attention to them the preacher gived theas papers to me and hit only cost 5 cents to send too home so I think that thay will bea worth that to the boys to read Mother I think that I will go to the Regt. this weeak if the docktors will let me go Mother there has bin severl death in the hospital since I have bin hear and there is men dieing now closte to me on the same row of beads as I am yet spared from death by the provedence of god I will try to serve him the balance of my days so I will come to a close...

James P. Crowder's stay in the hospital was longer than he anticipated. On 4 June, he wrote from the ward at Petersburg: "I am able to go to my Regt now tho I donte nowe when I will go it was in this mornings paper that the Yankes was a crossing the River a gain at fedricks berge." Hooker's Federals were making inconsequential demonstrations at the Rappahannock. The real story, however, was Lee's attempt to camouflage his Army's march into Maryland and Pennsylvania. But if Crowder knew of this, he did not write about it. On 22 June, still troubled by the patients dying around him, the young soldier admitted that General Lee wanted no more men at present.

Poplarlawn hospital Ward No 1
Petersberg Va
June 22, 1863
Dear Mother,

...[T]hay will not let me go to my Regt General Lee sente orders to the hospitals not to send no more men to him till he cald for them so thay wante let me go to my Regt now so there is no teling when I will go to my Regt.

Mother there is a grate deal of sickness here at this hospital there was one man died rite closte to me laste nite and his funerel was preach this morning at the hospital I here a sermon every day or too...

By late June, with Lee's army far behind Union lines, fears of a Federal attack on Richmond were so rife as to nearly empty the hospitals for the protection of the city. Actually, the Union Army of the Potomac, now under General George G. Meade, was too busy watching Lee to pose much threat to Richmond. Still, young Crowder was moved to strong patriotic defense of his nation's capital.

Poplarlawn hospital
Petersberge Va
June 28, 1863
Dear Mother,

...[A]s I have got back from town and eate my diner I will finish my letter...the hold town is full of excitement all the men that is in town is all on the streets and drawing guns to protect the citey it is sed in town this morning that presedente Davis orderd out every man in Richmond that cold shoot a gun for protecktion of that citey and this morning there came a order to the hospital for all the men that was able to go to there Regt for them to bea sente rite off with 5 days rashings so I will leave here in the morning to go to my Regt I have got orders to bea Redey...in the morning by ten o clock to go to Richmond so I will leave this place soon tho I do think that we will stop in Richmond and stay there a whyle tho I can not tell it is reported that there is a large forse of yankees coming on to Richmond and the people is very much scerd tho I donte think there is much danger yet if the yankes tries to take Richmond now thay mite get foold as bad as thay dide laste June [Seven Days'] for the streats will run with blood before the yankes dos get that place tho thay may get hit Mother there is a rite smarte of sicknes here tho not as much as has bin at present the men is all geting well very faste and a going to there Regt in every directions...

At the conclusion of the battle of Gettysburg on 3 July (and the siege of Vicksburg on 4 July), Crowder was still at Richmond, reporting no knowledge of his regiment's location. In fact, he said he had not heard from it in over a month. He was currently excited about the local defense of the Confederate capital.

Richmond Va
Saterday
July 4, 1863
Dear Brother G. M. Crowder,

...I am at Richmond this morning at campe lee the same place where I was laste 4 of July I rote yo all a letter laste year on the 4 of July in this same place tho I never thoght that I wood stay in the war this long then tho there is no more chance for me to get out now than thay was then I lefte the hospital laste thursday and come to this place thay will not let me go to my Regt and I have not herd from hit in a month or more and I dont no where it is there is a grate many men in camp lee that is able for dutey and thay are a drawing gones [guns] and forming in to company and going out to the breste works to defend Richmond the yankes has bernt severel briges in the laste fiew days a round Richmond.

There is no teling when I will draw a gun and go to the breste [works] hit may bea be fore nite I cante tell we will go as soon as the cap ten dos dray guns for us and that may bea before night it is sed that there is fiftey thousan yankes advancing on Richmond and if there is hit will take us all to scare them back thay take all the men that come from hospitals and puts all the Ala. men to gether and the Ga. together and Miss, and then thay all dray armes and go out to the breste works there is a grate deal of excitement in Richmond so there is no teling when I will get to my Regt now no teling when I will leave this place tho hit may bea before night...

By 12 July, Crowder had learned his regiment's hereabouts and of the "bige fite" at Gettysburg, in which Longstreet's corps had been centrally and controversially involved. Dreading the long march required for rejoining his company, Crowder (like most Southerners) did not yet perceive the full extent of the Confederate loss in

Pennsylvania. Gettysburg cost Lee 28,000 casualties, amounting to more than one-third of his army, a loss that would never be replaced.

Stanton Va
July 12, 1863
Dear Mother,

...I lefte Richmond yesterday morning and come to this place I got here this morning about day lite we are too miles above Stanton on the Winchester turnpike I will leave here this eavening at too o clock to go to the Regt tho hit will bea somtime before I do get there my Regt is in marelen and thay have bin in a bige fite and got cut all to peaces so I have herd I donte no how true hit is it is true they have hade a fite for there is a grate many woonded a passing the road a going to Stanton and thay say that the yankes got a grate many of our woonded Mother there will bea warme times in marelen as soon as Generel Lee getes his men that is a going to him there is about 6 thousan men a going to him thay all will get to him some time this weeake

Mother General Lee has captured a grate many cattle and thay have bin drove to Richmond in large droves the boys ses thay have fared well sence thay wente in to marelen thay get a plentey to eate thay say and that is good tho thay say that thay have fiting a plentey to do and that the yankes fites very harde Mother it is a long ways to the Regt and I do dread the walk hit is about one hundred and Seventy five miles to where the Regt is and the Capt ses that he is a going to march us all twenty miles a day so that will bea rite harde marching in this warm weather for men rite out of the hospital...

When young Thomas Barron wrote his sister on 27 July, he had been at Gettysburg. His letter communicates a type of shock. Sometime before 7 June, Thomas's father, G. C. Barron, had had "two of his fingers Shot off and a ball shot through his thigh," wounds which subsequently sent him home from Virginia. Thus Thomas had the burden of loneliness to add to that of homesickness. Then, in early July, his regiment lost heavily at Gettysburg.

In Camp Near Culpeper C. Hs Va
July 27, 1863
Dear Sister,

...I am Botherd a little with the Rhumatism here of late But I keep on foot...Sisey I have just put on clean cloths an wash the ones I pull off you aught to have seen me a washing I do all of my own washing when I am well for it is heap the cheapest when I have Soap for when I hires it done its not half done and then it takes so mouch money 25 and 50 cts per garment I have plenty of Soap yet that mother sent me it has save me of a heap of trouble an escspence but I have touted it amany a mile Sissey I entend to go blackberry hunting after I finish my letter to you if it do not rain it looks like it will rain sometime to day for it is thundering Mary I wish I was at home to go with you and siter for it would be so mouch pleasure for me to healp pick berrys for to make a pie I often think of the time when we live together We would hunt berryes an play to gether an be happy But as it is I have to go without you But it is pleasure for me to think of you an to think how happy I would be if I was with you I hope God will let us live to talk over our childhood happey days an I [hope] we may live to pay our parents for raising us so happy Sister take care of them till I come home for them Sister Edy & you are all my happaness I love you all dearly if I was a good writer I could not discribe how dear I love you & them I hope God will take care of them & you I feel more indebted to father and you all since he has happen to the luck to be shoten so badley for he will kneed my assistance the more and he shall have it if I live an do not happen to wors luck than he has Sister I do not know how long we will stay at this camp but I think that we will not remain long hear if we leave here shortly I will have to march barefooted for I have no shoes I wore them so completely out that they would not stay on my feet But there has been a repeort made out how many shoes was wanting in the company their are four or five more barefooted an severls others near bout in the same fix tell Pa all of the boys wants to hear from him...This is yankee paper it came off of the battlefield of Gettysburg Pa.

Barron was more composed in the next letter. Yet he was still concerned about matters of religion, death, and the privacy of girls' letters to soldiers.

Camp Near Orange C.H

Fall, 1863

Dear Mother,

...I still enjoy good health an fine spirits there is very little sickness in camp at present all of the boys seem to be in fine spirits an we have plenty of Rashons on hand an exspect to draw money in a few days I sent Father ten dollars by G. W. Taylor But he has not goten home yet.

Mother I am proud to hear of [those accepting] of God at home an Glad to hear of others joining the church you do not know [how] mouch it encourages the sinful soildiers to hear of the great Meetings at home it bouys them up to think that Some can get Religeon that God has not forsak our people Mother I wish I was a christon...you said you hope to live to see all of [your] children join the church of God an be babtise I hope so to dear Mother I hope to be a christen I do not care what denomination or church so I am a christen but I would join your church being as you belong to the mishionnarys for I want to be with you We still have meeting in camp every day an night tell Pa that Henry Burns an T. R. Moon has join the church Hery the Baptis and Roan the Methodis.

Mother I have no news conserning the enemy only that there is no endercation of a fight at present the boys seem to be in fine spirits an those that have not been home exspects to get a fouloug this winter I exspect to get one if old Gen Lee will [release] the company...Tell Pa his mess is well an all of them wants to see him they send him their respects an well wishes We get on fine in our famly We have the best mess in camp I recon wel mess together as long as the [war lasts] if we live it through...We hear here that people at home have been crettering stories told on us which they should not have don that is this that we exspose the letters we get from our friends an from young ladys Reason aught to teach them that it is not So Where is the young man that would stoope to so low an act as to be a showing his letters that he had receive from a young lady we think to much of them [and of] our selves than to let others read [them] if we get a letter from ou parents we then show one another if it contain no secret an only the news it contains Pa Knows this himself he never seen any letters from young lady an the boys would let him see there letters...

Thomas Barron's Fourteenth Alabama Regiment wintered near Orange Court House in preparation for the next year's hard contests with Grant at the Wilderness and Spotsylvania in 1864. Instead of James Crowder's having to go and find his regiment, it apparently met him in northern Virginia. The next time we hear from him, he is back at Port Royal with his company, once again watching the Federals who were camped across the Rappahannock. Now Crowder was rested and in fine form, except for the recurring pain of remembering one "Rebecca hammonds" back home in Chambers County, Alabama.

Porte Royl Va
Aug. 26, 1863
Dear Mother Sisters and brother,

...[W]e are camped in porte Royl on the Raperhanok. We have bin over the river for the laste three days tho we come back yesterday morning thay say that the yankes has come down there wher we was the 48 Ala Regt wente over there yesterday morning and the yankes run them back laste eavening Brother we have had a fine time down on the River we have bin down here some time a foregen and we get any thing to eate that we wante and a plentey of hit and that is good we have got a good many loads of corn from the other side of the river and a grate deal of forage of every sorte and...that is good tho we will stope now fore a while.

Brother yo sed that Uncle William [Andrews] was at home I was glad to her that he had got home I cold not here from since the getesburg fite and I was glad to here that he was at home for I thoght that the yankes had got him...mabea there will bea my time soon to get to come home I do wante to sea yo all very bad tho there is no chance yet I will wate patientley till my time...comes and I hope that wont be long tho let hit bea long or shorte I will do the beste I can for myself and for yo all I will draw money soon and I will send yo som if yo neade hit as soon as I get the chance to send hit to yo I wante yo to rite to me how much money yo have got.

...I donte wante...any close for the winter I can get good close here...tho I wante here [mother] to send me too pare of socks by the first one that does pass I do wante coton socks and nothing else...I wante yo to rit where Rebecca hamonds is a living and when yo saw here laste I can tell yo that ther is a grate many pretey Girls in Porte Royl and that are ceces [secession] Girls and thay like the sothern boys very well.

Brother I have bin in Virginia so long that I have got to liking the girls very well and I think that I will bring one of the Virginia Girls down south with me when I come home...I had the tooth ache for som days paste...

Brother there will bea a fite here soon the cannons has bin roaring all the morning u p toward fredricksburg and hit is the cavalry a filing I think so no mor at presant.

Altough Crowder expected to remain in Virginia indefinitely, that front was entering another period of lull as the Union government continued its search for a general who just might prove equal to Robert E. Lee's defensive abilities. President Lincoln eventually settled on U. S. Grant to fill this position. As the new general-in-chief of the Union armies, Grant issued orders to George G. Meade, who was left in command of the Army of the Potomac. Although Meade had fought well at Gettysburg, he disappointed Lincoln in his failure afterward to press and crush Lee's army, now safely back in northern Virginia.

Lincoln's selection of Grant to head the Union forces did not occur until March 1864. Grant took two more months for reorganization before initiating the massive Virginia offensive at the Wilderness in May 1864. Pending these developments in the east, James Crowder's regiment would be detached to the west as a part of James Longstreet's corps, whose first assignment was to assist Braxton Bragg's defense of Chattanooga against William Rosecrans's threatening army. But before all of this transpired in mid-September 1863, Crowder's concerns at Fredericksburg were the ordinary ones of everyday camp life.

Camps Near Fredrickburg
Sept. 2, 1863
Dear Mother sisters and Brothers,

...[W]e have come back to fredricksburg from Porte Royl and I think that there is some chance of us a camping near fredricksburg for some time...Mother there has bin meating a going in the brigad for the laste month ther is a grate many that has joined the church and there is to bea babtising this eavening and I am a riting in hearing of preaching now and I do want to get my letter don so I can go to baptising Mother being at meating makes me [think] about home more than I dide sence I have bin in the ware thn [will] Bare hit patientley till I can get to come home...the setlment boys is generaly well Mr. Smith has ben absent for too weeaks and no one noes where he is with out he is gon home so as there has come orders to clean up camps I will come to a close...

Smith's mysterious "disappearance" was not unusual, but Crowder would come back to the subject later, in November 1863, when he was petitioned on the line of siege at Chattanooga.

At the end of chapter 2, the Tennessee campaign was centered at Murfreesboro, where the Federal General Rosecrans had taken up a leisurely winter quarters, allowing his army plenty of time to heal its wounds before pressing on to Chattanooga. The next chapter rejoins Braxton Bragg's Confederate army in middle Tennessee as it awaited the next contact with Rosecrans's force.

4

Tennessee: 1863–1864

The year 1863 proved devastating for the Southern cause. That fact, however, was not always realized or acknowledged at the time. On 3 July (as noted in chapter 3), General Lee's army was repulsed at Gettysburg, Pennsylvania, forever ending the Confederacy's hope for a successful invasion of the North. As if Gettysburg were not enough, the fourth day of the same month brought U. S. Grant's capture of the Confederate garrison at Vicksburg. Vicksburg was a major Federal victory that opened the Mississippi River to complete Union control and effectively divided the western Confederacy from the eastern portion. This development significantly weakened the Southern military effort.

Less well known but almost as detrimental to the Southern cause was the Confederate loss of Chattanooga in November 1863. This chapter treats the halting defense of that city as it was reported by a few Chattahoocheans who were members of General Braxton Bragg's hard-pressed army. These Southern troops would wait in middle Tennessee near Murfreesboro until late June and then withdraw, only to do the same again as Bragg's army moved southeastward to Chattanooga and then beyond it, not really trying to engage the advancing force of General William S. Rosecrans until the battle of Chickamauga, 19–20 September, in northwestern Georgia. Here, Bragg finally struck back and, assisted by General James Longstreet's corps (recently arrived from Virginia), drove the Federals onto the defensive within the confines of Chattanooga itself.

Then for a moment in time, as wars go, it appeared that Bragg would actually trap and defeat Rosecrans's army in the city. Such was not to be, however, as this Southern commander, with characteristic tardiness, waited too long to strike, thereby allowing General Grant (not long from Vicksburg) and other Federal reinforcements to arrive at Chattanooga and relieve the besieged force. The renewed Union offensive on 23–25 November pushed the Confederates farther south into northern Georgia, giving the Federals a free rein in Chattanooga and parts of eastern Tennessee.

After General Bragg's failure to follow up the victory at Chickamauga in September, General Longstreet welcomed the opportunity to detach his corps once again, this time for a campaign against growing Federal strength in east Tennessee. Following an unsuccessful assault on Fort Sanders at Knoxville on 29 November, Longstreet moved eastward and spent the remainder of the winter at Greenville, Tennessee. The irrepressible James P. Crowder, optimistic despite frostbitten feet, served with Longstreet's army during the winter exile. Thus, Crowder's letters from eastern Tennessee are included at the end of this chapter.

It was, however, another Chattahoochean, one Thomas T. Bigbie, who early in 1863 opened this year's correspondence while Bragg's army was still in middle Tennessee. Bigbie wrote from Tullahoma in February. His letters began about a month after the Confederates had evacuated Murfreesboro in order to establish a defensive winter camp just south of that place. Thomas Bigbie was a native of Pondtown in Dale (now Geneva) County, Alabama. He was a member of Company G, Thirty-Third Alabama Infantry. Not surprisingly, the same regiment included his relatives, L. W. Bigbie (probably a brother) and G. C. Bush. They were later joined by Thomas Bigbie's brother-in-law, Will Lewis. In the dead of winter, Bigbie appropriately began the Tennessee correspondence on a very cold note. But there was plenty of food for the inactive army and enough money to pay the inflated prices for whiskey and clothing. Bigbie did not see anything wrong with some personal profiteering in an undersupplied market. He had evidently just returned from a furlough home.

Tullahoma Tenese
Feb. 3, 1863
Dear Wife,

...I got here to my [camp] yesterday and found the boys all a bought there is 25 of our company here at this [time] and they are all up [some] of them has bad cold it is mity cold here now wee had a right smart snow her last night wee have got Chimley bilt to our tents here and likely will stay here some time wee are at Tulihoma forty miles from murfes buro...here they boys has got plenty of monney they boys pays [$]15 a quart for whiskey socks and gloves is worth two Dollars a pair and they are glad to get them at that...I wish now that I had a brought all of my socks with mee when any of the boys comes that you send mee all the socks you can for it is an accomidation to them to git to by them here at most any prise they get a plenty to eat here now though it is mity cold wee do our one coocking and eating here E Miller sends his respects to all the girls back there and ses he wants to see them mity bad tell them to right to him some time for he is very ancus to here from them It is so cold here that I can hardly right it has bin snowing and sleeting for severul days Feb 6...we are in a mity mudy plase here G C Bush is sick to day I will have to go on guard in a few ours wee dont have to stand of a night when it is cold i will Right a gain when it gits Warmer...

In this same month, Lieutenant S. H. Dent and his artillerymen were in winter quarters at Shelbyville, a few miles north of Thomas Bigbie at Tullahoma. It was still a bitter, cold February when Dent wrote, expressing his stoic and newsy point of view. His stoicism was Christian, based on a providential concept of history. Moving down the Mississippi River, so to speak, Dent regretted the loss of Arkansas Post, feared for the safety of Vicksburg (which held out until July) and acknowledged the defensive importance of Confederate Port Hudson just north of Federal-held Baton Rouge. Criticisms by Bragg's officers of his mismanagement both during and after the battle of Stones River (31 December–2 January) near Murfreesboro had brought General Joseph Johnston, coordinator of the western armies, to evaluate the situation for President Jefferson Davis. Somewhat surprisingly, Johnston exonerated Bragg, perhaps because he did not want to risk being named Bragg's successor as commander of the Army of Tennessee.

Camp near Shelbyville Tenn
Feb. 6, 1863
My own Dear Wife,

...Yesterday morning I found it snowing very fast—it then hailed and snowed alternately all day—the ground was hard frozen this morning and for a short time at least we were rid of the mud and sloppiness of our Camp. To-day is clear bright and cold—and I hope we may have several days of just such weather...I hope some of our officers and men especially those who get behind clay-roots will take courage...and not be frightened at the whistling of the musket balls or the rushing and bursting of shells. I have always believed that God was with us—if I had not my arm would long since have palsied—and I now as firmly believe that when the end does come it will give independence and peace to our Country as I ever believed any thing. But I differ with those who think there will be peace in the spring. I can see no signs of it. The enemy struck us a very severe blow by the capture of Arkansas Post. I am afraid the silence from about Vicksburg is ominous. I fear the enemy will do us some great injury there. I had rather lose the whole state of Tennessee than be cut off in our communications with the trans-Miss dept. The bread question is an important one—our army here is eating corn bread and it is making them sick—unless they could sift it and have it ground finer it will continue to make them sick. We are however carrying flour from this country and I suppose are storing it somewhere. I heard yesterday that troops were being sent from here to Port Hudson—but I do not think it can be true. Braggs army has certainly been reduced enough before. I have heard nothing more of any further movements around here. We had a picket fight two or three days ago—did not amount to much...We are to be reviewed today by Genl Joe Johnston. It bids fair to be a fine day...

Lieutenant Dent's valid concern for Vicksburg makes this a proper place to consider another Chattahoochean's letter from that front. The following message was penned in March, about four months before the Vicksburg garrison of General John C. Pemberton surrendered to Grant's siege. The correspondent, George Washington Shealy, from Cusseta in Chambers County, Alabama, was a lieutenant (and later captain) in G Company of the Thirty-Seventh Alabama Infantry. He wrote while Grant's campaign was still bogged down in the swamps around Vicksburg. For the moment, Shealy was comfortable at picket duty on the Yazoo River. This Chattahoochean was both pious and pleased with himself. He was less proud of the army because of a recent execution and some soldiers' unsavory "wickedness" that, unnamed, he left to our imaginations.

Camps near Vicksburg, Miss.
March 9, 1863
My dear Companion,

Tonight I will engage in the same good pleasure of writing to you again, but how different it seems to me seated in a comfortable house to see the fire burning so pleasantly and around it some of our boys engaged in playing of cards. But I will take my pleasure in writing to my loved one. They said when I commenced writing that I had just thought of something good to tell you. They will play for fun in my presence, but they won't bet. Anything that I say is too bad they will not do. Ain't you afraid Gusta that I will be led off into these bad habits when so much of it is going on, or where most all engage but myself. Sometimes they ask me to play out of fun and tell me it is no harm, but my conscience tells me better. Any innocent fun they always insist on my taking part. Probably you have begun to think at what house I have been speaking of.

Our camp is up on the Yazoo River on picket. Close by there is a large plantation and we stay in the houses. My post is with the Regiment but Gus did not want to go and I went in his place. It is about one mile and a half from Camps the only way we can get here is to come up a large bayough in skiffs and small boats. We have one post to guard about a mile from here on the Yazoo. I had charge of the guards yesterday only three stand at a time it was my birthday. All through the day and night I could hear nothing save the waves beating her banks and the course songs of the sea fowls. [The boys have gotten into scuffle they call upon me to stop it]. You may imagine Gusta that I had a lonesome time of it...

This morning I will continue to write while the boys are off fishing. Last night it rained very hard, our house does not leak any. We are living fine at this time. We go over about one mile from here to a corn pen and get corn to make lye hominey, we buy bacon. Also have a plenty of fish most every meal. We have large kettles to boil the corn in, then we fry it. It eats splendid. When we are put up to it we can make a good many shifts to get along.

Last Friday which was your birthday I saw a man shot. Gusta it was a Solemn Scene. He deserted our army at New Orleans and was taken by us in the last fight at this place. He was an excellent looking man, fine appearance seemed to be a well educated man. Our Brigade was ordered to be present. The rules of shooting men in the army is a detail of twelve men. Their guns are loaded by an officer. Six of them have balls the remaining six blank cartridges. He was placed upon his coffin a short distance in front. A preacher talked to him awhile. While he was sitting there how solemn the scene was to me I could not help offering a prayer to God in his behalf though he was my enemy but I sincerely wished that he was prepared to meet his God. To see the missiles of death staring him in the face, sitting upon the lid which would soon hide him from this earth. Oh! Could we imagine his feelings knowing that his soul would be in eternal misery. Soon his doom would be sealed. Then there are no pardoning. The hour is past. The dye is cast, lost, lost forever...All around me seem to be delighted in the wickedness of this life. Often I go to myself and reflect [on] the...evils...

The Mississippi front also concerned Confederate troops in Tennessee, indicated by a letter from S. H. Dent. Port Hudson, near Baton Rouge, would hold out until 9 July, and the rumor that the Federals were leaving Murfreesboro was three months premature.

On picket Eagleville Pike 7 Miles from Shelbyville Tenn
March 18, 1863
My Own Darling Nannie,

...I am still on picket. The weather continues fine. I Have heard nothing more of the rumor about the evacuation of Murfreesboro by the Yankees...We have pretty good news from Port Hudson and I only hope the good news will continue. But it has been a little remarkable that in nearly all our fights we had the best at first. Such things make one suspicious...I heard that our cavalry in front were organizing a reconnoitering expedition to find out the truth about the evacuation of M. or what movements the Yankees are making. If the expedition went I presume we will hear something to-morrow. We have Genl [John A.] Wharton on this road...

S. H. Dent, the artilleryman, was no cavalryman, evidenced by his next letter. But he remained uncritically loyal to the controversial Bragg, who might have been removed from field command except for the support of Joseph Johnston. Dent was also prescient on the growing importance of protective works for soldiers in defensive positions. The increased amount of firepower and its greater accuracy proved to be more costly in lives than field commanders like Bragg had anticipated. Union General William S. Rosecrans would wait a while longer for better weather, reinforcements, and a near certain victory at Vicksburg before he moved against Bragg.

Camp near Shelbyville Tenn
March 24, 1863
My own Nannie,

I returned from picket yesteday evening late...I rode out this morning and took some cavalry exercise—but it came on to rain again and I left. I managed to cut my horse a little on the hind leg. I was cutting at what was supposed to be a Yankee's head while he [the Yankee] was lying down. It is the first time I ever exercised and I was rather awkward and my horse was shy. I am going to practice some and see how I can do. It will exercise me and that is what I need...If Rosenkranz had any idea of advancing which I doubt, this rain and mudj will delay him. I see the newspapers are full of the news of the evacuation of Murfreesboro. That may turn out like the report of the evacuation of Nashville shortly before the battle of Murfreesboro. In fact I can't believe a word of it...I am getting along very well with the Company—have very little trouble—and I must own that I have a very hard set of Men or at least some very hard cases. But of one thing I feel certain I can rely on them in a fight—well Darling I must go and look after my horses now. In a battery a horse is a great thing and I must have mine well looked after...I heard the other day that Genl Bragg had been relieved from command here and would go to Mobile or Vicksburg. I have not seen any one that knew any thing about it. I hope it is not so for no matter how much others may abuse him I like him as a General and I hope he will remain with this army. I would go into a fight under him with greater confidence than any other Genl—however able and distinguished he might be. There are a great many men who want to see him relieved and I expect it in some of them who have started the report. You see I still stand up for my old General. Genl [Jones M.] Withers returned last week—he has been absent since the battle of Murfreesboro and Genl [J. Patton] Anderson has been commanding the Division. I like Genl A. very much and think him a fine soldier...The Yankees are certainly moving very slowly. Rosenkranz has been seen forced with Twenty thousand men—but he does not seem to think these sufficient for his purposes. If we can hold this country three months longer I think we can hold it the balance of the year. In fact if we can stay here until the 1st of June I think we will not only hold this country but drive the Yankees back. The Yankees are working very energetically at Vicksburg. They work like beavers. The Yankees had rather work six months with picks and spades than fight one battle—while our soldiers had rather fight six battles than work one month. We have not worked enough with the spade. I wish our Genls would work more with them...

The reluctance of "Old Rosy" (Rosecrans) to leave Murfreesboro enabled T. T. Bigbie to write his wife about the life of a soldier: playing, eating, and drinking, each of which was satisfactory except the unrelieved prospect of battle. The Tullahoma area of Tennessee where Bigbie was camped was hilly, sparsely populated, and depleted by two years of occupation by Confederate and Federal troops.

Tullihoma Tenesee
March 31, 1863
Dear Wife,

...I came of guard this morning the ground is coverd with snow and the boys is now out in the snow a playing with the snow there is not less than two hunderd in the old field at this time we are in a mity poore contry here and there is verry few people lives here but I think i t is as good a place for us as wee could git to wee have plenty of wood and water and wee have ben gitting tolerbal plenty to eat though our meet falls rather short sometimes wee git plenty of meal the helth of our regt is improved a grate deal since last year our boys is all well...wee are well fortifide here there is not much porspect of a fight here good there is some taulk of fighting and some taulk of peece but I cant tell anything abought that...

Thomas Bigbie gave his father further details of snowball fights in Bragg's army.

Tullihuma
March 31, 1863
Dear father,

...[T]he boys enjoyes there self pirty I have just come in to finish my letter for I had to go out and take a play with them wee firs started the play in the camp then we devided the croud and had a grate play and then there came over fore other rigtments in a line of battle i can tell you that it was pirty sight to see tow or three thousand men in an old field at one time playing in the snow in regular battle form this is a grate plase for amusement and pass time L W [Bigbie] is on guard and misted the play but Dick and Lish plade a good hand for him I am verry anuis to see and to here from you all...

Soon S. H. Dent wrote his wife of one of his Sunday schedules during this long wait in Tennessee. He also joked about the intelligence report of Rosecrans's reluctance to leave camp, a piece of information that proved to be rather accurate.

Camp near Shelbyville Tenn
April 5, 1863
My Dearest Wife,

It is a lovely sabbath afternoon. Every thing is quiet and still. The noisy wagons and the busy hum of everyday life in camp has hushed. I have eaten my dinner and concluded I would spend an hour in writing to my Darling wife. I went to church this morning—carried Stockton and Brut on with me—went by for [Felix] Robertson and took him along also. I heard an ordinary sermon. The house was crowded. Robertson came out to Camp with us for dinner he has left and all the other officers are endeavoring to pass away the afternoon by sleeping. To-day looks as if Spring had commenced in reality. If Rosenkranz is waiting for fine weather he need wait no longer—a Yankee prisoner captured a few days ago got off a joke upon his General—when asked what news was stirring about his Camp when he left he said it was reported that old Rosy would advance in June. We have been here already longer than at any out place since I left Pensacola—when I say we I mean the battery and in fact we [the Battery] have been here longer than at any out place since we have been in the service—and the indications are that we will remain here sometime longer...My General officers are very much opposed to my leaving the command particularly Genl Withers and Genl [Zachariah C.] Deas. Genl Deas says he had rather lose any regiment in his command than my Battery...I heard this morning that [Confederate Cavalry leader John Hunt] Morgan was driven back from [Tennessee]—near Lebanon day before yesterday. He was attacked by a large force of [Federal] Infantry and cavalry. Every where else every thing is quiet...

Military inactivity allowed Hubert Dent plenty of time to write his "Darling Nannie." P. G. T. Beauregard was in charge of the successful defense of Charleston against Union attack. Ambrose E. Burnside, who had failed so miserably against Lee in Virginia, would on 2 September occupy Knoxville, Tennessee, where he backed up the Federal move against Chattanooga. There would be no Confederate reinvasion of Kentucky. Bragg's Army of Tennessee still waited for Rosecrans to advance from Murfreesboro. Dent's allusions to local "ladies" must have piqued his wife's curiosity. It is doubtful that he referred to the numerous prostitutes who followed the armies of both sides.

Camp near Shelbyville
April 8, 1863
My Darling Nannie,

...Things are moving on here pretty much as usual. There were some rumors of an advance of the enemy on the Murfreesboro road yesterday—but I heard nothing more of it to-day. In fact every one is taken up with the news from Charleston—news came this morning that the fight had commenced there yesterday and continued up to 6 o'clock P M when the enemy drew off. This evening later news came reporting that the fight had been renewed to-day and that one of the Yankee iron clads had been sunk and that our Forts and Batteries had sustained no damage. God grant that we may be successfull there. I think if we can succeed in holding the enemy in check there that it will do a great deal towards bringing about peace.

...I go out on picket next week again and will be gone until the following Monday. But Dearest you need not feel any uneasiness for everything here is quiet. There are a good many rumors of troops concentrating at Knoxville for the purpose of going into Ky. and a gentleman just from Tullahoma to-day said that Genl [John C.] Breckenridge's Division were under marching orders and it was thought Ky was there destination. There seems to be a good deal of doubt about where Burnside's corps has gone to. It is reported that it has gone into Ky. Some however seem to think that it is a ruse of the Yankees to get troops from Genl Lee and then try another "on to Richmond." I have been reading to-day some extracts from the speech of Ben Wood of New York. It is decidedly the most favorable for peace of any I have read from northern men. He speaks out boldly and talks plainly. The trouble is however that Lincoln is independent of Congress for nearly twelve months as long as his money will last. Southern victories are the only thing that will end the war. I have hopes that if we can be successful this spring and summer that the war will end this year at least come to such a stand still that it will end early next...April is passing away—the [nights] however keep quite cool and we have frost every night. It is cloudy to night and a little warmer and we may have rain before morning. I dread rainy weather for I am very badly provided against it. It seems [impossible] to get a tent—all the officers have gone in town to a party to-night. They are quite common. From what I have heard of the Ladies here I think there are very few whose society I would like even were I in the best sort of mood for enjoying such things...

Soon, Dent would be out on the picket line, away from town and the ladies. Meanwhile, he manifested the uneasiness that builds before a battle can assume particular form. Even as Dent feared, Rosecrans's maneuvers would force Bragg to fall back without a fight. Instead of leaving Mississippi, as reported here, Grant was merely shifting his army to a more advantageous position for attacking Pemberton's Confederate force at Vicksburg.

On Picket Eagleville Pike
7 miles from Shelbyville Tenn
April 13, 1863
My Own Darling,

...The company came out on picket this morning...The army here is a good deal excited over the news that the Yankees are evacuating the Miss and the impression prevails that Grant will unite with Rosecrans and try and drive Genl Bragg from Tenn. We may be reinforced by Pemberton but I am afraid the proportion will not hold out. What I mean by that is this. That Pemberton's army away from his Forts and breastworks will not be as much of a reinforcement for Genl Bragg as Grant's army will be for Rosecrans. Well it is our fortune to contend with superior numbers and we must do our best and trust in God for the rest. Genl Bragg and Johnston (I beg Johnston's pardon I should have named him first) were expected in Shelbyville this evening and a "big review" was expected to come off on Wednesday. We are digging ditches and building batteries somewhere in this country and the impression prevails that we must fight here or near here. I think the idea of ever falling back as far as Tullahoma without a fight has been abandoned unless "Old Rosy" endeavors to get on our flank and cut off our communications with Chattanooga...I have not drawn any pay for since January. The pay-masters have no money—as soon as I can draw some I will send you some. But it makes a big hole in a hundred dollars to feed myself and have my horse taken care of...I have just heard a musket fire and I must find out what it is about—we may have an alarm to-night...It is now Tuesday morning—nothing occured during the night...

A death in Anna Beall's family sent Hubert Dent to buy mourning materials for her. He was currently in financial straits but hoped a promotion to captain would enable him to replace the funds Nannie had been forced to use out of her own deposits.

Shelbyville
April 24, 1863
[torn]

...I received yours and Mr. Young's letters by Dr Bryan. The first thing I did this morning was to go down town "shopping" [all the artillery are camped together now and we are three miles from town]. I could find no black silk except some at 25 cts a skein...I could not find a single piece of mourning goods any where...All the goods here [are in] the hands of jews and I believe...[We] have a half-a dozen little shops here with each about a good shoulder turn of goods in them. That is all there is in Shelbyville—of course my own darling you were right to go in mourning. I expected it. I wish I could procure for you such things as you need. I wish I could send you some money but unfortunately just now I am unable to do so. I have money owed to me that I could very well send you if I had it—about a hundred and sixty dollars...You must draw on your deposits for the present. I will replace it in a little while—when I get to be Capt I will have a little more. This is the third letter I have written to-night—both the others however were on official business. The artillery orgainzation of which I have written has commenced—but is not perfected yet—when that is perfected I will not belong to any Brigade—we are however all camped together. I moved out yesterday on the Lewisburg [Pike] I have the best camp I have ever had. Tolerably convenient to both wood and water—and in a beautiful grassy place. If there is any thing that I can procure for you Darling do not hesitate a moment to call on me...

When Dent wrote in May 1863, he could not resist telling his wife about a picnic with the "Ladies," perhaps to tease her, possibly to reassure her of his fidelity. The comment about J. Patton Anderson and John C. Breckinridge at Murfreesboro pertained to Bragg's unwarranted criticism of Breckinridge's use of his troops at Stones River the previous January. It was Bragg's custom to blame his subordinates for any military setback.

Camp near Shelbyville Tenn

May 1, 1863

My own Darling,

This is the 1st of May and lovely day it is—clear warm and bright. Some of the officers of the artillry have gone to a picnic near our camp. The Ladies up here indulge in such things occasionally—although invited I did not feel like going and have remained in camp all day. As one of the Brigade of our Division has been ordered out here near our camp I expect I will go out on picket again on Monday. I thought when I was last there that I would not go again—but now I feel differently and I do not know how much longer we will remain here...An officer has just come by and pressed me so hard to go to the picnic that I have partially consented. I may go directly. I wonder what you are all doing at home to-day...Well Darling I went to the picnic remained about an hour and left. There were plenty of Gentlemen and not caring to push in I keep out and pretty quiet...I rode out yesterday evening in a direction I had never been before and I was struck with the appearance of the country. The scenery in some places was remarkably fine...How soon we may be called on to move I cannot tell but I expect pretty soon—our artillery organization is not complete yet. I do not like things at all as they now are. I hope they will improve. There will be I think a good deal of feeling about the promotions or rather the appointment of Field officers. I want to send you some money the first safe opportunity. I do not care to risk the mail if I can do better...I hope I will be able to get home this summer but think it doubtful. I expect to be on the move. I have read the official report of Genl Bragg of the battle of Murfreesboro. I think it well written—his tribute to the private Soldier is very fine and well-deserved—of his critticisms of the Generals I have nothing to say. From what my officers say I think Genl Bragg is mistaken about Anderson's Brigade checking the advance of the enemy after Breckinridges repulse. The enemy were checked when he arrived...

Hubert Dent might have been unable to send money home, but Thomas Bigbie could, at least for the time being, until inflation and irregular pay exhausted soldier funds. There was more troop movement now, in preparation for the Yankee offensive that was sure to come. The restless and irascible Confederate cavalry leader General N. B. Forrest could still harass the enemy and take prisoners to boot. Bigbie must have referred to Forrest's capture on 3 May of General Abel Streight's 1,466 cavalrymen in northeastern Alabama.

Tennessee Camp War trace
May 12, 1863
Dear Wife,

...I sent home sixty dollars by George pellam I sent it to pa as I thought that he would have the best chance to git it and I have got a bought sixty or seventy dollars more that I would like to send home if I can git a chance to send it to you I will sent it to you as I can and I want you to use it as you see proper...[Recently] wee had orders to cook rashings to leave the next morning...and a bought the time that wee got our cooking don the order was counter manded we are here yeat we have marched a bought 12 or 14 miles from where wee was there is a right smart movering a bought of the soldiers here but there is nothing of importance goin on here generl forrest taken a bought 15 hunderd or 2 thousand yankees a few days a go not fare from here...wee have got one of the best [revival] meetings a going on here close to our regt that I have ever seen anywhere...

Thomas Bigbie's situation did not change much from 12 May until the end of the month. Meanwhile, at Vicksburg, Grant had arrived and was beginning the six weeks' siege which would compel Pemberton's surrender. Against Grant's wishes, Rosecrans continued inactive at Murfreesboro. Still, the tension was building at Wartrace. Among Confederates in middle Tennessee, as elsewhere, revival meetings aroused greater interest in 1863 than in earlier periods of the war.

Ware Trace Tenn
May 31, 1863
Dear Wife and Mother,

...I can say to you that we finely made a little march since I rote to you the day that Atwell left here wee got orders to take our coats and blankets to go to a gap a bout 10 or 12 miles from here wee marched up there and stade to days and come back to our camp and is at the same camp yeat wee are a gitting a long tolerbul well yeut some of the boys complain a bought not having a nuf to eat but I have never suferd for something to eat yeat I give 50 cents for a canteen of milk and walk 2 miles after it and is a doing well at that there is a grate excitement a bout the vicksburg fight at this time but I dont think that wee will have any fight here soon we have got a very good meeting a going on here close to us and 1 have seen some of the best meetings here that I have ever seen...

Now Hubert Dent could report increased activity of both armies around Murfreesboro. He was still concerned for Vicksburg, where Grant's cordon was tightening. But Dent was misled in his hope that Bragg would launch a successful offensive against Rosecrans for a reinvasion of Kentucky. Confederate movement in Tennessee, when it finally came, was in the opposite direction. Meanwhile, in Mississippi, Johnston was trying futilely to assemble a Confederate army large enough to attack Grant and relieve Pemberton's 31,000 besieged troops at Vicksburg.

Camp near Shelbyville Tenn
June 5, 1863
My own Darling Wife,

...I received orders last Tuesday to be ready to march at 5:30 A M next morning with two days cooked rations—and left accordingly going out on the Unionville and Triune pike. Two Brigades of Wither's Division Anderson's and Deas' went out. We went on the pike as far as Rover and then turne off towards Versailles and Salem. We camped Wednesday night Twenty-one miles from our Shelbyville camp—went three miles farther next morning and within about eleven miles of Murfreesboro—our cavalry went three or four miles nearer to M and found a considerable force of the enemy just beyond Salem—too strong for us to attack when we retraced our steps. I arrived in Camp just about Sun set having marched Twenty-seven miles. I left the Infantry behind. They could not keep up with me. [The artillery had horses.] It had been rumored for several days that the enemy were evacuating Murfreesboro and this advance was made in order to ascertain if the report was true—advances were made on the other roads at the same time. The enemy have drawn in their lines a long distance—but are still occupying M. in force...The news from Miss is pretty good—but we always want things better than they are. I have heard that Genl [Franklin] Gardner had repulsed [N. P.] Banks at Port Hudson. I hope it is true. Then let Bragg be re-enforced so we can push Rosecrans back and invade Kentucky again. If Genl Johnston could dispose of Grants army so effectually that he could start a column of men towards Memphis it would force Rosecrans to fall back and perhaps we might get Nashville and go up as far as Bowling Green—and bring the war to an end during the fall. Oh! how I wish my hopes may be realized...I have sent you now three hundred dollars since I came back [in January]. I promised you fifty Dollars a month and I will try and save it and send it to you and if I ever get my commission as Captain I will try and make it more. My horse is a great deal better and if I had not rode him on this last march we made I think he would have been well. I have made application to buy one from the Battery if I can get him I will keep him to ride until my horse gets entirely well and then try and send him home to you to sell—horses must be high there...I see by the papers this morning that Grant has been heavily reenforced and has renewed the attack on Vicksburg. I don't like the complexion of affairs at all and what is singular I see also that Gen Breckinridge's Division has been sent back here. I hope Genl Johnston has not been deceived...The citizens have reported that the Yankees were leaving Murfreesboro and that old Rosecrans had his Hd Qrs in Nashville and the con[cen]tration of the enemy's lines gave some color to the report. Some thing has been going on up there—but what it is no one knows accurately...I have only about two things here in the Company to love—one is George—the other my horse. I have had my horse so long and he has carried me safely through dangers and over so many miles that I have an affection for him—and he knows me so well. I turn him loose sometime in camp and it is very seldom he will let any one catch him except myself—horses are frequently stolen in the army—well I am never afraid of any one getting my horse when he is loose for he will not be caught away from Camp...

The Federals under Rosecrans at Murfreesboro did not move in force until 24 June. Still, rumors of an earlier attack persisted. Hubert Dent's worst fears for Mississippi and Louisiana would soon be confirmed. Meanwhile, he had stopped visiting the "ladies" for the duration, or so he reported to Nannie. Dent's estimate of Joseph E. Johnston's troops was inflated, but others also wondered why the Confederate general was so slow to move against the Federals at Vicksburg.

Camp near Shelbyville Tenn
June 9, 1863
My own Darling Nannie,

...Genl [Frank] Cheathim's Division has gone out to the front and ours was ordered out but the order was countermanded yesterday evening. It is

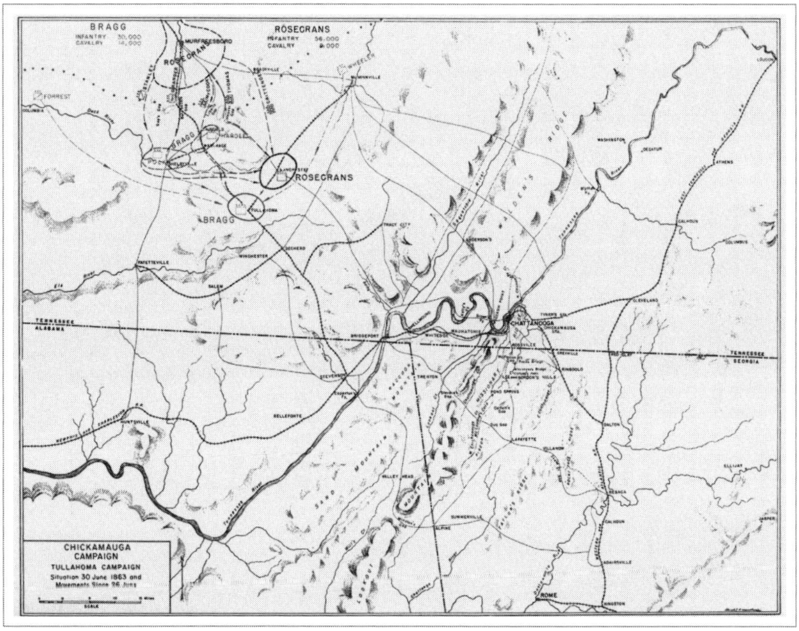

CHICKAMAUGA CAMPAIGN, TULLAHOMA CAMPAIGN, 1863

currently reported that "Old Rosey" is advancing cautiously. I expected when I wrote my last letter that we would have been gone before this time but "large bodies move slowly" and old Rosey's army seems to be verifying this old adage. Well when he does come I expect Genl Bragg will give him the best fight he can. I can't pretend to predict the result. I do not like the long silence from Miss and La. I am afraid the Yankees will burrow Pemberton out of Vicksburg and if they get that Port Hudson will go. I can't imagine what Genl Johnston is about—he ought to have from thirty-five to Forty thousand men under him and ought to be able to commence operations on Grant's rear. I think a great deal is at stake on the result of Vicksburg. I believe I would rather give up more of Tenn if that would save it. I await the result with great anxiety. Now is the time for every body to be in the field...There is a Lady visiting Mrs. [Henry] Fields [the widow] named McLaughlin [pronounced McLocklin] who has a son in my company. I would be pleased if you would call on her...I have altogether retired to private life—and do not expect to appear in public [among the Ladies] any more while the war lasts...I intend keeping all the cloth I have and having me a full suit coat pants & vest made in regular artillery style. I have some idea of keeping them here to be made but am not certain yet what I will do. It is right nice cloth and will make me a finer suit than the one McKenna made for me which is showing the effects of the sun already. I think I will get the trimmings here but do not know what they will cost...I hope I may be able to visit home before September but to be candid I fear I will not. I look if not for activity certainly for vigilance during this summer. I think a great deal is at stake and I feel that I must do my part the best I am able. I wish I could get some horses for my battery. I need them very much—and in fact the battery is hardly efficient without them...

While R. E. Lee was moving toward Gettysburg, Pennsylvania, and Pemberton was languishing at Vicksburg on the Mississippi, prospects for a fight in Tennessee seemed to be lessening. It was, however, the lull before the storm. Veterans like Hubert Dent probably realized this even as he assured his wife to the contrary.

Camp near Shelbyville Tenn
June 11, 1863
My own Darling,

I...have been busy receiving ordnance stores and never got through until dark. I am tired—but...I am very well...I believe the idea of an immediate fight is all blown over. I send by Mr Spurlock my coat & vest I will keep my cloth here and have it made up—and will then have as many clothes as I can carry...

Thomas Bigbie continued sending money to his family. His view of battle prospects was similar to Dent's.

Ware trace Tenn
June 11, 1863
Dear Wife,

...I will right you a few lines just to let you no that I have not forgot you yeat...I am very ancus to see you and I could tell you a grate deal that I cannot right to you...I sent you fifty dollars...wee have draud our monney a gain 1 have got fifty dollars more that I can spare I want to send it to you the first chance that I can git to send it saf wee are not a fairing a[s] well as wee did a while...but I have never suferd for something to eat yeat I do not think that wee will be apt to have a fight here soon wee hear a grate deal of very faverbul news from vicksburg...

In the limbo of waiting, S. H. Dent left an interesting description of General Joseph Wheeler, the Confederate cavalry commander. In Mississippi during June, Johnston believed he lacked the manpower necessary to attack Grant and raise the siege of Vicksburg.

Camp near Shelbyville Tenn
June 13, 1863
My own Darling,

...This is certainly a fine climate...One year ago we were sweltering under a Miss. sun and suffocating with Miss. dust. It is very different here now....Every thing has quieted down here to the same old thing. Genl Bragg has concluded I think that old Rosey is not ready to pay him a visit yet and another Brigade from this army has gone to Miss—[Genl Preston Smith's]. They keep taking troops from Genl Bragg. I do hope that Johnston will succeed in doing something great and telling in Miss. He must be collecting a fine army and it seems is taking his time moving. We have no late news from Vicksburg or Port Hudson. The wires were not working yesterday and I have heard nothing to-day. I think I will ride into town this evening and see what I can hear. I expect both armies in Tenn are watching with great anxiety the result of the operations on the Miss. It was reported in the newspapers a few days ago that Genl Kirby Smith had Millikens bend about Twenty-five miles above Vicksburg and had Grant's supplies cut off. I can't [understand] how he can cut off Grants Supplies without heavy batteries and then not effectually. It has been some time since Grant made his first attempt on Vicksburg and it seems now that he has commenced digging ditches and preparing to take the place by regular siege approaches. Unless Genl Johnston can compel him to raise that siege the provision question might become an alarming one. A great deal I think depends on Vicksburg. I hope and pray we shall be successful there. The newspapers in Virginia throw out mysterious hints of what Lee is doing—but I pay very little attention to such nods & winks. I have long since found out that they amount to nothing...Well darling I believe I will get ready and go down town and call on Genl Wheeler this evening and finish this to night....I have returned from Town—no news from any quarter. I went to call on Genl Wheeler he was out of town about three or four miles on the Fairfield Pike. I however rode on out to see him found him pleasantly situated at a good farm house. Talked with him a short time and rode back in a hurry as there was every appearance of a thunder storm...I think all idea of an immediate fight is over in this quarter—and every thing has resumed the same old routine. The only change I have heard is that Genl Withers moves out of Town nearer our trenches. I suppose this is done to place him nearer his Division. Genl Wheeler reminded me this evening of the time [in July 1861 when] I was so anxious to get home to see my boy from Pensacola—and asked after you and the boy. He is a very pleasant agreeable gentleman and the sort of man I think you would like—modest and retiring especially before Ladies and a gentleman in the old acceptation of that term. He does not look as well as he formerly did. He is a small man and not good looking—but I like him very much...Since Genl Withers has moved it would not surprise me if we were to move out nearer the trenches ourselves. I hope not for I have a very pleasant camp and would dislike to give it up. We have been around Shelbyville a long time and I feel sometimes like I would like to change. I wonder if we will go back to Murfreesboro this summer...

During the month that transpired before Dent's next letter on 11 July, the Confederacy was defeated at several strategic points. In the long run, these defeats marked the Southern cause as lost, even though the conflict would continue for two full years. The war then was far from over when Lee was repulsed at Gettysburg on 3 July and Vicksburg fell to Grant the following day. The surrender of Vicksburg was followed by that of Port Hudson on 9 July. These last developments opened the entire Mississippi River to Federal forces and irreparably divided the Confederacy like so much pie.

Meanwhile, on 24 June, when Rosecrans was certain of Union victory in Mississippi, he moved out of Murfreesboro against Bragg, flanking the Confederate line of defense and forcing another humiliating retreat that did not stop until it reached Chattanooga. Now, suddenly, most of middle Tennessee was in Union hands, and Chattanooga became the last means of securing Georgia and eastern Tennessee for the Confederacy. No wonder Dent's stoicism was weakened as he urged his wife to remain at home during these uncertain times.

Camp near Chattanooga Tenn
July 11, 1863
My own Darling,

I should have written to you yesterday—but was busy all day riding round to see if I could find a place for you to stay when you come up here—and I am sorry to say I could find none. Col [H. D. Clayton] and myself rode around town—out in the country in the morning and in the evening I went up on Lookout [Mountain]. Every place was full. There are a great many refugees here and the public boarding houses are full and private houses are full. I suppose you might be able to stay at the Hotel but it is not a suitable place for a Lady to stay & I had rather you were at home than here and compelled to remain at the Spencer House—more especially as I could not be with you constantly...For the present Darling I think you had best remain at home...I expect you all have the blues over the military news. I am getting accustomed to it—and do not feel dispirited either. I only think the war is certain to last a long time yet and that of itself makes me feel badly. I do not know what this army will do—wait here I suppose until Rosecrans develops his plans—and then try and protect Georgia.

Genl [William J.] Hardee's corps is going to Tyners Station—where we were last summer. Some rumors of troops going to Miss—but I hear nothing definite. Grant seems to be pushing on after Johnston and Miss is pretty much at the mercy of Yankees. North Alabama is in the same condition. I expect Genl Lee will wind up his agressive [Pennsylvania] campaign [back] in Richmond pretty soon and things resume the old style only a little worse. Well I do not know what a few months may bring forth. Fifteen months ago affairs were as gloomy as they are now and we redeemed them. We may do it again. Let us hope for the best...I am tired of Chattanooga already and wish I was some where else. Plenty of whiskey about here and plenty of drunkenness. I think some times the country is ruined any way whether the Yankees get it or not. This army must be badly demoralized and three months of inactivity will only make it worse...

The Confederate retreat from Tullahoma and Wartrace to Harrison (near Chattanooga) was a trying experience because of the rough, mountainous terrain, inadequate roads, and the torrential rains that fell for days without respite. Thomas Bigbie was deservedly proud of the physical strength that brought him through the ordeal. The unrelenting rains also had the effect of delaying for several weeks the Federal advance.

Harrison Hamilton Tenn
July 12, 1863
Dear Wife,

...I have bin on the pad for the last 14 or 15 days wee have bin marching wee have come back from wartrace to this plase five miles from where wee was last year when I was taken sick when wee left Ware trace wee lef in the rain and went to bell buckle where they was fighting...I was five days and nits that my close was not dry on me...and my blanket was not dry and it rained all most all of the time and wee did not git much sleep when wee got to tullahoma wee stopped and rested and wee got to sleep wee stade there two days and nights and wee then started for chattanooga I went on a had when wee left tullahoma to cook and they was a holling our knap sacks and they throud them out and I lost mine there was severl of the boys lost theirs I have no clos only what I had on I had my coat with me but I lost my best pants but one conselation I did not have them to cary there was severl of the boys that all most give out some had to be hald and some of them fell out and come up in a day or to there was three compines of our regt that was in picket that fought the Yank all most all day and we was a bout one hunderd and fifty yds from them and the bulets whisled over in thick I heard the bulets whisle and the bums bust and expected to be in it ever minit and there was not one of our men got hurt...we had to leave there to ceep from being cut off I stood the march first rate all of the rain and wee marched through the mud in the night and it from shan quarter to half nee deep in the night and wee waded creeks and mud holes a wee come to them and it never hurt me I never new what a man could stand till I come here when I got here I was just as good as I was when I started or a little better...

After every hard march, which meant discarding extra baggage, the Confederate soldier usually required new clothing. Sizing was a problem, especially when the sewing was done at great distances. T. T. Bigbie also showed that money and food were growing scarce. There were, however, vermin aplenty.

Harrison Tenn
July 15, 1863
Dear Wife,

...I was glad to get my close from home...my shirt dos fine but my pants was way too little I put them on and ever time I stoop down they busted I could stand up in them but I could not stoop down in them my socks just fild the bill I will ceep them...thirty Dollars...is as much as I can well spare at this time for I have to buy a heepe to eat there I have bin so that I could make monny a nuf to pay my way wit out what I draw but I cant do that now wee live pirty hard here...but wee make out the best that we can...we live from hand to mouth I have all ways heard of ones living from hand to mouth but I never new just how it was till I come to the ware wee dont git a plenty to eat here but wee make out and I have never sufferd myself only when wee was on the march and then wee could not git any thing to cook in nor to cook...I will need some winter close some that is warm...a wolin shirt ant any worse for lise that any other sort I recun that you would like to no how me and the lise makes it now I have never bin bothered with them but very little since I come back here when you make me another shirt put pockets in it and then it will just suat a solger I lost my gloves you may send me another pair if you can...I am going to rite to pa to come out herethis fall for I no that he can come wee will pay anyboddy expences that will come and bring is some butter and eggs close and so on and wee are glad to see them any how...

In setting his parents' minds at ease, Bigbie boasted of physical prowess. But where did he get the money to purchase extra food at such inflated prices?

Harrison Tenn
July 16, 1863
Dear father and mother,

...I am well though I have a bile on my [foot] so that I can hardly walk today...but I Stod the march first rate I can asure you that I have seen sites since I left home I have seen the bums burst and heard the bullets wihisel I marched through the rain and mud with but little to eat though I stood it all pirty well if I coud see you I could tell you a grate deal that I cant rite i want to see you all very bald...our rashings has bin redust and wee did not git any to much before but I made out very well for I go out in the cuntry and buy when I can finde any thing to buy ever thing is mity high ires potaters from 15 cts to 300$ a peck a canteen of milk is worth 50 a chicken 100 to 200 $ a head of cabege 50 cts–$100 wee are a guarding a little town here at this time our deuty is lite now it is not worth while for me to try to rite you the ware news...

The Memphis and Charleston Railroad crossed the Tennessee at Bridgeport in northeastern Alabama. This was Rosecrans's logical point of crossing the river in order to flank Bragg out of Chattanooga. Lieutenant S. H. Dent and his battery were near Bridgeport on the south bank of the Tennessee. He hoped the Federals would not cross at this place. But Rosecrans's forces would do just that within a month of this writing. Meanwhile, Charleston, South Carolina, the symbol of secession, was still holding out (under Beauregard) against the bombardment directed by General Quincy Gillmore. Gillmore was very much alive, despite the Confederate picket's claim to the contrary.

Camp near Bridgport Ala
Aug. 1, 1863
My own Darling Wife,

...There has been a good deal of Excitement down here for the last two or three days. The Yankees are as thick as black berries on the other side of the river and are quite impudent. They have a high bluff and two good earth works and some eight or ten pieces of Artillery—some of them heavy pieces. And I can't say how many men. In position they have a decided advantage over us and if they attempt it can make this side of the river very uncomfortable—they may even be able to cross the river. I have no idea what they intend to do—but I hardly think they will cross the river and try to reach Chattanooga from this point. Day before yesterday in the evening Genl Anderson came to me and told me to go down to the river and select positions for two guns and open on the enemy at daylight next morning. Accordingly I went down selected the positions and took two guns down that night—about 11 o'clock I received orders not to fire without there was some pressing necessity. My guns are still there—but no prospect of firing them soon. The Yankees come down to the river bank and shout across to our men and ask them a great many questions. One of our men told them in reply to "what was the news from Charleston" that "Genl [Quincy] Gilmore was killed." Is that so said the Yankee—certainly said our man. They offered to give coffee for Tobacco & &. They seem to be planting some heavy guns on the heights on the other Side of the River...Have you read Genl [D. H.] Hill's address to his corps. He gives it to the exempts—calls them "worthless creatures" and "poltroons" who have skulked from the field under the provisions of the exemption law...I have had eight men to desert since we left shelbyville and I expect others will do the same thing. But that does not trouble me at all now—my company is getting gradually smaller and unless more men are given to me I will be compelled to give up two guns and make mine a four gun Battery like every other Battery in this army—except one or perhaps two...

Suffering from another failure of nerve, Braxton Bragg did not fight at the place that would have given him his best advantage, Rosecrans's river crossing at Bridgeport. Thus, by 9 September, the Federals were across the Tennessee and threatening Bragg's southern line of supply to the extent that he felt compelled to evacuate Chattanooga, thereby giving the city to the Union without a fight. From his position south of Chattanooga at LaFayette, Georgia, Bragg watched Rosecrans send his army in pursuit through the mountains in a way that divided the Federal forces and invited a counter attack by the Confederates. This occurred at Chickamauga on 19 and 20 September, though not until after Rosecrans had concentrated his forces. By now Bragg was reinforced by generals S. B. Buckner from Knoxville and James Longstreet from Virginia.

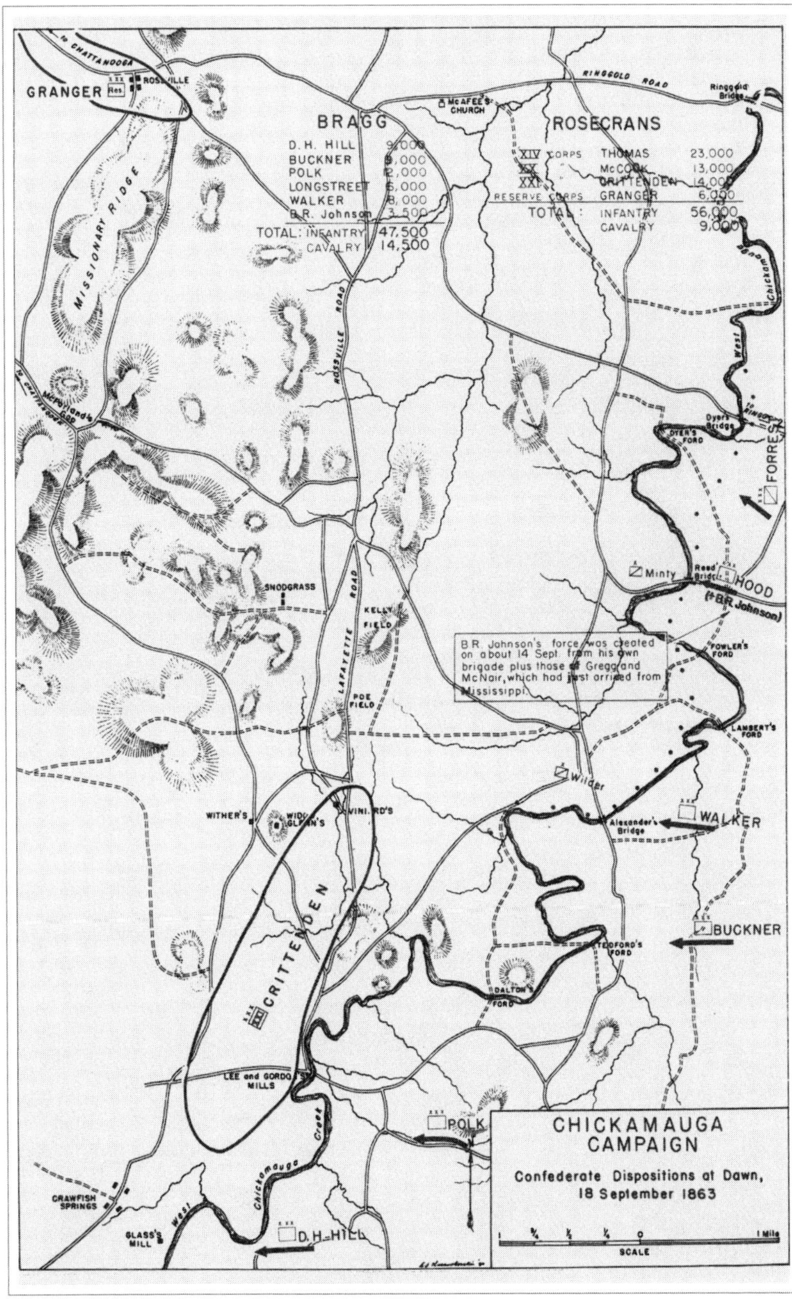

CHICKAMAUGA CAMPAIGN, 1863

The battle of Chickamauga was a much-needed Confederate victory that drove Rosecrans onto the defensive within the confines of Chattanooga. Only the heroic stand of Union General George H. Thomas (the "Rock of Chickamauga") prevented a complete rout of Rosecrans's army that day. Thomas Bigbie's Thirty-Third Alabama was one of the regiments that suffered heavily in the Confederate attack at Chickamauga.

Camp 33 Ala Regt
Sept. 22, 1863
My Dear Wife,

...I am just out of the titest place that ever I have bin in wee have had a very hard fight here on saterday and Sunday I went through it un hurt dos seem that nothing but the finger of God could cary a man through such a seen wee suferd a grate deal on saterday wee [his company] got fore wounded...one kilde...on Saturday even wee routed the yanks and drive them two miles and on sundy wee [attacked their] brest work and faild to take them the first time late in the evening wee drove them back from there brest works and they left that night wee have advanced five or six miles and it is said that they are in full retret and I am in-hops that is so and I think that wee will keep them a going wee have got a reinforcement from Verginia and I think that wee will push them through we lost a heepe of men and they lost a keep also I walked over some of the battle field and I seen at least five of the enemy to one of our men but I did not go over where most of our men was kild James Bugh helpt to berry them and he ses he thinks that they got the most men kild...he has a better chance to no wee captured seventy five or eighty peaces of artilery and horeses mules wagons and wee made them drive their one peaces of artilery out wee may have to fight again soon I cant tell God has blest and protected me so far and I pray that he may continue his protection...I have...no ider when I will git the chance to mail this I am in the woods a sitting by a big post oke wee will leave here this evening some time if you git any chance this fall send me a suat of winter close I give elbert a pair of socks last night wee have bin on the pad for a month and I stand it very well so fare...

James Crowder was among the reinforcements brought from Virginia to Chickamauga by Longstreet. This was one of the longest troop movements by rail during the war (843 miles). Longstreet's Confederates left their trains at Ringgold just in time to break through a gap inadvertently left by the Federals in shifting their position, and thus became a decisive factor in Rosecrans's defeat. Although the battle ended on 20 September, skirmishing continued for days. Crowder described to his mother the plundering of supplies from slain Yankees in the aftermath of the battle. The big battle predicted by Crowder did not come until 23–25 November, and the offensive was taken by Grant rather than Bragg.

In line of battle near chatnaga, tenn
Sept. 29, 1863
Dear Mother,

...I was on picket laste nite close to the yankes I had to set up all nite and thay was a fiting all nite and are still at hit this morning Mother we have bin in line of battle for the laste ten days and there has bin a grate deal of fiting all the time there has bin 8 woonded and one kiled in our company I wood rite there names tho yo will here hoo hit is by the time yo get this letter I wood a have rote before now tho I did not have the chance the bige fite come off last Saturday and Sunday tho the fiting is not done yet there will bea a nother big fite soon hit may come off to day or tomorrow for all I no tho I cante tell yet when hit will come off.

Mother I have not fared as well sence I lefte Virgina and come to Tennesee as I did before tho I think I fared very well to get out of the fite safe the boys had a fine time a plondering the yankes nap-sacks I got me a good napsack and too pare of socks and three packs of envelops and severel other tricks too teadios to mention yo rote to me to send yo som neadles tho I am at a place that I cante get them I have got some that I got out of a yankee napsack that I will send to yo in this letter...I have got me a good pare of shoes thay coste me twelve dolars thay was made at lafayett and thay are a good pare and I got me the best blanket of ave [off of] the battle field that I ever saw so I am fix up for the winter so I will close and rite agane as soon as this fite is over if I live to get through safe...

In another letter of the same date (perhaps misdated) Crowder explained the speed with which Longstreet's corps departed Virginia. He also noted the ease with which men could be separated from their companies, by design or mistake. A "sutler" was someone who accompanied troops and sold food, drink, and supplies.

Campe Near Chatanooga Tenn
Sept. 29, 1863
Dear Mother and Sisters,

...Mrs. Smith wanted to no what had beacome of Mr. Smith I will tell her what I no about him whyle we was camped at fredricksburg Va one morning Mr. Smith and Robert Adams got left to go to the texas Suttar [sutler] and get them som things and whyle thay was gone we got orders to go to porte Royl and we started and we left several of the boys in camp sick and we lefte there things there and after we had bin gone about one hour thay came back and thay took there things and started after us all Robert Adams had a gun and Mr. Smith never had nary one and that is the laste that I have heard of him I have not heard of nary one of them sence that is all I no about them and that is the truth...I can get close here cheaper than yo can make them...I wante yo to send me som potatoes and union [onions] and some little vegatbles that is if we stop closte to the railroad I will rite to yo when to send them so as I have to go on piket to nite I will come to a close and eate my supper and get ready to go.

Although the Confederates had Rosecrans's army on the defensive in Chattanooga, Thomas Bigbie was showing the strain of vigilance and short rations when he "lighted" into some unknown miscreant who had tattled falsely to the folk back home.

Camp 33 Ala regt
Oct. 3, 1863
My Dear Wife,

[I]t is strange to me that men [will] pretend to be something and be a nother...I cant see why anybody can want to rite any thing back home that is not so or be a tatling but I just a low to let all of that go for what it is worth and that ant muct rite to me all a bought it but I shall not try to rake up any bodys tales for it won pay I just want to no for my one sats faction I intend to make the best of this ware that I can for it is bad a nuf the best one can make of it but I dont complane like some of the boys do our rashings is pirty short and men here is liek children they want to eat all of the time...they will quarl till they get more it seems like they have a craving appitite and cant be satisfide unless they are eating their has several diserted lately they was three in a compiny going out last nite and their is servel thretning to leave but I am in hops that it is more taulk than [action] we are in 3 miles of Chattanooga and has bin ever since the fight.

While Bragg continued the siege of Chattanooga, Thomas Bigbie was distressed by Confederate desertion. He vowed he would never desert, even though his superiors made it virtually impossible to get a furlough except by obtaining a recruit. This particular incentive caused Bigbie to agonize over his relative Will Lewis's entering Confederate military service. Will was apparently the brother of Thomas's wife. Bigbie was impressively realistic in his evaluation of the army's camp life.

In camp
Nov. 1, 1863
Dear Wife,

A Gillmand...is going home on furlow and he ses that he will bring anything back that you have to send if you will send it by neuton or to Daleville he lives a bought 5 miles from Nancy I need a sute of close but if you have not got a coat redy made you need not send one my coat is to little for me but I can draw one I recon send my [?] jacket.

I lost my vest and am with out any now I want my pants linde it is a gitting mity cold up here wee need thick warm close here if you have them ready pa can cary them to him and he will bring them saf to me their is severl gitting far los now Bragg has ishiurd an order that anyone that will git a recrut to join their compiny that he will give them a furloe for not excedon forty days and their has [been] severl ritting for the boys that is nearly eighteen to come tell Will that I want him to stay at home if he can and not git to the ware untill he is a bought eighteen nohow if he has to go I had rather that he would come here waring is bald a nuf any where but I had just a bought as live risk it here as any where tell him not to go off for no body just to git them home a little while I would advise him as a brother and had rather he would stay at home if he can do it onerbuly I dont recklect how old he is and if he findes that he will have to go to the ware and he will come here I can git to come home 30 or 40 days but I would not have him to come for that unless he hast to come any how...last tuesday they was severl kild and wounded wee are a fairing tolerbul well at this time wee have a heepe of guard Deuty to do wee stand picket in hunderd yds of the yank but we have quit shootin at each other it rains a most ever day here but we have got so we stand the rain pirty well I want to see you all mity bald but I cant tell when I git to see you a gain this ware dont close fast there has severl of our regt diserted and I recon...gon home but I think that is making a bald matter worse for I never could ly in the woods I am not deceived in the ware it is just what I expected it to be it is no worse than I expected it to be when I first started...

Instead of pursuing Rosecrans's army and destroying it, as generals Longstreet and Forrest advised, Bragg had laid siege to Chattanooga and waited for hunger to win the battle for him. But reinforcements reached this Union army before starvation, and Bragg finally found himself pitted against the forces of George H. Thomas (who replaced Rosecrans), Joseph Hooker, and William T. Sherman—all under the command General U. S. Grant.

Bragg's reluctance to attack apparently stemmed from his natural indecisiveness and genuine belief that his lofty positions on Lookout Mountain and Missionary Ridge were impregnable. But while Bragg sat and waited for the "inevitable" surrender of Rosecrans's army, Grant opened a new supply line and prepared to take the offensive.

Meanwhile, General James Longstreet, incensed at what he called Bragg's mismanagement, was dispatched into eastern Tennessee with orders to relieve Knoxville of the presence of General Ambrose Burnside and his Union troops. Bragg's overconfident sense of a secure position helps explain his misguided decision to detach Longstreet's army at such a critical moment. James Crowder was still with Longstreet on the way to Knoxville when he wrote from Cleveland, Tennessee, about the mixed blessing of warm winter clothes, which were welcome but exceedingly heavy when one had to march.

Camp Near Cleavelin
Nov. 10, 1863
Dear Mother,

I got the things yo sent...tho the eavening that I got them thay started to march and I had to toate the things and thay marched all day the nexte day after wards and I had to toate them all day tho we are all camped now and expect to take the cars this eavening tho I donte no where we will go yet tho hit is sed that we will go to sweeatewater on the easte tennessee roade some seventey five miles from heare so thay say Longstreets corps is a going up there.

I wante yo to rite woord whether yo got hit [the money] or not Mother I have got some money yet to send yo tho there is no prospect of us a geting any money soon and I will ceape hit till I draw so as I have not had no brakefast yet I will come to a close.

With Longstreet still moving north, other Confederates were just now drawing into position outside Chattanooga. One of these, Israel Wade Prather, from Marcoot, Chambers County, Alabama, wrote his wife, Elizabeth, from the Confederate lines near Chickamauga. He described the siege positions on Missionary Ridge and Lookout Mountain as well as the scene of death on the weeks-old battlefield at Chickamauga. Uncharacteristic of his nonliterary type, Prather ended the letter with a little philosophy and some poetry.

Chicamauga, Tenn.
Nov. 14, 1863
Dear Companion,

[W]e landed here last night a little after dark. We will leave here this evening or in the morning and go 5 or 6 miles and take up camp. There is a heap of mountains about here and our people have breastworks on all of them. General Bragg, himself, is on a mountain called the Mishonary Ridge, 5 or 6 miles from here. They can see the Yankees very plain from there. There is a heavy firing going on over there somewhere now, probably some of it from Lookout Mountain. The cannons is firing now like five hundred. We can see the smoke rise from the cannon from here. The probability is that we will fight here soon. Gen. Longstreet is moved, gone from here up into Tenn. to try and flank the Yankees. We are close by the place where they fought before [Chickamauga]. There is some of the Yankees dead bodies lying on the battlefield yet. They buried all they could, they could not bury all, they stunk so bad. I am on guard today, guarding the baggage of the rest. We are 140 miles above Atlanta, the climate is a great deal colder here than there. If times do not get too excitable I intend to apply for a fourlough before long, but if there is a fight expected soon, I will not apply, for it would be useless to do so.

You must not trouble yourself about me, if a man is born to be hung, he will never be drowned. I expect to try to do my duty as a soldier and to serve God whose hands I am in, and whose will we all have to submit to. You must serve the Lord and do the best you can. I would be mighty glad to get a letter from you. When this you see, remember me, though many miles apart we be.

S. H. Dent was also near Chattanooga, on Missionary Ridge. His letter of 16 November shows how this long, somewhat secure wait had indeed dulled the hard-edge fighting readiness. Dent was a loyal Confederate, as devoted to the cause as anyone. But while besieged Federals in the valleys below were hardening themselves to do the impossible, the Confederates had fallen into the trap of waiting for a victory, which was not to be. Thus, Dent was not preoccupied with a forthcoming battle. Instead, his plans for winter camp turned around the assumption of semipermanence. In this letter, it would have been impossible for Dent to suggest that General Bragg would be falling back on Georgia in fewer than ten days. Yet that is exactly what happened.

Camp on Missionary Ridge
Nov. 16, 1863
My own Darling,

I have brought my table in my tent and have a comfortable fire and if nothing interrupts me I am going to write you a long letter. It is cloudy and cold and looks like it might snow. I have been busy for three days past working to put up a shelter for my horses, and I am afraid now that it will snow or rain before I finish it. I am a little nervous from cutting wood and can scarcely write. I spent a very quiet day yesterday. Every officer left Camp except myself. I shut up my tent—made a good fire—took a thorough was[h] put on clean clothes & spent the balance of the morning in looking at you and reading my bible. It seemed more like the sabbath than any I have passed in the army in a long time. After dinner I read my bible again and Thompson came in and I read several chapters aloud. I felt really better when night came. I wish I could spend all my Sundays in that manner. I was sitting by my fire last night thinking of home...But leaves of absence just now are not granted as liberally as they were a short time back—and there is some talk of reorganizing those men who reenlisted at Pensacola if any thing of that Kind is going to be done I will be compelled to remain here and look after it as I might go home and come back and find myself without a company. I feel satisfied that I can stay and Keep the company together or enough to make a company. I received one recruit this morning under Genl Bragg's order of giving a furlough for every recruit. I think I will get one or two more soon. I will take them just to Keep my company full I have nearly as many men now as some of the Infantry regiments. Most of the new men who have been transferred here seem to be very well pleased and if I could get rid of about a half a dozen of the old crowd I would have a well behaved company—and I do not know that I ought to complain...Affairs here are going on pretty much as heretofore—occasional shelling from batteries on both sides—our Troops have built sheds and shanties until nearly all of them are comfortable—very few have tents—but as long as they remain here they are independent of them—one can see...every variety of style & structure by riding along our lines—"necessity is truly the parent of invention." The assignment of General Hardee to this corps gives great satisfaction in our Division—now if Genl Anderson could only get the Division—but I am afraid he will not. I very often go over and see him when he has nothing to do and find him very agreeable and entertaining. He has lived in nearly every state in the old Union—that is extravagant but he has lived in several and Knows a great many persons. I go over and play chess with Capt Barth occasionally at night. I can generally beat him too. In fact I am victor so far over all my competitors in the chess line—not that I can play so well either for there are plenty of men who can beat me. It commenced sleeting a few moments ago...I have bought me a silver watch lately—found I could not get on well without one. I am ashamed to tell you what I gave for it...Our rations are improving some very much to my gratification. I hope Congress will do some thing for officers—our month's expenses for this month including the box Mr Young sends me will be about one Hundred dollars for each man—pretty heavy on 2nd Lts who get only ninety—and ordinarily it will run up to sixty or seventy. Well Darling I close for to-night...I was aroused this morning about day light by a heavy artillery fire on our left which created some excitement. I Jumped up myself and was about to dress when I happened to think that I heard yesterday that Robertson was going to take a Battery up on the left and open fire on a Yankee camp—so I laid still again. The firing soon ceased. Robertson either could do them very little damage or they soon got out of the way...I wish I had my stable covered—but it will take me a week to get the boards out. Breakfast is ready so I must close. I expect I will send Richardson to Atlanta after ordnance stores. But I do not intend to let him remain as long as he did before—ten days this time.

On 23 November, the Union offensive from Chattanooga began with George H. Thomas's troops advancing in the center, and on the following day the forces of Joseph Hooker pushed up Lookout Mountain during a foggy drizzle that caused their fight to be named "battle above the clouds." On 25 November, while Hooker was still advancing on the Federal right, Sherman on the left was supposed to take the northern

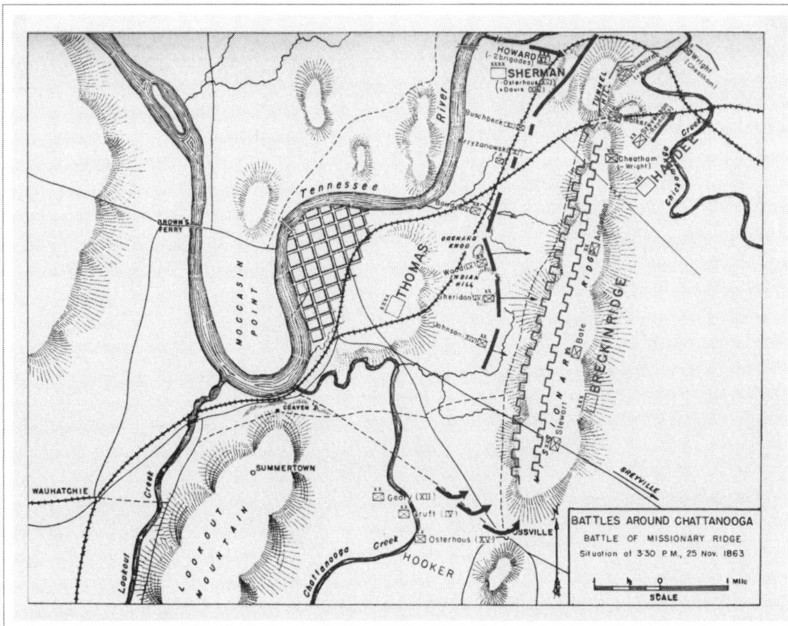

BATTLES AROUND CHATTANOOGA, BATTLE OF MISSIONARY RIDGE, 1863

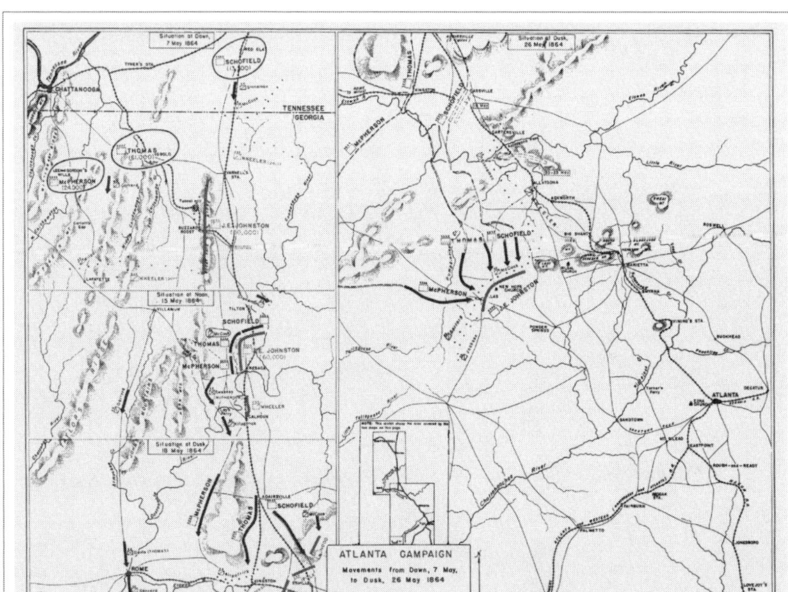

ATLANTA CAMPAIGN, MAY, 1864

end of Missionary Ridge. But Sherman's troops could not budge the strong defense of General Patrick Cleburne. Thus, the Federal advance stalled until Thomas's Army of the Cumberland (in the center position) took matters into their own hands and rushed up the Missionary Ridge and captured two miles of the mountain directly in the middle of Bragg's defensive line. With his center split and routed, there was nothing Bragg could do but draw off into Georgia. Some Confederates had fought badly, but Bigbie's Thirty-Third Alabama, a part of Cleburne's command, did not panic. Later in orderly retreat, the Thirty-Third was "part of the wall of fire that checked the exultant Federals at Ringgold Gap." Georgia. L. W. Bigbie, Thomas's brother, wrote his sister-in-law, Mary Jane, of these events. The fighting had been hard enough to make any man think of deserting, though both Bigbies abhorred the idea of it.

Camp 33 Ala regt
Dec. 3, 1863
Dear Sister,

[W]e have fell Back from Missionary ridge & is at Tunnel Hill Georgia we hade Som verry hard fighting Before we left the ridge But our regt was not in the hard part of the fight we was lying off Be hind Som Brest works no near a nuff to do any Shooting that night after the fight we taken up the line of march & fell Back to ring gall Ga & Stade thare till the Yanks com up & then gave them a Decent floggen [21 November] we onley lost two men killed & 8 wonded out of the regt Sis the night Before the [Ringgold] fight we waded a creek that was a Bout 3 oclock in the night when we cross Well Sis I want to See you verry Bad But I dont no when I will get a chance to com horn I cant do like Wess & pervis did Desert I dont want to See you nor none of the rest of my People Bad a nuff for that I think that things will work round for me to get a furloh Between this & next march if not I will com home when I Serve my time out which will Be 12 monts from next march Si...I would a rote to you Sonner But I have Ben on a march So I couldent.

Four days later, Thomas Bigbie expanded his brother's account of the battles and told of General Bragg's removal from field command on 28 November. W. J. Hardee agreed to take the command temporarily until Joseph Johnston could come to Dalton and assume the responsibility. Bigbie was still thinking that his relative, Will, might volunteer for Confederate service and thereby provide him a furlough home. But

Bigbie miscalculated the casualties, which were more like 1,000 Confederates to 6,000 Federals.

Camp Near Tunihill
Dec. 7, 1863
Dear Wife,

[W]ee air campt a bought a mile from tunilhill wee have had a nother fight near chattunooge [25 November] our regt did not suffe in the chattunouge fight but wee fell back to ringale and wee had a pirty hard engagement [27 November] and wee drove them back and kild a right smart of them with a small loss on our side no body kild or wounded that you no I am off on guard to day a bought a mile from the regt I may stay here some time if I do I will have a easy time here the boys is all out to day building brest works but I dont no wether wee will make any stand here or not the yanks has drove us from chattunooga but they lost a grate deal the most men in the fight our loss is estimated a fore thousand 4000 while theirs is said to be 15,000 they had to fight us in our brest works and I think that it was mis management that caused us to have to [retreat] their general Bragg has bin releived from deuty and general Hardee has bin assinde in his place I expect that they will make the matter better or worce and I cant tell which it will bee...Their is severl of our men gitting furlos but a furlo that one gits without a recrute is so short that they ant hardly worht going home with tell Will that I say that I will rite to him when to come if he has to go to the war that he can stay till spring.

Even though Bragg was finished as a field commander, he could now go to Richmond to advise President Davis on military affairs. Despite harsh criticism of Confederate soldiers at Missionary Ridge, some had fought well there, especially Cleburne's men, who consistently repulsed Sherman's attacks and then effectively covered the retreat. Thomas Bigbie, under Cleburne's command, was sure he had done his "deuty."

Dec. 15, 1863
Dear Ant Ann,

[W]e are campt at tunelhill Ga wee had a little fight at the [Missionary] rige and had to leve This [there] our regt was not in the fight at the rige but wee was close by wee was in site wee stood and seed the yanks charge our men severl times in their brest works but they drove them back ever time and kild a large number of them withe a small loss for wee had the advanteg of position but they finely broke our line and wee had to leave their wee was in the rear and they folered us and on the 27 [November] wee stopt at ringole and fought them untill our wagon trane could git a head and wee kild a grate many of them our compiny did not git any man hurt our regt got 2 kild and 8 wounded they whipt us at the rige but wee give them a dicent whipin at ringole wee have built us rite good winter quarters here but I cant tell how long wee will stay here for it semms that the yanks has got so much advantege of us that I have no ider what they will do they have driven us from the strongest posion that we have got just because some of our men is so tiard of the ware till they wont fight a tall it is said [that] Brigade gave way and that broke our line and wee all had to leave I intend if we ar ever run over and subjected it shall never be because I did not do my deuty...

Once again a hard retreat from a losing battle rendered Confederate clothing in short supply. The winter was bitter, and Thomas Bigbie wanted "brother" Will to come, but would not ask him to do so.

Tunilhill Ga
Dec. 11, 1863
Dear Wife,

Eli Hendrix is going to start home in a few days So I will...rite a few lines by him Gilman did not bring my close to me he said that he enquierd at Wilkesons for them and that he did not see Carmical so I have not got them yeat and I am needing them if you have sent them to Newton you will have to send after them and send them to me the first chance that you git...their is severl gitting to go home Eli has got a recrute and has a 40 days furlo if you don't...send my close before he will bring them...Will rote...some thing a bought comeing to the compiny tell him that if he has to go to the ware that I would be glad to see him come here if he comes here I can git a 40 days furlo but he will have to stay if he has to come he can come back with Eli I would have ritting to him to come before now but I [wanted] the wethe to...git warm before he come I want to come home mity bald but I dont want to pursuade will of before he has to go I want him to use his own plesue tell your father I sent him a pound of pouder by...Wm Moss and I forgot to say anythng a bought it in the letter...I will send him some caps and I want him to have me a dride venson ham when I come home or send [me] one...

On Christmas Eve, Thomas Bigbie tried to be cheerful. The war could wait, at least until the new year. Confederate morale was poor after the several disasters of 1863.

Tunilhill Ga
Dec. 24, 1863
Dear Wife,

I have not got a letter from you in a long time I shall have to quarl a little if you dont rite oftine than you do George said that I had to rit a few lines so that he would have a good excuse to go and see you hee ses that he is going hom to git marrid and he has envited me over as it is rather in conviniant for me to go over you will have to go in my place and then you must rite me all a bought it you must send me a big sausage by some of the boys I am a going to try to come home my self before long fo I want to see you mity bald tell will I am a going to try and come after him some time between this and spring m y best love to you all I must close I still remain your husband till Dth...

It was difficult to receive things from home exactly as they were sent. Large parcels of food and clothing were more apt to be left somewhere en route than small ones of letters and money. Thomas Bigbie appreciated his new clothes, despite the tight fit.

Tunilhill Ga
Dec. 25, 1863
Dear Wife,

Mr Collins got her last night he got my close through safe but he left my meet at Marieter where Oin Williams was he fergot to take it out of the box and left it I am a going to try to go after it but it will take me three or for days to git leave of absance for 36 hours it takes as long to git a leave of absance as it would to git a furlo I am acting Ordly sergent at this time and it is a bald chance to git off but I think...that I will go...I will tell you something a bought my clos I was proud to git them fer I needed them my pants was to small in the waste the next you make you must make them larger in the waist and a cross the puckets you have fergot how large I am I way 160 lbs and is in as good health as I ever was in my life but I can wair them the rest of my clos fit and seuted my very well the pants is worth 50.00 dollars here...socks and Gloves is worth 1.00 a pair here I found a knap sack with a good pair of socks Gloves and new shirt in it that some body had throwd a way...The ringane [Ringgold] fight...helpt me out a bought cloths rite smart...

Thus for Thomas Bigbie, 1863 ended in a cold winter camp Tunnel Hill. He was on one of the forward lines of Joseph Johnston's army, which was headquartered farther south at Dalton. But Bigbie's spirit was buoyant, reflecting the indomitable resilience of the Southern yeoman.

Camp 33 Ala Regt Co G
Dec. 31, 1863
Dier Wife,

L K L Adams is agaoing to start home this morning so I will send you a few lines but I have nothing new to rite to you wee are a gitting a long a bought as common it is rainy wether and we air sitting in our huts around the fiar tawlking over what wee want to bee and what...wee want to come to pass the heart of it all is the ware to close I want you to send me a string of pepper and some sage and some sowing threed and if you need anything rite to me and when I come home I will try and git it for you send it the first chance that you git their has so many gon now that I think you want be bothered much to send any thing...

Bigbie's dream of going home would not be realized until his relative, Will Lewis, voluntarily joined Joseph Johnston's army.

In the meantime, James P. Crowder was spending the winter of 1863–1864 with Longstreet's command in east Tennessee. Crowder's letter of mid-January from Morristown, Tennessee, told of bare feet, frostbite, and of a short march along the French Broad River. Obviously neither side was fit for fighting in this dismal effort that amounted to little more than a freezing stalemate.

Campe Near Mrestown Tennessee

Jan. 15, 1864

Dear Mother Brothers and Sisters,

I am yet in the land of the living and enjoing good helth every way more than my feate is frostebiten tho not bade...I am nearly crasy to heare from home for Mr. Smith sed that when he lefte home Brother George was very sick...

...[T]his morning before hit was day there come a order to cook up three days rashings and bea readey to move at twelve O clock and for the sick and the bare footed to stay in camps and there was three bare footed in our company and too sick and me my feate was sore and Dr. Burton sed that I shod not go I juste came in off ave picket laste eavening I had bin gone for 4 days and hit was very bad weather all the time and the roads very mud and my feate got very sore tho thay will bea well in a fieu days if I can stay in my winter quarters and I recon that I can for Dr. Burton sese that I shod not do no more duty this winter if my feate donte get well J. Th. Walls can tell yo what sorte of a fix my feate is in thay are like thay was laste winter more than thay are worser than thay was laste winter thay got froste biten at Winchester Va. this last fole was one yeare a go and thay do ceape a geting worser tho I have got good shoes yet tho when thay are gone I donte no where the nex is to come from

...[As for] the Regt having to march thay started at twelve O clock and all the Brigade wente and hit is a general move thay are a going down on french bread [Broad] river to run the yankes back the yankes has got too sasy to soote old general longestreete and thay will have a fite before thay come back if the yankes does not run and I donte think that thay will the laste 4 days when I was on piket there was fiting on the line all the time onley piket fiting, so I will stop the fiting [story] Mother there has bin the moste cold wether for the laste too weeaks that I ever saw hit did snow...there is some of the men that does neade close very bad we drew some close and shoes this morning and I cold a have got a coate if there had bine arey one large a nuf for me We have not got no money yet...I have to go and cut wood and make me a fire as hit is very cold I will come to a close...

In these meaningless skirmishes (many of them between cavalry units), the Federals would advance and the Confederates would repulse them, or vice versa. In this situation, a major source of Crowder's dignity and self-respect was his

responsibility as cook for his mess, a task he took quite seriously. He was still at Morristown when he next wrote home.

Camp Near Morestown Tennessee
Jan. 16, 1864
Mother,

[L]aste nite there was a [scare] in camps and all the men that was in camps was caled out thoght that the yankes was a coming...[but they did not].

...I will have to stop riting since I have sat down to rite there has come one days rashings to bea cook up and sent to the Regt and I have got three mens rashings too cook up and send hit to them so as hit is a giting late and the lite is bad and thay are a holring for me to come and get my flour I will have to come to a clos by saying rite soon...

Longstreet was astride the Virginia and East Tennessee Railroad above Knoxville. This made supplies accessible from the north, but the continued presence of Burnside and other Federals required uncomfortable moves. Thus, by February 1864, Crowder's regiment had left their warm winter quarters at Morristown for a cold temporary camp nearer Knoxville at New Market. The effect was not salutary. But Crowder would warm himself with thoughts of girls back home.

Camp Near Newmarket
Feb. 9, 1864
Dear Brother,

[T]here is some little fiting today there is some little canonading today and hit is very cold today and we have lefte our winter quarters and have all gone out of dors and that does not go well with us at all we are camped near newmarket on the railroad and the cars runs rite where we are camped and on down the road to strawbery planes and we will get any thing that we wante in a fiew days tjiere is a grate deall of clothing coming to the army and there is more shoes than you can shake a stick at I have got me a new pare of shoes and nearly all the hole army has got new shoes.

Brother as I am very cold and I have no more nuse to rite I will close by saying rite soon and rite all the nuse and rit all about the girls and how thay are a geting along and hu all is mared I heard that betty gates was mared and that there girls all dide want to mary the worse sorte and that there was a good many mared...

Moving nearer to Knoxville at Strawberry Plains, Crowder's concern for his family's well-being was both genuine and touching. As the oldest child of his widowed mother, he tried to be a father to the younger children, even at this great distance from home.

Campe Near strawberry plans
Feb. 18, 1864
Dear brothers,

I was glad to hear that yo had got a hors to plow and that...yo had got yo a sow and I was glad to hear that mother had pade Ives McKnight for the land and that she had desided to stay where she is and I was gld to hear that yo was a geting a long so well with your crop or that yo was a geting read to go to work at hit Brother I want yo [to] woark hard and make a good crop brother I will send yo all some rings I have not got one a pease tho I will send yo all that I hav got and I wante yo all to ware them hoo ever thay do fite...I will send yo 5 dolars...

Brother I will send Mother too pare of sisors by Lieut Bentley...I have nothing to send to yo all tho I will send thomas fiftey cents in confedirt money and I will send yo all some money be fore long if I donte get to come home tell William that I cante get him nary Knife heare...poket Knives is worth from ten to fifteen dolars a pease and none to sell at that in camps...

Crowder also wrote to a fellow Confederate acknowledging the mixed quality of camp life. Nearness to an operative railroad at Bull's Gap facilitated supply. But Longstreet's hopes for a Kentucky campaign were unrealistic.

Campe Near Buells gap Tennesee
March 2, 1864
Mr. J. H. Walls,

[H]oping when theas fiew lines comes to hand thay may find yo well and able to come to the regt tho yo had beter stay home as long as yo can for there is some talk of us all a going to cain Tuckey soon. We are camped at buells gap and have bin camped heare from some days and hit is sed that General [?] will bea back heare tomorow and hit is sed that Colonel [?] will bea in heare tomorow and will tak comand of our Regt and then I will bea glad and hit will all bea right General Buckhanan [?] is in command of [John B.] hoods division and he is a fine man and all the men does like him he dide have division review a fiew days ago and I can tell yo that old hoods division is a whale hit is as larg as I ever say hit since I have bin in hit.

John I can tell yo that we have had some hart times since yo lef us and then on the other hand we have had some of the beste times sence we have bin in the ware up hear in Tenessee and we have had a plentey to eate...moste of the time we have kild hogs...we are camped clost to the railroad...Give my best respect to all enquiring friends and to all the girls and accept a potion of hit yourself I want yo to rite to me how my gal is getin along...

Crowder's lack of a furlough was troubling the family. He tried to explain the situation to the homefolk. While this Confederate's personal patriotism was now more vocal, he also discouraged his brother's joining the army until he was forced to do so.

Camp Near Buells Gap Tennessee
March 13, 1864
Dear Brother,

I was sory to hear that Mother was sick and more so to heare that she is in bed sick. I would like to come home the best in the world tho there is no chance for a whyle for me to get off. The 10 of this month our company got too furlows and then all the men in the company had to draw for them and I miste hit by one draw thay give furlows to us for expresing our determination to fite this ware tell the laste and all of our Regt is in for the ware only parte of too companys thay refused to stay for the ware tho hit fuse like thay could a have done hit for thay will hold them for the ware. Brother I wente in for the ware and I do expect to fite till the last for fredom. I know that the mose of people is whiped at home or at leaste the moste of them is tho I can tell yo that the soldiers in the Army is not near whiped I can tell yo that as longe as General Longstreet has a body of soldiers as good as he has got now the Yankes never can whip them at all I am proud to say that I belong to the army of east tennessee hit is the flour of the confederate states army and can whipe twiste its number of the yankes with our galiand leader that is before us Brother we have bin camped heare on the railroad between Buells Gap and Grenville ever since the 26 [of last] month and I donte no what to think for hit I donte think that we have ever bin still this long since we have bin in service before at one place and some think that peace is a going to bea made and others thinks that we have stoped to recruite the army to make a rade in to caintuckey and some think one thing and some a nother tho hit is one thing shore that there is something up for thay ceape giving furlows to the men the cars comes heare once a day and some times more to and thay are all way loaded with men when they come down that is a coming from home on furlows and when the cars goes back to Bristol thay are loaded with men a going home on furlows General Longstreet is a furlowing ten men from every [regiment] and as soon as thay get back he sends some more and I hope that hit will bea m y time soon there is ten men in my company that has never bin home since we lefte there and when we get a furlow to our company we all have to draw for hit...hit will not do for me to come home without a furlow for thay have had the gard house full of men for the laste month for going home without leaf and I donte no when thay will get out so I had drather stay heare till the ware ends than to go home in any such a way so I have rote yo the truth and God knows it is from my harte.

Brother I no yo all think that every body else comes home only me tho hit is not so for there is a good many heare that has never bin home since we lefte and there is some good many mared men heare that has never bin home since we lefte there tho for all that I do all that is in my power to get to come home Brother yo rote in your letter that thay was a taking them [in the army] from 17 to 50 [years old] tho I wante yo to stay at home as long as yo can and when you have to go I want yo to do as yo plese come to me or go to where yo please tho I can tell yo not to get scared and leave home till yo are [drafted] to go do the beste yo can with your crop for fear yo do have to go soon I wood like to have yo with me if yo have to go tho if yo can go where yo can fare beter than yo can heare yo had beter go so I will have to close for the wante of paper...I have got me a new hat that will last for the ware.

During the month of March, three Union corps tried to close in on Morristown. But Longstreet's "flour of the confederate states army" held out until the Yankees withdrew in early April. Perhaps recurring attacks made it more difficult for Dr. Crowder to go home. Finally, his mother wrote his captain urging a furlough for her son, but to no avail. The winter had been one of unrest and uncertainty. But now it was April, and spring, while slow in coming, would mark the beginning of active campaigns when furloughs would cease. Crowder's regiment was already moving northeastward following the railroad to Bristol on the Tennessee-Virginia state line.

Campe Near the Railroad Below Bristol, Tenn.
April 9, 1864
Dear Mother,

[T]he Capt [received] that paper yo sente to him and he sed that he was wiling to give me a furlow tho the head men wante sine hit at all in that case thay say that I will have to wate tell them men comes back from home and then draw for hit. So I have done all that I can to get to come home at presant tho I will ceape a trying untill I do get to come home if I ever do I think that I will get home soon. Mother, Bentley lefte the things yo sente by him in lafayett so he ses and he got moste all the things that he started with stold from him as he come on so he never broght me nothing only the letter I wood a have rote as soon as he come tho we ware a marching when he come to us we have bin marching for the laste seven days and hit has bin the worste march that I have ever bin on hit as rand and snowd moste every day since we started and the rods is moste nee deape in mud and all of our bed close wet moste all the time and we come from Zolacofer today to this camp distance some 5 miles and hit is some six miles to bristole McClain division is gone to Bristole and hit is sed that thay are going to Richmond tho I donte no how true hit is thay say that we are camped heare for a few days till thay can get off on the car and then we will go too. Mother our Brigade has bin transferred to General [S. B.] Buckner old division and Uncle Jo Crowder is in [Archibald] grades Brigade in Buckners division and thay are camped closte to where we are. Saw Uncle Jo Crowder about one hour ago and he is well and I am glad that I have got closte to him he does drive a wagon and I can sea him moste any day.

...I donte wante yo to send me no close at present only some socks and send them by the firste one that dose past tho donte send any thing else in the clothing line for moste all that anybody starts with thay do get hit stolen from them before thay do get here if yo do get a good chance yo may send me something to eate tho yo neadn't to cook hit at all for I am as good a cook as yo ever saw so let me cook hit in my way...we may come back to georgia before longe for no one noes when we are a going yet I no of

...I am very tired and worn out from seven days march we have stoped here for a day or [two] to reste and let the rods get dry...I have to stretch my tente and bild a fier I will come to a close by saying I remain your truly sone untill death so good by...

The message of 9 April was truly "good by," so far as Crowder's extant letters are concerned. Rumors had his regiment returning to Virginia and going back into Georgia. Soon, now, General Longstreet's corps would return to northern Virginia, even as their position at Bristol might have indicated. From Bristol, it was a relatively easy trip by rail to Lynchburg, Charlottesville, and on to the Wilderness. Crowder, with Longstreet's corps, arrived at the last place in time for the Confederates' terrible defense of that area against General Grant's determined invasion on 5 and 6 May. Although the battle cost more Northern than Southern lives, a gunshot wound at the Wilderness proved fatal to Crowder.

Although the Southern cause was dying, many Johnny Rebs were not willing to admit it. Among those still hopeful were Thomas Bigbie and other Chattahoocheans at Tunnel Hill who continued to wait with Joe Johnston's army for "old Sherman" to begin his advance into north Georgia. The year 1864 promised to be the harshest one yet in this war.

5

Georgia: 1864

As the fourth year of war began, the Confederacy was faltering. Yet her armies, while forced to a defensive role, were still lethal. In Virginia, Lee would hold his own against Grant's overwhelming numbers for another year. And in Georgia, Joseph Johnston's skillful defense made William Sherman's goal of capturing Atlanta a difficult and costly task.

Contrary to some opinions, then and now, the Dalton-Atlanta campaign was not easy for either side. Sherman had good reason to respect his opponent. And with an army about half the size of the 100,000 Federal troops in and around Chattanooga, Johnston was usually wise not to attack the invader head on. It is true, however, that the Confederate commander was overly inclined toward a defensive role. Thus, Johnston would entrench his force in strong positions between Sherman and Atlanta, slowing the Federal advance and forcing a flanking move. Beginning his offensive move from Chattanooga in May, Sherman soon learned that direct assaults on Johnston's strong defensive works would cost too many Northern lives.

Once the Yankees began their flanking movement, however, Johnston would withdraw and take up a new defensive entrenchment between the Federals and Atlanta. This classic maneuver was repeated again and again until mid-July, when Johnston was removed from command and his replacement, General John B. Hood, took the initiative and attacked Sherman, only to lose Atlanta to the Federals on 2 September. That outcome was probably a foregone conclusion with or without Hood, but Johnston's defensive abilities were not always appreciated.

Following the fall of Atlanta in September, the Confederates reinforced Mobile and reinvaded Tennessee. Instead of pursuing Hood back into Tennessee, as Southern leaders had hoped he would, Sherman chose to cut his line of supply and follow a largely unobstructed route of pillage and destruction from Atlanta to the sea at Savannah. This chapter tells of a few Chattahoocheans who helped resist Sherman's advance to Atlanta and then moved to reinforce Mobile and reinvade Tennessee.

While awaiting spring and Sherman's advance, Johnston had to transfer some of his troops to places where provisions for men and forage for horses were more plentiful.

Allen Hunter Merrill, of Eufaula, Alabama, and the Eufaula Light Artillery was one of the Confederates who were ordered from a comfortable winter camp to Kingston, Georgia, where new quarters had to be built. Kingston was far to the south of the first line of defense at Tunnel Hill near Dalton. Merrill, an "only brother," must have found a sympathetic listener in his sister at home. Perhaps she was older. His letters to her reflect an understandable quality of self-centeredness.

Eufaula Light Aartilery Kingston Geo
Jan. 23, 1864
Dear Sister,

[W]e have left our camps and all our winter quarters to my great grief I was making a window in my house when the order came that we were to leave for this place in the morning I let the anger drop you may know how I felt after taking so much pains and having every thing so nicely fixed the next morning the bugle blowed before day we all rose and you may conceive the confusion some packing some cooking others loding the wagons and after getting to the depot we had to wait until nearly night before we got away the train being delayed then we stayed all night in Dalton there Herbert and myself slept in an old box car next morning we ran down to Kingston the boys hollowing at every body they saw after arriving here we stayed two nights in town then moved out our camp groun being pcked out by the officers we are ordered to build winter quarters again and I would be at work now but was not able to get boards all the boys being at work with the axes We and all the rest of the artilery is sent here to the rear to forage the horses they being very poor we are encamped near six or seven battery and in the morning I can hear bugles all over the woods the others companines are also building and the axes are going incessantly...Well Sister I must trouble you again I reckon you think I am great trouble I want 2 two pair of draws and three shirts any sort of cloth will do...it being hard to get washing done and you know that I have but two pairs of draws please get them done as soon as possible...

At Kingston, Merrill needed drawers. Thomas Bigbie, farther north at Tunnel Hill, Georgia, had more basic wants in food. As might be expected, soldiers, when idle, were more demanding of homefolk.

Tunnill Hill Ga
Jan. 25, 1864
Dear Wife,

W W Hathaway is a going to start home in a few days he will carry this letter for me...Hathaway ses that he will bring anything fer any of us that any of you wants to sen...I want you to send me a bought one side 20 [pounds] of meet and any tin jug full of surup and some eggs and a big potater home baked and sume sawcedges an egg is worth 50 cts a peace here I rite fer what I would like to have and you can send what you can wee all send fer a bought the same tell your pap that if any of them will help Hathaway to the river with the things that wee will pay them for thir trubile I want him to see that they air sent I would rite for some butter but I no that you have not got any fix the things up in a bun and marke them...we have bin fairing pirty well for a while for I went down to Marieter and I got one ham of the meet that you sent to me and I bought some more and we have got a little of it yeat and when that is out it is just to do with out only what wee git from home I had like to fergot I want some white peas send me a half bushel or a bushel of them I hav to give 1 Dollar a quart for them here and wee dont git any greens and so mity bald after peas send what you can and do the best you can I hate to send home for anything the rest is sending...rit to me all a bought my hogs and how many their is of them...

While Bigbie, a married infantryman in northern Georgia, dreamed of food, Merrill, an unmarried artilleryman, continued o construct a new camp, clear the grounds, and think about "Valentines" and other "pictures." Even as Merrill was describing the drudgery of camp life at sleepy Kingston, General Sherman was about to initiate a rapid raid from Vicksburg to Meridian and back to Chattanooga, all of which foreshadowed the destruction of his summer's Georgia campaign.

Kingston Geo
Feb. 5, 1864
Dear Sister,

I would have answered your letter before this but did not have time being so busy building the stables then after that was finished we had to sweep and rail all between our houses clear a place for dress parade which takes place every evening then camps are police every morning they seemed determined to keep us at work when we finished one thing they find an other; but now we have cleened up on both sides of our houses for a hundred yards and hope that we are done anyfway! for the present. I forgot to state in my last letter the receipt of the socks...

...I wish I were in Eufaula this February to send Valentines up here we can get none if we send any they will be written ones...P.S. I enclose jennies picture as I dont wish to keep any pictures attall...

Despite Richmond's urging, Joseph E. Johnston refused to attack the Federals at Chattanooga. Confederate morale was improving under the new command at Dalton, yet boredom was a problem. So much so that Thomas Bigbie even welcomed the opportunity to hunt deserters. He does not state that he found any but his loyalty was unquestioned. Long letters from home also relieved the tedium of waiting.

Tunnill Hill Ga
Feb. 13, 1864
Dear Wife,

I have just bin out three days a hunting fer some diserters their was seven of our camp diserted a feu nights ago and the cornel sent fer me and gave me a horse and sent me with som men after them I was gon three days and I had a fine time and faird first rate I just got back late yesterday evening...L W has got a furlogh and is a going to start in a few minits and he can tell you a grate deal more than I can rit to you...I have thought that I would git to come home some time this spring but I dont see much chance at this time them fellows diserting has stoped the furloing for a whille if nat all at the time is seems to be an un avoidable sercumstance that the inisant must sufer fer the guilty but I am a fraid that some of them will have to suffer a penilty that no body can suffr for them if they air caught...I will come as soon as I can never will you see me ling in the woods when you see me you shall see me hold my head up I will be a man...rit to me a lette[r] that it will take me a long time to read...

For those at home in the Chattahoochee Valley, the briefest of letters could bring the best of news: that one was still alive. Thus Andrew Jackson Garner's abbreviated letter to his father, John Garner, in southeastern Alabama (evidently Dale County), must have been welcome.

Camp Near Dalton Gorgia
Feb. 13, 1864
Dear father,

It is with plesher that I Seat my Self to in form you that I [am] well at this time well I hope that these few lines may find you all the Same I have nothing of importance to write I am getting a long as well as could Bee ex pectted I will get the chance to [draw] A furlow when [?] gets Back we have Dull times in camp [but] we have purty wether now for the time of year you must not look for me un tell you see me Mother you must think of me and pray [for] me when you pray for your Self father I want you to rite Soon So I will Clos by Saying [I] remain your loving Son Until Deth...

In contrast to Garner's reticence, Thomas Bigbie was verbose and explicit, though not always on camp life, which was, as Garner said, presently dull. Bigbie was still hunting deserters, thinking of food, and mindful of the provisions his "Dear Wife" sent.

Tunnill Hill Ga
Feb. 14, 1864
Dear Wife,

I recieved the letter and the provisions that you sent to me by elli Tomblin last night and I was verry glad to get them they come unexpected to me for I had heard that Hathaway was not a going to bring any thing back with him...I rot to your pap some time ago to send me a venson ham tell him that he must kill him better dears than the one that he did kill the boys sais that if he had a bin usd to eating our pore beef that he woul of thought it was fat and of packet it home...

On 9 March, three days before Thomas Bigbie's next letter, U. S. Grant was named general-in-chief of all Union armies and called east to deal with R. E. Lee. Sherman received top command of the western forces and would direct the invasion of Georgia. Meantime, Bigbie wrote of his brother L. W.'s furlough. Thomas was also ready for Will to enlist so that he could go home.

Dalton, Ga
March 12, 1864
Dear Wife,

L W has got back I received the letter that you sent by him I have sent up two furious and has not got ary this time...tell will that if he wants to come here he had better come on fer he will have to go some where soon if he ant already gone it looks like nearly every boddy will have to take a hand in this ware that can...a bought your money you had better try and send it and have it redeemed if not redeemed in one year it is not worth any thing...I am glad to see that you improve in riteing...L W ses that will sais that he want to come here if he has to go to the ware so I will send him a discriptive list so that he can come without it costing him anything if he is at home and he wants to come tell him to go to generl Shiels at ft Gains [on the Chattahoochee] and he will give him transpertation here...I understand that Governer [Thomas H.] Watts [of Alabama] has ordered all from 16 to 50 in the servis I want Will to do as he think best and as his pa and mother sais for I am not calqalatid to advise him...till Warron that I have got a rite smart of led if I could git a chance to send it to him...If it was not for the waite of it I could send him 4 or 5 pounds the boys has to walk from ft Gains and they have more to carry than they can...L W ses that you cant all read my righting you must spell and gess at it...

Camp inactivity had the positive effect of allowing time for Allen Merrill to visit relatives who were in the vicinity, even crotchety "Uncle Henry," whom the war had happily mellowed. By now Merrill had moved from Kingston northward and forward to Dalton, the site of General Johnston's headquarters.

Camp Near Dalton
March 30, 1864
Dear Sister,

[D]ont be too confident of my return home in July for all furloughing may be stoped and then you will be disappointed there are great many men in our company who have never had a furlough I went over to see Uncle Henry yesterday he seemed very glad to see me was quite sociable and gave me a bottle of molasses when I was going to leave which was very acceptable: the war has changed him for the better and a good many for the worst he even asked me to come and stay all night with him...

The weather has been very bad for the last week rain has fallen in torrents and now it is so cold that I have to leave my writing to go to the fire every now and then, it looks very little like spring as there is not a bud on any of the trees and April will soon be here...remember me to all of aunt Rena's family tell all the negros howdy...

While Grant and Sherman were polishing to coordinate their pring offensives in Virginia and Georgia, Confederate artilleryman Merrill continued writing from Dalton. Greetings to the blacks appeared in most of his letters. He wanted to go fishing for pleasure and to supplement uncertain rations.

Near Dalton Geo
April 12, 1864
Dear Sister,

Now as the weather is getting warmer I want to participate in the pleasure of fishing not only because it is a pleasure but it helps to fill up our rations, so please look in the secertary draw of my bookcase in the little draw to the right hand and send me the fish-hoocks that you find there if they are not in that draw look in all the other small ones, I hope you have put away all my schooll book as I requested you to do for I would not have one of them lost for any thing. It has been raining all day which makes it very disagreeable having to stay under our folys [sic] all the time.

...Give my love to all kiss Baby for me remember me to all the blacks...

As the fateful month of May began, Thacker Howard Owens, a native of Cottonton, Russell County, Alabama, who was a private in Companies I and G of the Thirty-Fourth Alabama Infantry, described the frustrations of picket duty on the north Georgia front. He also noted frequent moves and countermanded orders, especially those that required much useless cooking of rations. With so many false starts, it is little wonder the Confederate soldier was sometimes unprepared for battle. False starts, yes; but Sherman's army was yet to move southward from the Chattanooga vicinity.

Camp near Dalton
May 1, 1864
Dear Sister,

I have just got in from on picket. I was on twenty four hours it rained last night but I did not get wet we had an old house to stay in. We moved about 6 or 7 miles from our old Camp last week. We are now living in a house with no chimney we cook out doors but this is good soldiering. I reckon I know it is better than staying out doors. I hope we will not move any more soon but I reckon we will. We were out in the woods the other day getting boards to make a bunk too sleep on and Matt Newble came and told us we had orders to move we went back to our Cabin and thought we would have to move immediately you ought to have seen us Cooking. We Cooked about three poans of bread apiece and quit they told us to carry our Cooking utensils to the wagon and when they got there they had to come back the order was Countermanded and we were glad of it...

By springtime, as S. H. Dent's letter showed, the army's winter camp was "ripe" with the odor of filth and plagued by clouds of flies. Such a place needed to be abandoned for a new and cleaner location. Dent, however, was wrong about General Johnston taking the offensive against Sherman. As usual, a Dent letter surveyed the military situation on several fronts. He wrote from Dalton.

Dalton, Georgia
May 1, 1864
My Darling,

Well Darling May is upon us—but this morning did not look much like it had arrived. Instead of a bright clear pleasant day—we had wind and rain enough to make it cool and a fire decidedly comfortable. It had been so warm that we had knocked out a great deal of the chinking and taken off a good many of the boards of our cabin—so last night and this morning we are blessed with plenty of air. I cant say however that it is very wholesome for we have too many old camps around us. Maj Courtney is talking of moving our camps and Beckham says if we move that he will put the entire regiment nearer together—while I would have not much objection to moving I am not anxious to get into a camp with so many horses. The flies are innumurable here and the greater the number of horses the greater the number of flies. I am glad my box has arrived

[home] safely. I expect to need the articles again next winter. About sending my horse or rather sending a mule in his place the suggestion may be a very good one—but the difficulty would be in getting the mule—none worth any thing can be procured here for love or money. I can send home a very good Mare and colt in his place if that would do any better by waiting some weeks yet...I have not been to church since I have been in Dalton and I ought to feel ashamed of such neglect. But I never did enjoy going to church in a strange place and among entire strangers. The excitement about an advance of the enemy has all quieted down—but many are under the impression that we cannot remain quiet much longer. Well Darling I have had dinner. The good things of our boxes are all gone and we are coming down to plain meat and bread a gain—well we can get along on it as well as the remainder of the army. We hope to get some coffee soon and then we will be all right for the Campaign. We have received no money yet and what is worse we don't know when we will. The soldiers are needing money now about as badly as they ever have since they have been in the service. I have no money at all. I had to borrow to send the two glasses I sent by Express a few days ago. So you see you are not the only one who is suffering from exhaustion of the pocket—well I have a good many postage stamps and a small quantity of paper so I will not need much money...Genl Johnston is receiving reenforcements and many think he will take the offensive if the enemy does not very soon. I see by the "Spirit [of the South" of Eufaula] that horses were given to two of [H. D.] Claytons staff...Lt. Col Bondurant of our Regt has been moved to Mobile. That creates a vacancy in the Regt and as Maj Courtney is the senior Major he may be promoted—and then possibly the senior Capt may be made a major—when all this is done I would be second Capt in the Battalion. Capt Kolb has been trying very hard to get Napoleon Guns But has not succeeded yet. He threatened to resign a day or two ago unless heavier Guns were given him. He has four howitzers. I hear nothing more about transfers from my company. Genl Johnston was my friend and disaproved all the applications. He calls mine a confederate Battery. To all appearances the men are contented...Troops are coming up here from Savannah—at least such is the report. I have not seen any of them, and it is reported that Genl [S. D.] Lee Commanding the cavalry in Miss—is on his way here—all this looks very much like our Generals expected this to be the scene of active operations. Genl Beauregard was at Wilmington [North Carolina] a week ago—and the capture of Plymouth is attributed to his prescence. There were very few troops in

Charleston when Thomasson was there—all had left for other fields...

By 3 May, Allen Merrill (as well as Dent and others) was quitting his creature comforts such as books, baggage, and blankets. Merrill had sent these items home in preparation for the summer campaign. In fact, skirmishing had already begun as each army flexed its muscles, impatient for contact.

Dalton Geo
May 3, 1864
Dear Sister,

I received your letter...relating to the books that I wrote for, you need not trouble yourself about them for I dont want you to send them as our Library is broken up, we have to carrie all of our bagage and blankets now consequently I have sent nearly all of mine home, which I suppose you have received ere this reaches you. I recon you heared of the excitement that we had lose Friday, in the morning about nine oclock the battery being out at drill we heared cannomradig in front and the long roll was beating in every direction and the infantry were marching out to our brest works then very suddenly the Battery came rushing in Capt [M. D.] Oliver hollowed out for us to pack our bagage and get ready to leave for the front immediately every thing was bustle and confusion but soon the gunners formed their detachments and we moved off in a gallop when we reached the brest works we took position on a high hill to wait until the yankees should come in sight but soon we heared that they had been driven back with our cavalry and we returned to camps, yesterday the same thing took place again except that we advanced about two miles toward Tunnel hill, but we are again safe in camps once more...

Already under marching orders, Dent did not need the distraction of stampeded artillery horses. And as noted, he was both right and wrong about the coming engagement. Testing for a frontal attack near Dalton on 7 and 8 May, Sherman, on finding the Confederates strongly entrenched at Buzzard's Roost, chose to flank them rather than sacrifice his troops. Similarly, Johnston chose to retreat rather than be outflanked. Dent's wife, Anna Beall, had visited him in camp during the winter at Dalton. Now the image of her goodness encouraged his piety, a major source of strength on the eve of meeting the Yankee foe.

Camp near Dalton Ga

May 4, 1864

We have just received orders to be ready to march at any moment—and as I promised yesterday to write you to-day I want to do so—although I am suffering so severely from sick headache that I can scarcely hold my head up. I sent my horses out to graze yesterday and they were turned loose near the Raisle Road—a Train came along stampeded Capt Garrity horses that were nearer the track than mine.

His horses ran through mine and the whole were stampeded. I have lost five permanently I fear. I have been riding all morning looking for them and it is the effect of the sun that has affected my head. It is a serious loss. Garrity lost six. I have some men out still but I have but little hope of finding them...I cant imagine what the order to be ready for action on short notice means. I have not heard a gun to-day or yesterday and as far as I Know every thing was quiet. But the two armies are so near together that a few hours any time can bring on an engagement. Since I have commenced writing...I have heard of four of my horses and if I get them I will be pretty well satisfied although I dislike very much to lose a single one. They are so scarce and hard to get...Nearly every one thinks that the collision so much talked of here connot be postponed a great deal longer. I can not think that the enemy will attack us in front. They may attempt to pass one of our flanks and if they do I think Genl Johnston would attack them. Be cheerful Darling about the result. I think Genl J. will be victorious when he fights and I trust the same kind Providence who has hithirto protected me will continue to do so. I feel Honey that your visit to me this winter did me a great deal of good. I believe I am a better man than I was and Darling to you I owe it all under Heaven. I am reading 2nd Kings also—I will read to morrow morning beginning at the 21st Chap. I do all my reading in the morning as I am unable to procure any candles now—You Know commissaries are not allowed to sell anything to officers now. We will be annoyed now constantly with orders to be ready to move until this fight is over. I do not feel at all like moving this evening but if I am right well in the morning and I hope I will be I don't care how soon we move out. Well Darling it is now Thursday morning. I feel much better—but my head is very sore. I hear this morning that the enemy have retired from our front and a good many think the order to be ready to move means that Genl Johnston intends advancing. If this news be true I think we will be moving in less than three days—all our cavalry are coming up from our rear I saw a good deal moving yesterday. I have recovered all my horses but one...

Moving around Dalton, Sherman had hoped to outflank Joe Johnston's army at Resaca. But when the Yankee advance rider under General James B. McPherson arrived there on 9 May, they found too many Confederates already dug in and others arriving by the minute. McPherson hesitated and Johnston reinforced Resaca. Now, like Buzzard's Roost at Dalton all over again, it would cost the Federals too many lives to make a frontal assault. Thus, after two days of limited skirmishing (14–15 May), Sherman began his flanking movement once more, forcing Johnston to retreat from Resaca down the Western and Atlantic Railroad to Adairsville.

By keeping his troops between Sherman and Atlanta, Johnston was behaving much like R. E. Lee in Virginia, proving himself a capable defensive commander. But this fact was not always recognized by Southerners, especially Georgians, who believed that Johnston's small army could simply attack and defeat Sherman's superior numbers of veteran troops. Until he reached Kennesaw Mountain, Sherman would not assault Confederate trenches. And Johnston refused to attack against such risky odds. Thus, Confederates continued holding and retreating in an orderly manner from Adairsville (17 May) to Cassville (19 May) and on to New Hope Church (25-27 May).

Shortly after New Hope Church (and Pickett's Mill, 27 May), one of Johnston's troops, Thacker Howard Owens, acknowledged the stress of this defensive campaign.

Sunday morning
May 29, 1864
My Dear Sister

...We have been going three weeks almost when...we were not marching we were in our breastworks and the bullets and shells coming part of the time I have stood the march very well part of the time but my foot hurts me now it does not hurt bad enough for me to stop though...Jim Chapman did not stay here long before he got wounded. I was broiling a piece of meat the other night and I heard some one say Oh Lord and as soon as I heard it I knew some one was wounded but did not know who it was. I heard Matt say Chapman is wounded. I ran where he was and thought he was dead but he was not he was laying down with his back to the breastworks and a stray ball came along and wounded him. Cousin Jimmie Carried him to the hospital he said it was just a slight wound. Cousin Jimmie got two of his fingers shot but it did not hurt him much. I hope this fuss will soon be over for I am tired of it but I am afraid it will not end soon. I went over the battle field this morning. I saw a good many dead yankees and took my breakfast in ten steps of two this morning. All of the boys are well...

In May, Will Lewis finally came into Johnston's army, thus enabling Thomas Bigbie to obtain his long-sought furlough home. On 21 May, shortly after Bigbie's return to the army, he wrote, "When I got to the regt it was in a line of battle a mile from town and our compiny was three miles of on picket." Once Bigbie rejoined his group, he found that "Will keeps up but he is not well I carry his close for him and help him all I can." Will would have been an unusual recruit not to have been shaken by immediate combat and retreat before an army of more than 100,000.

Writing again on 29 and 30 May, Thomas Bigbie described Pickett's Mill where Patrick Cleburne's crack Confederates stopped a Federal offensive on 27 May, inflicting heavy losses on the attackers. The struggle continued as Confederates tried to stop Sherman's flanking move to the east toward Marietta and the railroad near Kennesaw Mountain. Even then, Will Lewis was still unarmed and thus trying to stay out of the "fight."

Camp 33
May 29, 1864
Dear Wife,

[O]n friday 27 wee went through as hard a fight as wee have ever had and I am still spaird and numbered a mong the living our loss was heavy our compiny got 2 kild and 5 wounded sevrel struck with bullets that is not disabled...but I never have seen the like of yankeys that was kild in one place I could of walked 2 or 3 hunderd yards on the bodys of the ded yanks this I seen with my one eyes I was in 50 yards of them wee helt the battle field and beuried our ded and carred out our wounded.

May 30 since yeasterday wee have moved to miles they fought all night last night and everything is still to day the left end of our regt and some cavrley run 3 hunderd yds through a field and broke their line but wee had to git back on the back on [of] the line our regt suferd worse than any one in the division Will was not in the fight he has an ax and when I seen that wee was a going to fight I told him to fall out and take the best cear of him self that he could so I did not see him in to days he has come up ses he faird verry well wee have heepe of them and never lost but too men kild and 11 wounden till last friday wee have got a plenty to eat I must close I thank God that I am spared this fair...send me some paper and envelops this is my last paper.

Shortly after Pickett's Mill, William P. Lewis wrote his parents explaining his initiation into army service.

Camp 33 Ala regt
June 7, 1864
Dear father and Mother,

[T]his will in form you that I am up and a bought at this time I have bin puny for some time but I ceepe with the compiny yeat I have bin a marching nearly every day and night since Thomas come back and I git a long very well if it was not for my bouels they bother me a grate deal but I am in hops that I will git well some time I have seen a heepe since I have bin here I was not in the fight that we had [on] the 27 of May I [have no] gun to carry I have an ax to carry so when they started in to the fight they told wee to stay that did not have a gun I have bin withe they compiny the most of the time I have seen severl men kild since the fight commencts...

Thomas Bigbie on 9 June added a note to Will's letter of 1 June in which he stated, "Dear Wife this will in form you it I am tolerbul well Will keeps up [Brother] L W is gon to the hospital he is not sick [but] had a risen on him so that he aid not march."

Compared with the "green" Will Lewises of this war, S. H. Dent was a veteran, seasoned several times over. He was also nearly a captain, having been promoted to head "Dent's Battery." Captain Dent clearly understood Sherman's flanking strategy when he wrote his "Darling" wife on 7 June. At that point, the two armies were still maneuvering for control of the Western and Atlantic Railroad, this time just north of Marietta. Dent's identification of the location of the corps commanders is not the one usually given. But he had heard correctly; Sherman would finally risk a frontal assault at Kennesaw Mountain on 27 June.

Meanwhile in Virginia, General Grant's force had, as Dent noted, moved closer to Richmond at the costly battle of Cold Harbor on 3 June.

Dent's Battery Johnston's Army
June 7, 1864
My Darling,

I wrote you a letter on the 5th Darling—we are in the same position. I do not believe our lines were formed when I wrote to you. Genl Hardee occupies the right—Hood the center and [Leonidas] Polk the left—our left rests at the foot of Lost Mountain. The right extends towards the rail road. We are about seven miles from Marietta, The enemy are following us up...The left fell back at Lost Mountain...I was interrupted here Darling to ride out in front of our works to see the Country to know how to use my guns. I went as far as our picket lines. It is reported that the enemy are moving to our right towards the Rail road. I am afraid we will [miss] them here. [I have my line positioned and prepared to fight them.]...I heard a rumor this morning that we had captured one of Sherman's couriers with despatches for Washington stating that he had driven Johnston as far by flanking him as he could and that to get him further back he would be compelled to fight him. I think probably the conclusion is correct but I do not believe the report about the capture of the Courier. The weather is very warm. I have not felt summer until the last few days. To-day the sun shines but very powerfully—and the only shade we have is artificial. I have not seen or heard directly from the relief committee. I heard a rumor that they were in Marietta—but I have not seen any one that has seen them. I would like very much to see them—but I hardly think they will venture out so far in the mud and I Cannot go down there. I am afraid our people will use up a great deal before the battle actually takes place and perhaps not be so well prepared as they are now. In My own opinion this campaign will continue all summer a good deal in the same manner that it has been carried on for the last thirty two or three days. Sherman is evidently very Cautious and I have very little idea that he will attack us in our works—I expect some morning to get the order to move forward and fight the yanks in their position as they do not seem disposed to fight us in ours.

Every thing seems to be going on well in Virginia athough Grant has reached nearly the same position that McClellan held two years ago [at Fair] Oaks—no one seems to be frightened. I think however that a great many are moving out. Mrs Courtney has left there she came as far as Columbia So. Ca. Maj C has sent for her to come to Atlanta or Marietta I feel very sorry for persons whose homes are in the hands of the enemy. I have seen some very distressing sights on this campaign. I hope I will get newspaper to-day. I want to see if any thing is going on. By the way the Black Republican Convention meets in Baltimore to-day and from the common newspaper statements—there will be very much such another scene as there was there four years ago when we were there...

Johnston's army, exhausted from strenuous marching in heat and rain, needed rest. By 21 June, Dent's battery was located a few miles west of Marietta near Lost Mountain. Although jaded by incessant contact with the enemy, he could write of soap and newspapers as though they were his major concern. Perhaps such subjects were designed to distract Nannie. The relief committee must have been from Eufaula or Barbour County, Alabama.

June 21, 1864

My Darling,

You would have been amused to have seen me a few moments ago darning my socks. You know I do not like to wear socks with holes and as he pair I had was in that condition I got out a small round used for carrying powder and regularly darnid my socks. We moved again on yesterday evening Darling and passed through Marietta and are bivouaced I expect about west from that place—going towards our left—we are on the powder springs road. It is reported that the enemy are in force about four miles from us. Genl [Carter] Stevenson's Division is passing now. I expect we will move as soon is that passes...I spoke to Maj Courtney of your kind offer and he desired me to thank you very heartly for your kindness and attention but that Mrs C. had effected arrangement in Columbia SC and expected for the present to make that her home. But that if in any way that arrangement should be broken up she might then avail herself of your offer. [Major] C. tried yesterday to get a Twenty-four hours leave to visit her—but it has not returned and I expect this move will defeat him. We are having a damp drizzly morning...I stopped as I passed through Marietta yesterday evening and took supper with the relief committee—and they gave me a piece of soap which I needed very much as some one stole the last piece I had a few days ago. I do not Know when they will leave. I have no idea Darling what is going on. In fact I never Know certainly what is going until I see the newspapers and when I see them I Know how to make allowances for what I see stated as actually occurring and then guess at the truth. It amuses one who Knows all about these things to see the highly wrought and highly colored pictures which are presented in our newspapers. It is raining faster and I think we will have another rainy day. It is worse than it was on the retreat out of Middle Tenn—last summer and that was very bad...

Dent's nearly illegible letter of 22 June was full of news about the box he had received from home. The Western and Atlantic Railroad to Atlanta was still in Confederate control. Sherman had the northern route to Nashville as his line of supply.

Dent's Battery Johnston's Army
June 22, 1864
My Darling,

I received yesterday the boots and letters together with the Testament and book you very Kindly sent me by Mr Starnes. One of the Eufaula Artillery passed my camp late yesterday evening and told me they were in Marietta. I immediately went up after them. Darling I am very glad you sent me the Testament. I shall carry it about with me and try and read it regularly. I shall get along ways behind in my Bible reading with you. The book sent I have glanced at and I think I will find it very interesting. I was very glad to get the boots one of my feet had been nearly on the ground. Yesterday morning however before I Knew the new ones had come—I got my shoe maker and went to my cooking wagons and sat down and waited until he mended them. They will last probably a month longer—as long as it is so muddy I shall wear the old ones...I hope the sun will continue out all day. Genls Johnston and Hood have just passed going towards our front. I think we will be very apt to move today. We do not often remain in bivouac longer than two days and rarely as long as that. I can hear skirmishing going on now. [Reuben] Kolb is in position and had three men wounded on yesterday. I do not think he has been on our front lines until recently. He has four Napoleon Guns now and I expect is very proud of them. The Eufaula Artillery is just below me on this same road. I saw Genl [Alpheus] Baker yesterday—he was visiting the relief Committee.

Allen H. Merrill was also suffering from Johnston's rapid responses to Sherman's quick flanking movements. Such response had the effect of extending the Confederate lines. The continuing heavy rains annoyed and impeded both Federals and Confederates. The "College examinations" were the commencement festivities at the

Union Female Academy in Eufaula, an opportune time for young men with courting on their minds.

Near Marietta
June 22, 1864
Dear Sister,

I received your letter on the eighteenth and I will tell you where I was when I got it, on the morning of that day about light we received orders to move after marching awhile it began to rain very hard soon we were wet through still we moved on to the left about ten oclock we stoped and the mail came up and in it my letter I was very glad to hear from home while there we built big fires and dryed as soon as we were comfortable we had to march back nearly to the same place we started from that day and got soaked again but I dryed off and had a very comfortable nights sleep. I would like very much to be a[t] home during the college examination as it always such a busy time and then the concert which I expect will be a good one I hope the audence will pay a little more attention to the music than they did before. Tell Miss Ann Green that it is getting time for the old maids to enquire after me as none of the young ones will do it...Enclose in your next letter an envelop and sheet of paper...I have pape at the wagons but gant get it at present.

Monday, 27 June, dawned clear. The rains were gone, but lingering moisture made a steamy hot day for Sherman's assault on Kennesaw. The mountain was near the center of Johnston's defensive line. Federal cannon opened fire at eight, and an hour later, George H. Thomas's Army of the Cumberland challenged Frank Cheatham's strong defensive position, but to no avail. The Chattahoochean Allen Merrill was on the edge of the Kennesaw battle, which he described, but less adequately than he pictured the trenches and breastworks that protected Confederates. By now, the Confederates were so adept at building defenses that Federals accused them of carrying breastworks on their backs. Combat disrupted payrolls and other aspects of regular army life.

Near Marietta

June 28, 1864

My Dear Sister,

[A]t present my health is very good never having been sick but three or four day[s] and then I had nothing but slight fevers and one dose of oil put me to rights again. We are on the left wing of the army and have been for the last day or two camped in a beautiful oak grove near the house where Ben Flake was marrie[d] the line of brest works run through the yard and our guns are in position in the garden it makes me feel sad to see every thing destroyed like they are here, for instance this beautiful place all the fence is all torn down some of the out houses also to make brest works some of the old magestic oaks that have stood for centauries are cut down but it is all done to stop the progress of our enemies and should not be murmured at.

There has been heavy skirmisheing going on in our front today and yesterday, not far to the right has been some cannonnading, and on Kenesaw mountain the booming of the cannon is a continiuous thing, yesterday there was some hat work done the yanks charged Gen Cheatham on our right, they were repulsed with heavy loss and some few prisoners captured. As one half of the detachment have to stay up at the gun all the time and now as it is my time to go I will close untill I return. I resume my pencil as everything is quiet in front of us. The clouds I think have drained themselves for we have very prettie weather now although it is extremely hot and the days seem very long to me as I have nothing to read and nothing to do as you know we have not marched any lately that is for the last day or two I had almost forgotten that this is one of the days of the Colledge examination and I expect while I am writing in one of the negro houses (for that is the case) you are in the Chapel surrouned by many other prettie faces all faning for I know it is hot there as well as here; I only wish I were with you. Dear Sister I am again reduced to the necessity of writing for money please send me twenty dollars in as small bills as possible, you must remember that I have never drawn a cent of pay since I came in service that washing is high and is often in my power to buy chickens and such like when we are marching through the contry though it is very seldom, I hope It will not be any trouble to you if it is dont do it as I can wait untill we are payed off which I have been looking for a long time...

The Bigbies, in the infantry, had seen heavy fighting, probably at Kennesaw Mountain. Thomas was wounded, but as L. W. told his sister, Mary Jane, he and a physician conspired to keep young Will Lewis away from the worst dangers of battle.

July 1, 1864
Dear Sistr...

[W]e are yet in line of Battle lying Behind our Brst works Thorn & Will is Both at the iospittal Tomey was Slightly wounded & Will was Sick Will was not Bad off a tall he was able to go a bout But not able for lots & the Docters Sent him off where he would Be out of Dainger tomy was Wounded one morning Be fore he got up...I will ell you that dick miller Was kild a day or to a go he vas kild a Skirmishing he was Shot [in] the head & died Right off...

Thomas Bigbie's wound was not serious. He soon wrote his wife about himself and the severe Union losses, especially at Kennesaw. There, Sherman finally risked a bloody frontal assault that was repulsed with 2,051 Federal casualties before Johnston resumed the more cautious strategy of flanking and maneuvering his army ever backward, however slowly, upon Atlanta. Bigbie's optimistic calculations for the Confederates did not include President Davis's removal of Johnston from command.

Marietta Ga
July 1, 1864
Dear Wife,

God has spaired me to rite you once more I am in verry good helth at this time on thursday 23 of this month of June I got slightly wounded a bullet strikeing me on the ankle it will be well in a few days I am at Marietta at this time and is a fairing verry well I shall got to my Co in a few days I have bin going a bought all of the time but my foot is too sore to wair my shoe so I am a gitting a little rest...since I came back here [from furlough home] I have bin in severl fights...L W has got back well he went to Mongomery Ala my wound was not bad a nuf for me to git a furlough I am truly glad it is no worse than it was it is all most un crettibul to tell how wee have kild and slaurterd the yanks and still their seems to be fight [left] in them wee have got them drove back and they as though they dreded it now I beleive that wee air bound to whip them in this fight though wee have fell back and lost a good deal of ground their is a rite smart of sickness in our army at this time their has bin so much rain and bad wether wee have mity pirty wether at this time I have don more and see more since I left home of hard solgrering than I did in the two years before this is the way to winde up the ware and I wish how soon it may be if sherman will push as hard on us for the next 2 monts as he has the past tow I think that wee will winde him up O that this cruel ware could end and wee could all git home...we have not got any money yeat but wee git a plenty to eat nothing more remember me and pray for me oftin I am as ever your Husband till Deth...

Under heavy artillery fire from the Federals after Kennesaw, Johnston's army continued its Fabian retreat. Early in July, the Confederates constructed defensive works on the north bank of the Chattahoochee River, halfway between Marietta and Atlanta. Captain Hubert Dent described this position and naively hoped conditions would force the Federals to an early peace. No sooner had Dent finished writing than Sherman sidled again, and Johnston promptly abandoned the river defense that he said would detain the Federals for sixty days. General Leonidas Polk, the Episcopal bishop and Confederate corps commander, had been killed 14 June at Pine Mountain, near Kennesaw.

July 7, 1864

My Darling,

We are in position about half a mile north of the Chattahoochee have a very good position. We never went in position until yesterday evening. We were subject to a very heavy artillery fire yesterday morning—while building my works I had one man killed and another wounded who went to the Hospital—besides a third slightly wounded...Out of ninety men who enlisted at Pensacola two and a half years ago—we have less than forty men left—and some of them are disabled by wounds. A man came back to the Battery a few days ago who was wounded at Chickamauga—in fact two came back—neither of them fit for duty...I expect the Yankee Batteries will open again to-day. Sherman seems inclined to make this fight with artillery. Well Darling I have had my breakfast. The Yankees have commenced shelling again this morning but not so furiously as they did yesterday. I can hear some artillery down to our left and across the river. Stevenson's Div. is across the river—and Garrity's Battery of our Battalion—we are pretty near the river. [Alexander P.] Stewarts Div. is between us and the river—most of our wagons and ordinance trains are across the river...Notwithstanding our prospects just now do not look very bright I cannot help believing that there is a good prospect for peace by the end of this year. I do not think I have ever before believed as strongly that peace was so near. It may be that the wish in this case is so strong that my belief is the result of it...Have you heard that [H. D.] Clayton was a Maj Genl? Well he is and takes command of Stewarts Division. Stewart goes to Polks Corps.

Clayton has risen rapidly and I think he will make a good Major General. [John C.] Brown was strongly recommended—but Clayton got ahead of him. [Thomas C.] Hindman who had hurt one of his eyes and gone to the Hospital has returned and Brown has been sent back to his old Div. Some Alabamaian will be made a Brig, to take Clayton's Brigade—Holtzclaw I expect. There is one piece of news that I must write. The man who was taking care of the mare & colt back at the wagons—has been missing since our last fall back and some fear he has deserted and taken the horse off with him. I will not think he has yet. But I cannot help wondering what has become of him...Well Darling it is now past 5 o'clock P M. The enemy [is] shelling again quite furiously. This is their usual custom every evening...

On 8 July, the same day Sherman's flanking move would force Johnston's army to retreat across the Chattahoochee, L. R. Byron wrote from the north bank of that river. Byron, apparently a member of D company of the Thirty-Ninth Alabama Infantry Regiment, wrote for himself and other soldiers from Eufaula. Byron did not foresee that Sherman would flank the Confederates to the northeast farther up the Chattahoochee at Soap Creek. Like the Confederate government at Richmond, young Byron was ready for General Johnston to attack the Federals. Few realized how little time Johnston had remaining as commander of this army.

In line of battle on Chattahoochee River [northern Georgia]
July 8, 1864
Kind friends,

We arrived at this place on the morning of the 5th of July we formed line of battle ten miles up and down the River and a better position we have not had since this campaign, the enemy was in full pursuit of us and got here about the same time we did, we did not get the line of battle formed before they commenced shelling us, & they have been shelling ever since. Our Soldiers have had a hard time for the last month and a half, and need the simpathies and good wishes of our friends at home. We are battling for freedom for every thing that is near and dear to us.

Several of our boys have fell in this campaign their lovely faces never more to be seen by their parents and loved ones at home, still we are cheered on by the hope that be the prayrs and true sympathies of those at home that after a while we will come but victorious and gain a complete victory that will give us peace. This campaign has been on hand better than two months and our loss out of our Regt has been upwards of Seventy, the loss of the whole army more than ten Thousand, that of the enemy has been considerable more. Our gallant Lieut Grantham fell a victim to the invading foe he was shot while out on Picket through the left breast by a miney ball. We moarn the loss of Lieut Grantham as a good officer and soldier [his remains] ware buried in Marietta Ga on the 30th of June I think it likely that we will not have to give back from the enemy any further. They may flank us by the way of West point [to the southwest] but that is the only way, if they should attack us at this point there is no doubt of our success. Our troops are in high spirits more so than they have been putting confidence in our position and works we feel confident of success. Our commanding Generals & our privates I think have been driven as far as they intend to be. And erlong I think you may hear of a complete victory by the success of our armies at this place. I would like to return home to see my friends and relatives. I would like the best in the world to go fishing again I think I could enjoy myself finely...

S. H. Dent described the artillery bombardment and flanking moves of 8 July, which persuaded Johnston to retreat across the Chattahoochee to new defensive lines. For the first time, Dent was openly critical of his commander. By now, the persistent Federal advance was on the outskirts of Atlanta. General Johnston would later claim that he was finally ready to risk his army in an all-out attack on the Federals when they had to divide their force in order to cross Peachtree Creek.

July 9, 1864

My Dear Darling,

Gov [John Gill] Shorter wrote...that the [relief] committee would locate yesterday at Clayton's Division Hospital. I also Darling received the box of vegetables. Every thing came very well unfortunately the stopper came out of the bottle of pure vinegar and it was lost. The pepper vinegar is very good. The

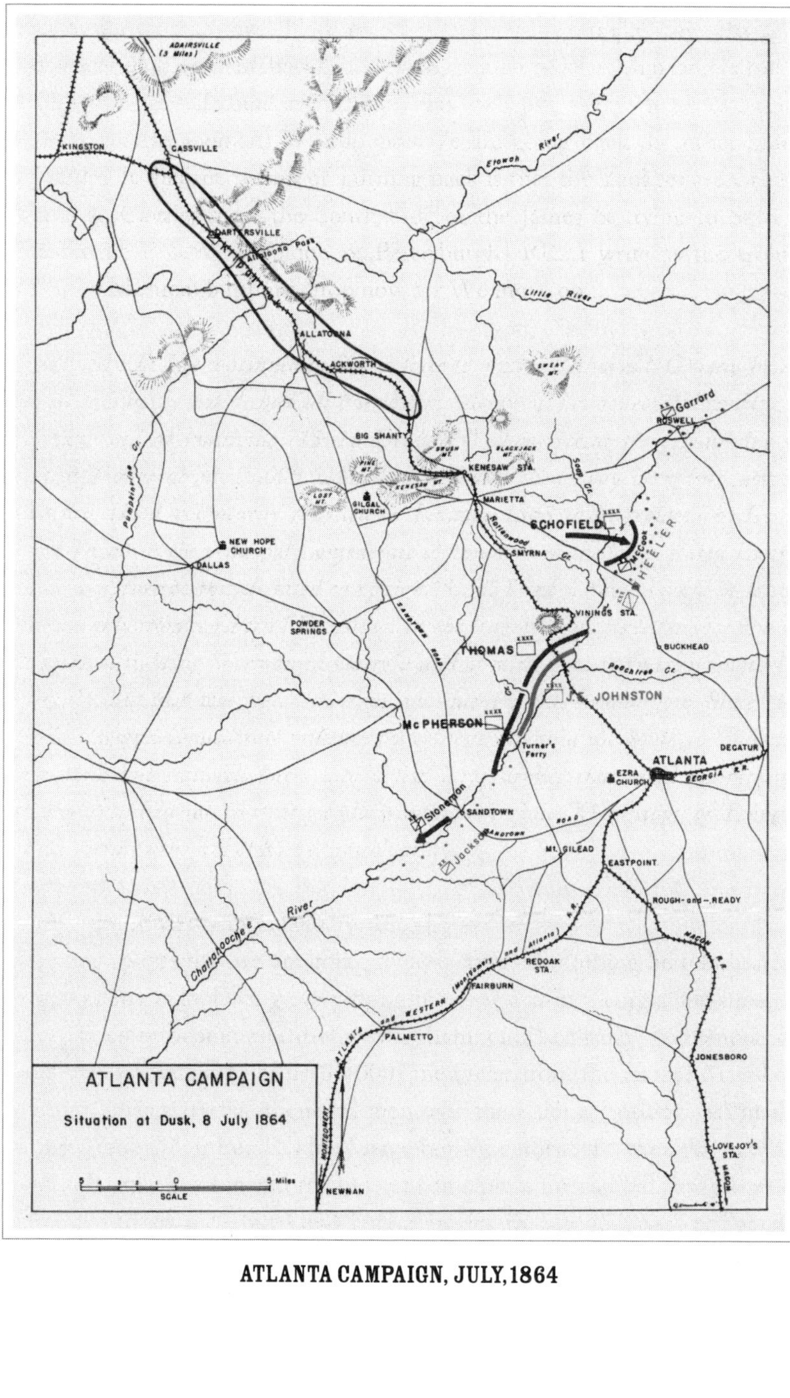

ATLANTA CAMPAIGN, JULY, 1864

beans potatoes and corn all of which we have tried we have found very good. The cucumbers did not appear very fresh but they tasted first rate—we keep our wagons across the river and have our cooking done there—and as we have to trust to others altogether, I had the catsup and Jam put by until such time as we could enjoy them better...We have been under a very severe artillery fire ever since we occupied our present position—a fragment of a shell entered one of my embrasures yesterday striking the face of the piece injuring it slightly and slightly wounding six men. I had to send the gun to the rear to be repaired. It was marvellous that it only slightly wounded six and seriously hurt no one. Three of them have gone to the hospital. The others did not go at all. None of them are from about Eufaula. It was a chance shot—and I hope they will not repeat it—we are not allowed to fire at the Yankee Batteries—ammunition too scarce. But about sunset on the 7th we opened on all the Batteries and kept up a heavy fire for a few minutes. The enemy replied with all their guns and the uproar was almost deafning. Their fire has not been so steady and constant since—but they still keep up a heavy fire—about every two or three minutes a shell comes screeching over—we have been quite fortunate lately in getting quiet positions. But we have one uncomfortable enough now to make up for all past favors. The weather is very warm—sultry—and the only shade we have is a brush arbor in our ditches—very little air can reach us—but still the company is quite healthy—one section of my Battery has been moved about three hundred yards further to the right...The enemy are demonstrating on our left and trying to cross the river. It is thought that we will finally cross the river. Stevenson's and Cheathims Divisions are already across—and perhaps others that I know not of. I have no idea that will be the result—But fear that Atlanta will be given up. If Johnston can be flanked out of every position from Dalton here I do not see why he cannot be flanked out of Atlanta. But I hope not. Every thing of a permanent character is being moved from there [illegible] I think this whole army will be pretty well tanned in this campaign...The artillery fire has ceased here—but the pickets keep popping away. I hear an occasional piece of Artillery on our right...I have just finished my dinner...The enemy are still firing—and a little more briskly. It will be apt to increase as the evening comes on I wish the Quarter masters Dept would get some money. I have not drawn any pay since I returned from home. They owe me for four months and at the end of this month will owe me for five months which will be seven Hundred Dollars...PS—we cross the Chattahoochee to-night good by. I will be on the...[other] side of the river before morning I think...

Neither Captain Dent nor the Confederate government at Richmond knew of Joseph Johnston's alleged plan to strike Sherman's army at Peachtree Creek. Johnston was popular with his men, but he was a poor diplomat and had consistently refused to divulge his plans to civilian leaders, particularly President Davis, whom he disliked and distrusted. He had also consistently retreated, giving the Confederate government no reason to think he would stand and fight for Atlanta. Thus, on 11 July, President Davis, with some reluctance, removed Johnston from command and replaced him with the battle-maimed General John B. Hood. No great intellect, the courageous and "gallant" Hood was a known fighter.

It was then no surprise to either side when Hood attacked the Federals at Peachtree Creek on 20 July. Here, just north of Atlanta, the Confederates fought well but were too uncoordinated to stop Sherman's larger force. Dent's letter was written between the clash of Peachtree Creek and the battle of Atlanta, fought near Decatur on 22 July. Dent's sense of being removed from the conflict reflects Hood's relatively limited use of artillery at Peachtree Creek.

In the field
July 21, 1864
My Dear Nannie,

We have been expecting all the morning that a fight would take place. But excepting some skirmishing which has taken place on our right, I have heard nothing like fighting. Stewarts corps with a portion of Hardee's drove the enemy on our left yesterday and from all I have been able to gather had quite a severe fight with them. Yesterday was quite a busy day with our immediate command—we moved into position about day light yesterday—went to work to fortify about 12 oclock left and went to the left—remained there ibout an hour or more—were then ordered back to wr first position—before we got there however were ordered on futker to the right and finally went nto position and fortified—finished our work early his morning—and have been awaiting for the fight which was expected to take place to-day—the third anniversary of the battle of [first] Manassas. But it is now after 12 O 'clock and no fight yet. Hood seems disposed to fight. The Yankees are getting all around us and it is getting time we were doing something. I expect the Columbus people were reatly excited when the Yankee raiders [under Heneral Lovell Rousseau] tore up the track on the Opelika and Columbus [rail]road. They seem disposed to destroy every thing through the country and it seems impossible to prevent such things. The Yankees have possession of the Augusta [rail]road nd consequently no communication in that direction. I do not think it will be long before the fight comes off. Hood is treading a dangerous path. This Army [of Tennessee] has killed A S Johnston laid Beauregard and Bragg aside and now Johnston (old Joe). So you see He [Hood] is the fifth Commander his army has had. I hope Hood will [utilize] his opoortunities better than any of the others. The yankees are at their old game of shelling. But not as continuously as they did when we were on the other de of the Chattahoochee....The Yankees have been throwing throwing a few shells into Atlanta. But as far as I have heard did no harm...Genl Cheathim Commands our corps—and Brown our Division. I have been expecting that Hindman would return so as to get command of the Corps being the Senior Major Genl in it. But he has not returned and Cheathim has been sent here from Hardees Corps to command us. Brig Genl Stevens of [W. H. T.] Walkers Division was Killed yesterday also Major Preston who commanded a battalion of Artillery in [Edward C.] Walthalls Division. He was formerly chief of Artillery for Genl Johnston—afterwards Inspector of Artillery. I expect you heard me mention him while you were in Dalton last winter. I heard of no other casualties and in fact have not heard any other particulars of the fight—just now every thing is remarkably quiet. I cannot even hear a stray picket fire. I saw Capt Macon Yesterday. He returned a few days ago. He is still with the Brigade. Clayton will make an effort to get him with him as soon as he can. As soon as this fight is over I am going to try and get a week or ten days furlough. I could spend several days at home by getting ten days leave...

On the day of the battle of Atlanta, Dent noted the necessity for his artillery to retreat inside the citadel of breastworks surrounding the city.

July 22, 1864

Well Darling we fell back last night inside the works immediately around Atlanta. I suppose it may be formally announced that the siege commenced. I am already in position...

But Hood's army could also come out of the citadel, as they demonstrated on 22 July when William Hardee took his Confederate corps on a flanking march toward Decatur just to the east of Atlanta. Here, he surprised James McPherson's Union force. Hardee's troops might have carried the day had not the Federals fortuitously extended their left flank before the attack. A. H. Merrill described some of the Confederate troop movements in this battle of Atlanta. This was the second time Hood's army had failed to defeat the Federal force that threatened the city.

Atlanta Geo.
July 23, 1864
Dear Sister,

I have put off writing to you longer than I intended doing but it is owing to our constant movements, it was not our good fortune to remain quietly in camps long, we moved over to the east side of Atlanta and are now in the suburbs of the city in line of battle night before last we left a line which is now about a half mile in our front while there we were under constant fire frome a yankee battery. The evening before we left very unexpectedly as we received orders to...move the guns was striped the men were told to leave their blankets and everything else at the caissons one man was to carrie an axe in his hands, all expected a grand charge we had not moved far before we halted, and it was accertained by our Generals that the enemy were massking their troops in front of us and it was all given overs that night we moved back to our present position and yesterday morning we that is our Battery with others opened on the enemy lines, shelling every place we saw a squad thrying to work and made one battery move its position, but that evening we could hear the rattle of musketry far off to our right and as it grew later it drew nearer, and then the troops around us were formed into three lines of battle and moved to the front to charge the enemy soon nothing could be heared but musketry and cannon our battery did not go to the front but was under a terrific fire from the batterys in front of us, the sum and substance of the whole was that Gen Hardee's corps charged them on the right captured a number of prisoners and some artillery. Occalionaly the yanks throw a shell over into the city and we can hear it burst among the fine houses it is a great pity to see them riddled by the shell I expect the [Yankee] rascals glory in it...I recon you were a little afraid of being visited by the yankee raiders [of General Lovell Rousseau] as they came so close to you and that is the cause of

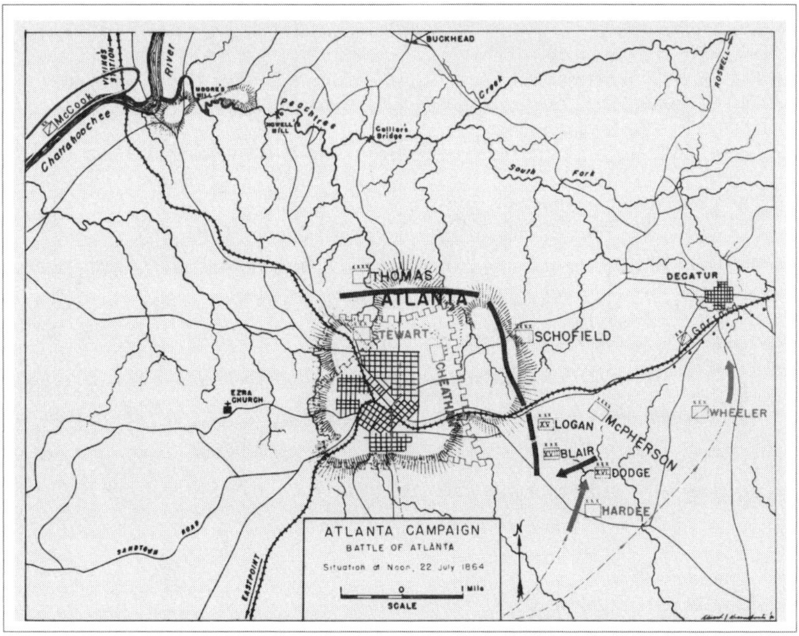

ATLANTA CAMPAIGN, BATTLE OF ATLANTA, 1864

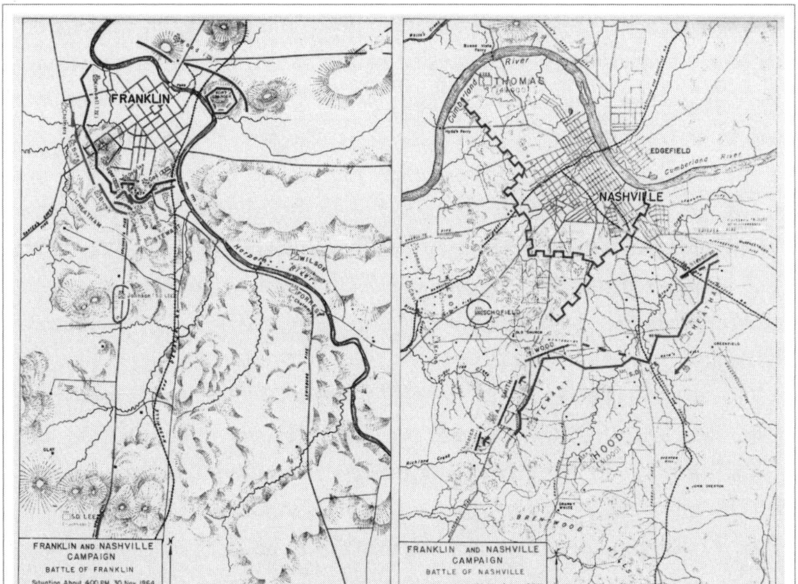

FRANKLIN AND NASHVILLE CAMPAIGN,
BATTLE OF FRANKLIN, BATTLE OF NASHVILLE, 1864

your not having written or the communication was cut as our mail comes by Columbus now...

N. B. We have been shelled prettie heavy this evening we had one man wounded...

With Atlanta momentarily secure behind its defenses, Sherman began extending his lines west and south of the city in order to cut the Confederates' rail connection with Macon and Montgomery. Hood tried to stop that move with an attack on Ezra Church, Georgia, on 28 July, but the Confederates were repulsed again. The Federal siege and bombardment continued. In this depressing situation, which took Confederate lives so arbitrarily, it is no wonder that A. H. Merrill, within the citadel of Atlanta, was short of temper and terse in prose, even when requesting clothes from home.

Atlanta Ga.
July 30, 1864
Dear Sister,

Sadness and gloom pervades the camp and there is truly a cause for we have met with a loss that cannot be replaced yes but such is the fate of war and death seems to pick those most needed in the world, day before yesterday just before it happened I and he was talking together when Leut McAll of another battery came by and asked him to walk down the lines he consented, they had not gone long before one of the boys came running down and hollowed out that Capt [M. D.] Oliver was killed I hastened up there and behold the man who but a few minutes before was a picture of health was laying in the agonies of death the ball had passed through his head and death was necessarily the consequence, Lieut McKenzie tried to send his body home but could not and they buried him in Atlanta.

There was some very hard fighting on our left day before yesterday our Division was engulfed but we were not Uncle Henry came out safe but his Division lost [a] good many men. I have ask you several times if you received the bundle I sent by express if so write me [about] my overcoat I want you to make Cler fix it as it is too small in the waist tell him to let in a peice in the back the arm holes are too small also there was a peice like the coat left please have it done right away, my boots also have them repaired the best you can don't mind expences for I want it done well, the winter bigins sooner up here than down there...

During August, General Hood, while still holding Atlanta, sent Joseph Wheeler's cavalry against Sherman's line of supply in northern Georgia and eastern Tennessee. The Confederates hoped this would force Sherman to fall back to the north. With Wheeler gone and with incomplete cavalry intelligence, Hood's information about Federal movement was inadequate. Thus, when Union soldiers began abandoning camps north and east of Atlanta in order to continue moving southward against the Macon railroad, the Confederates mistakenly believed Sherman was retreating north across the Chattahoochee. Merrill reported one of those Yankee withdrawals as a welcomed respite from artillery bombardment. Enjoying the prizes of an abandoned Federal camp, he could only hope that Sherman was truly retreating.

Atlanta Geo
Aug. 1864
Dear Sister,

[Y]esterday evening late we were surprised by a yankee Battery opening on us as several days had passed without their shelling us, and we could see clouds of smoke rise along the line as though they were burning ammunition but sister the picket kept up their same old banging away untill about midnight when it gradualy cease, every body was awakened highly elated that the yankees were gone for such it was reported by the pickets; well next morning at sun rise I with several of the boys started over to their works we reached there and found that they were truly gone from our front but I still hear firing on the left, report says that Sherman is recroosing the [Chattahoochee] river but its hard to tell as we hear so many false rumors, when we reached their works we proceeded to examine and see what they had left; canteens old cloths old hats and a few blankets were strown around some of our boys came back dressed completely in yankee uniform; they had a very prettie camp well fixed up as though the[y] [plan] to stay a long time: chess and draught men also cards were conspicuous, apparently they were men fond of amusement, I picked up some papers which you and I know Uncle Bertran will be glad to see...

But Sherman was not gone. And the fruitless shifting, rebuilding, and heavy work within the Confederates' besieged lines around Atlanta took a heavy toll on the morale of Hood's army. Confederate desertions were high. But for the moment, S. H. Dent was more concerned with the false report his death, which had reached Eufaula and disturbed his wife. He had been confused with Captain M. D. Oliver of the Eufaula Light Artillery, whose death Merrill reported in his letter of 30 July. Mobile Bay was opened to the Federals on 5 August 1864, but the city held out until 12 April 1865.

In The Field
Aug. 11, 1864
My Dear Nannie,

The siege of Atlanta is dragging its weary lenghts along and thus far I can see but little change in the situation. It will soon be a month since Genl Hood took Command of the army. It has already been a month since we crossed the Chattahoochee. We have done much fighting in that time and I do not think the enemy have gained much. The enemy shelled Atlanta very serverely yesterday and from the sound of cannon Kept up after night I think. I do not Know what damage they committed. It is now reported that the enemy are moving back to our right. They however are still in our front over here on the left. I had one man painfully but not seriously wounded on the 9th and another severely wounded on yesterday—both by minnie balls. Genl [William B.] Bate was wounded nearly a mile in rear of our line yesterday by a minnie ball. I do not Know how seriously. I hear nothing else of interest. I received your letter of the 5th Darling and am sorry that such a report ever reached Eufaula. It was current in the army—and I think it arose out of the fact that Capt Oliver was Killed. Nearly all who Know me Know that I am from Eufaula and Oliver being Captain of the Eufaula Battery somehow the idea got out that I was the man Killed...I am very well Honey—but poor. You would be amused if you could see my bunk with logs put up at the head to Keep of minnie balls. But discretion in this instance is the better part of valor. I have another Gun in the place of my disabled one—so I have four Guns again. The weather continues cloudy with some rain. I have seen no paper lately—am uneasy about Mobile. The surrender of Fort Gaines [Alabama] seems to have been a disgraceful affair. Anderson must have sold out...

D. M. Denny, from Randolph County, Alabama, and a member of the Thirty-Seventh Alabama Infantry, while "In Trenches Near atlanta," was so glad to get letters from his wife, Sinai, that he would run through a storm of lead to receive them. Even now, Sherman's design on the Macon railroad was not very clear to Confederates.

In Trenches Near atlanta
Aug. 24, 1864
Dear Sinai and Children,

I am gratified to Say that I received your verry kind letter of the 14th & 15th yesterday which gave me verry great Satisfaction to hear from you...I was on Picket when I Received it it came to the next Post to me & the boys hollarred & told me that [they] had a letter for me I got out of the Ditch and ran threw the whistles of minys and the bursting of Shells to get my letter...we Still hold atlanta but I fear we will loose the Westpoint & atlanta road but if we do we can send letters Round by Columbus & Macon Rail road we will look for Capt Welch in afew days now we are gld to See him at any time to get letters and othir things...The vegetables you Sent me has done me a great deel of good I have a Small peice of my ham yet it is very good to mix with midling and Beef...all the boys are in pretty good health...

Shortly before Atlanta fell, Denny and some of his fellows, part of General Alpheus Baker's brigade, were transferred Mobile to reinforce that city's defenses. During the removal, Denny reported that he was ill, not from battle or camp fever, but from eating too many sweets sent from home.

Opalaca in Rout to mobeil
Aug. 27, 1864
Dear Sinai & Children,

I rote the day before we left Atlanta I am not as well off as I was when I left atlanta but still up Well I supose it was oing to my treatment eating fruit Pound cake and other goodies...about half of our Co left us last knight [for home] they will tell you more than I can wright...

The last days of the Atlanta campaign were very confusing. Sherman's secret concentration of troops at Jonesboro south of the city threatened the Confederates' remaining rail connection, which was with Macon. Emerging from a fog of certainty on 30 August, Hood finally dispatched S. D. Lee and W. J. Hardee to Jonesboro to protect the railroad. Hardee engaged the enemy at Jonesboro on 31 August, but to no avail. With Hardee dug in around that place, Lee, on Hood's order, started toward Atlanta to assist Hood and A. P. Stewart in the defense of the city against what was erroneously believed to be a large Union force to the north. On 1 September, Hood finally realized that Sherman was concentrated south, not north, of Atlanta and that the Confederate army was dangerously divided. To relieve Hardee and reunite the army, Hood and Stewart evacuated the city on the night of 1 September, met Lee's corps, and turned them around for a successful reunion with Hardee. It was this confused marching to and from and back to Jonesboro that A. H. Merrill, a member of Lee's command, partially explained to his sister. The Federals occupied Atlanta on 2 September, but they had failed to capture Hood's army, which now formed a defensive line on the railroad from Jonesboro to Lovejoy's Station.

Mt Carmel Near Love joy Station
Sept. 5 1864
Dear Sister,

I received your letter [of 22nd of August] before we left Atlanta but after I tell you what I have been doing you will excuse my long silence. I was sorry when we received orders to leave our old stone house to move to the left which took place the day after the yankees left our front, well we did not march long before we took position on the line there we stayed until night when we moved out for Jonesboro marching all night and half of [the] next day we reached the town and rested until about four oclock, when we started in a great hurry as the line of battle had been formed and we could hear the fiering soon we got into it but it did not last long our men charged and were repulsed, George Williams was the only man wounded and it was slight we also had several horses struck, next morning at daylight we moved out again toward Atlanta while passing through Jonesboro the enemy heared the artillery moving and opened a battery on us, the shells flew around prettie thick, and one came and bursted just as our battery was passing it killed James Chandler that shell killed and wounded thirteen men and two horses, we marched all day toward Atlanta in the hot sun tired and worn out about night we stoped and stayed until morning when we started from Atlanta and then we knew that the great gate city was evacuated, of course we felt bad but it soon...passed off and we are now as hopefull as ever, that morning we again started and another long hot day found us truging through the dust and sand, horses breaking down men giving out it was the hardest marching that I ever done, several of our men are now missing but I expect they will come up in a day or two every body says that they never saw so much stragling in their lives, although we did not draw any rations. S[t]ill we lived well on the whole trip upon potatoes and pork and then there was any quantity of chinees shugar cane and sometimes apples all of which we enjoyed very much...

Captain S. H. Dent and other officers blamed the loss of Atlanta on the troops' unwillingness to fight at Jonesboro (31 August). Given the odds against the Confederates and Hood's confusion, the troops were only a part of the problem; furthermore, these gray backs would again fight well before the war was over. U. S. Grant and the Lincoln administration shared Dent's view that Sherman was missing a good chance to crush Hood's army. But the Federals were momentarily resting in Atlanta. Dent was near Lovejoy's Station.

Sept. 7, 1864

My Dear Nannie,

Yesterday morning it was discovered that the enemy had left our front again—rumor says thay have gone towards Atlanta and are destroying the rail road as they go. We have not yet moved—my Battery on the evening of the 5th relieved Douglas' Battery on picket and we are still in the same position. Genl [S. D.] Lee yesterday had each Division of his corps assembled and made a little speech to Clayton's (I expect) and Stevenson's—just as he was about to address our Division the rain bust upon us and he had to postpone it. He is trying to get up a better feeling in his corps. He told them of the poor fighting they did at Jonesboro on the 31st [August] and talked to them very plainly about what they ought to do and how they ought to fight. I heard nearly all he said to Stevenson's Divisions and I presume he would have said the same thing to our Division. The spirit of our troops is very bad and unless they do better I do not see what is to prevent Sherman from going any where he pleases. If we had been successful at Jonesboro we would have held Atlanta now and there is no reason why we should not have been successful. The men did not fight and Hood ought not to be blamed for that. I feel badly over the result of that fight. It is a new thing for our men to refuse to fight or what is the same thing to fight with no spirit—our cause here is not in a good condition and I am sorry to see it...the army P O was destroyed at Atlanta with the mails and no arrangements had been made then for distributing the army mail. I shall send down again to-day. It has been two weeks since I had a letter from you. Well Darling what do the people about Eufaula say about the [Democratic] nominees of the Chicago convention. I can't say that I hope for much unless we can check the enemy and even if we succeed in doing that and they are elected we will have another thing to fear and that is the disposition of our people to accept peace on any terms. I do not want to see the Confederacy go back into the Union on any terms. We are separated from them and I want to remain separated. If [George B.] McClellan is elected and refuses to recognize our independence I believe he and his party would be worse enemies to our cause than Lincoln himself. The army is a good deal faded and needs rest and severe discipline. It was very much disorganized in our last retreat. If the enemy have returned to Atlanta we may have a few days of rest. I think Sherman made a great mistake in not following us up vigorously—we could have made but a poor resistance. Sherman from Atlanta can threaten Montgomery Augusta and Macon—three important points. It was reported yesterday that a prisoner said they were going back to Atlanta and move out on the Augusta road. I do not think however that Sherman will move the bulk of his army far on that road. I saw Capt Garrity yesterday just from Mobile. He says the people there are tolerably quiet but that we have very few troops there and he thinks a land force could take the city as the force now stands. [Alpheus] Baker's Brigade and a few battalions being the only forces we have there besides the militia and I tell you Baker's Brigade would not fight up here I hope it will do better at Mobile.

The bitterness of defeat temporarily clouded Hubert Dent's naturally sunny disposition. Upset at the troops' poor fighting at Jonesboro, the captain was now able to see some mismanagement by the generals. For him the increased prospects of a long war were not encouraging. Sherman's recent occupation of Atlanta would help assure Lincoln's reelection in 1864 over General George B. McClellan.

Camp near Lovejoy's Station
Sept. 10th 1864
My Darling,

The sun is not yet visible above the horizon—but as I intend to start a man to Griffin quite early this morning I want to finish a letter to you before he leaves. You Know we have had no mail for ten days or more...I expect a letter for me was destroyed with the mail at Atlanta when we evacuated. So I hope to get two or three today. There is some talk here of troops going to Virginia but it may be all talk. It is expected that Sherman will send troops to Grant and if he does I suppose Hood will send some of his to Genl [R. E.] Lee. What do you all think of the fall of Atlanta and our fighting at Jonesboro. For my own part I cannot think of it without shame and mortification. I will further say as I am writing to you Darling that I think there was very little generalship shown either by Hood in sending their forces there as he did or in Hardee making the attack as he did. It seems to me that if Hood felt strong enough to attack them at all that he ought to have attacked them in their rear instead of in front—and Hardee instead of making a general assault with weak lines all along their ranks ought to have massed on some good point and taken that and pushed the enemy out on the right and left. But it is all over and I must hope it happened for the best and that we will do better next time. Hardee lost eight guns there. Just the number he captured from the Yankees on the 22nd of July. This loss however occurred on the 1st Sept after his corps had left and the enemy making the attack. It is said they suffered very severely but succeeded in breaking our lines and carrying the works. Hardees corps is about Jonesboro now. Stewarts & Lee's are just below Lovejoys station on either side of the railroad—all the troops are resting and we will rest for several days. My horses needed rest very much and they are looking better already. We have very heavy dews now—the sun shines out clear and warm during the day. The company is generally in very good health—my own is very good. Capt Garrity has returned to his company. Since he left on the 28th May he had lost every one of his Lieuts...Bond wounded and killed by a rairoad collision on his way home. I have seen nothing of it in the newpapers but from what many persons tell me it must have been a very serious collision. About thirty-three were Killed outright—besides a good many wounded. I was in hopes I would have been able to get off home for a short time—but no chance—no leave of absence to be forwarded except on surgeon certificate. If there was a place for you to remain any where near me I would ask you to come up but there is no place nearer than Griffin and that is fifteen miles off and I could only see you once or twice a week. I do not feel as sanguine about peace now as I did a month ago or less. The fall of Atlanta will cause great rejoycing in the North and Lincoln to give greater effort to it reducing the draft to one hundred thousand men I expect he apprehended some trouble in enforcing the draft for the full number called for and therefore reduced it to one hundred thousand. He plays his cards very adroitly and he had better for the campaign will soon end and I do not regard his election as altogether certain. The truth is Darling I cannot see the end of this thing. If Lincoln is reelected the war will go on. If Fremont is elected the war I think will go on. If McClellan is elected there is no certainty that we will have peace and the Yankees will be so much inspirited by the fall of Atlanta that they will take new interest in the war. If I did not believe that there was a providence in all these things I would be entirely disheartened. But I cannot believe that our Father in Heaven intends that we shall be subjugated by such a race of people as the Yankees. But suppose Lincoln should overrun the Country—what else could he do—our Southern people would not stand and see their lands go into the hands of enemies tamely and making no resistence.

No one supposes that life or property would be safe and the horrors of Mexico would be repeated. I cannot believe that our land will be given over to such punishment—God grant it may not be. There is a good deal of complaint against Genl Hood but that is natural. Some are wishing for Joe Johnston others for Bragg. Some men have lost all hope others take the fall of Atlanta and the retreat of the army as matters of course. For my own part I do not mind the fall of Atlanta half as much as the way our troops fought. If they had fought well I would not have cared half so much—but to think we lost it by the timidity—nay almost cowardice of our own troops. I heard from Genl Anderson a few days ago—he was doing very well—but could not talk yet—his lower jaw was fractured...

With Sherman's army in Atlanta and temporarily inactive, Captain Dent found time to rest, recuperate, and regain confidence in the Confederate cause. And soon this artilleryman was full of plans for repairing a gun and getting home for a visit.

Near Lovejoy's Station
Sept. 13, 1864
My Darling,

I went to call on Genl [H. D.] Clayton yesterday found him very well—but feeling pretty blue over the condition of our affairs. He is very anxious to get off home for a few days—but his application was refused. He gave me a note to an acquaintance of his to see if I could not get board for you but the house was full and it was refused. I went to other places but all had excuses. I have no tent or you might come up my way for a few days. The principal objection is the want of something to eat—we are only drawing beef now—very poor at that—get no bacon and have no grease. We have flour but can't use it. I am going in a few minutes to army Hd Qrs on business and while there I intend to see if there is no possible chance for me to get home. One of my guns needs a new vent piece and if it is sent to Macon I intend to try and go with it and if I get off will go home. But this is very uncertain. The nights are becoming much cooler and I caught a severe cold last night which effects my head a good deal. I thought the relief committee had gone home—but Clayton told me yesterday that they were in Griffin...Clayton is pretty nearly whipped. I dislike to see such feelings among our people. While I regard the fall of Atlanta as a great and serious blow to us I do not think it renders our cause hopeless...We have a review of our artillery tomorrow evening. I heard that Genl [S. D.] Lee reviewed his corps to-day. The Infantry part of it. I am very well fixed up now and my Battery is in very good Condition...

General Grant wanted nothing less than the complete destruction of Hood's army. But this was easier ordered than done. When Sherman finally tried to catch the Confederate force, now heading northward, Hood's 40,000 veterans eluded the Federals and began preying on the Union's line of supply along the Western and Atlantic Railroad in northern Georgia. Captain Dent, still not far from Lovejoy's Station, wrote about the beginning of this move.

Near Fayetteville [Georgia]
Sept. 18, 1864

We are on the march—have been all day and will start at 4 o'clock in the morning...I do not know where we are going to in the end—but to-morrow we are to march eighteen miles to Fairburn on the Westpoint Rail Road—where next I do not know our corps [S. D. Lee's] and theirs [Stewart's] are both moving in the same direction. I have not heard whether Hardee's is moving or not. I am very well physically but feel very much annoyed at not receiving letters and a great deal of anxiety to hear from home...There are rumors that we are going to Blue Mountain [near present-day Anniston, Alabama]—and various other rumors...

With Hood planning a harassment campaign against Sherman's supply line, D. M. Denny, a member of the Thirty-Seventh Alabama Infantry and Alpheus Baker's Brigade, arrived in Mobile in time for the fall fevers. Denny's regiment was stationed at Spanish Fort, Alabama, before it was sent into North Carolina for the final phase of the war in 1865. Perhaps Denny had been slow to return to his company; someone sent for him.

Camp 37th Regt Ala vol
Oct. 3, 1864
Dear Sinai,

I am heeled with fishooks This leaves me in about as good health as I have been in Since I came to mobeil the Co Still has Chills and fever I dont think I will take the Chills oing to my Pewny condition and thin Blood Our Co is off Some three miles from this place on duty as I wrote you before I hardly Ever See any of them Save the Sick as they was Taken and Sent back I was down thare day before yesterday to See them it is not worth while for me to under take to give you a list of those having Chills it is So common here they are hardly noticed thare is but two of the boys here with me now and we will go down the Bay, the Regt was ordered and went down last evening we will go tomorrow if nothing turns up rong nor breaks thare has two of the Co just got here after us to assist us to The Co...

In late September and early October, while Hood was harassing the Federals in northern Georgia and Sherman was trying to persuade Grant to approve the Atlanta-Savannah campaign, S. H. Dent managed to get a few days at home Eufaula. This was possible since he had taken one of his artillery pieces to be repaired, apparently in Columbus, Georgia, where his return was delayed long enough to write about the recent trip home.

Columbus Geo
Oct. 6, 1864
M y Dear Darling,

I am still in Columbus—will leave to-morrow morning. I could have remained twenty four hours longer in Eufaula and I feel very much annoyed that I did not know it...I shall go to West Point I think—my Gun will be ready this evening. I could not have succeeded in procuring my photograph except by staying here as I have done. I get them this evening and will enclose the best looking one to You I am a little afraid that I will have some trouble about finding the Company but will find out when I get to West Point...I was unable to procure any cloth for my officers.

About three weeks before General Sherman began his destructive march from Atlanta to the sea at Savannah, Joel Aycock, Company C, Third Georgia Reserves, wrote from Camp Lawton near Millen, Georgia, where he was a guard in the Confederate prison. Millen was along Sherman's future line of March. Aycock's reference to "Anderson" probably was to the controversial Confederate prison at Andersonville, Georgia, from whence most prisoners had been dispersed for safekeeping against Sherman's invasion.

Camp Lauton
Oct. 23, 1864
Dear Ma,

I am well once more. Nor we dont have as much duty to do as we did at Anderson but we dont draw as mutch [food now] we draw one days rashions of surrope & one of beef, we generally eat all of the beef at one meal that we draw for one day...we draw surrope ever other day. Ma Dr Harrison was not one of the board that examend me when I come from home. I will get to come home by march if not before, as soon as all the boys gets furloughs that hasent binn home the rest of the company will draw for it Ma we look for the capt next Thursday.

Lutenant wats has come we havent elected...no lieutenant yet. Ma we have not drawed any thing at tall yet nor I dont know when we will, we dont draw any pays. Ma this maks the third letter I have wrote home I sent one by hand. Orders was read out in dress perraid that all that could go home in one day would get seven days furloring & if it takes too days we will get nine-days. I will close by asking you to write soon...

By mid-October, Hood was ready to leave Georgia for Alabama, where he planned a rapid march into Tennessee. Instead of pulling Sherman after him as hoped, Hood was opposed by Federal generals George H. Thomas and John M. Schofield. This left Sherman and half of his former force to press almost unopposed from Atlanta to Savannah. Meanwhile, up in Tennessee, as S. H. Dent explained, Hood lost heavily at Franklin on 30 November. And the forthcoming disaster at Nashville on 15 December resulted in General Thomas's virtually destroying Hood's army in the field, perhaps the most complete destruction of a Confederate force battle during the entire war. In both contests, Hood was courageous but foolhardy. His troops fought heroically in these battles, especially at Franklin, where they charged across open country to assault impregnable defenses.

Near Nashville Tenn
Dec. 4, 1864
My Darling,

Since writing to you we have fought a fierce battle and are now within sight of the tall steeples and glittering spires of the City of Nashville. The fight occurred at Franklin on the 30th ult. We lost very heavy in officers—our loss in men too was quite severe—among the Killed are Maj. Genl Cleburne—Brig Genls Strahl, Granberry, Adams and I think some others...It was the most desperate fighting I ever witnessed. The enemy were strongly posted behind works. I think the losses on each side nearly the same—we may have lost a few more killed than the enemy—but we captured more prisoners. But when we remember the Genl officers killed our loss was much the more serious. Genl Cleburn's loss is very hard to repair. We had some skirmishing at Columbia in which we damaged the enemy a good deal and pressed him very closely on his retreat from Columbia to Franklin. I think Genl Hood did not think the enemy's works at Franklin were as strong as they were or he would never have rushed upon them as he did. They only reached Franklin a few hours before us—but their works were already built. Johnston's Division of our corps was all the troops Lee had in the fight. It fought very finely and was highly complimented. The loss in the Division was not very heavy—my own loss was one man seriously wounded—he could lose one if not both of his eyes [Another] was struck just over the region of the heart but he had a book and several other things in the side pocket of his coat and it saved him from a serious if not a mortal wound. We have a good many remors as usual among others that [J. C.] C.J Breckinridge has whipped [S. G.] Burgridge very badly and is on his way to unite with Hood. We have a rumor also that Sherman had been whipped out in Georgia and was on his way to Nashville. I hope he has been whipped. I heard just now that Forrest crossed the Cumberland last night and had captured a transport with 160 mules on it. Our lines were advanced yesterday and I hear are to advance again this evening. I am ready harnessed to advance if needed. I regret that Col Beckham our chief of artillery was mortally wounded at Columbia. We regret his loss very much. Maj. Courtney is still absent. Richardson's resignation has been accepted and he is no longer an officer of Dent's Battery. He talks of going to the trans Miss. Dept. I expect heavy work before Nashville fall if it fall at all and unless Hood is going to take it or try I do not know what he means...But the great feat remains to be accomplished—the yankees are decidedly afraid of us. They say they never saw such fighting in all their lives—and I do not believe such fighting was ever done before by any troops in the world...I am standing the campaign well and in fine health...I have just heard that Sherman was at Milledgeville. I think it reasonable that he may be. I hope he will not get down in your neighborhood. We are fighting part of Sherman's army up here. He cannot have a very large force with him...

Confederate losses at Nashville in December 1864 were larger than Dent anticipated, with about 4,500 falling captive to the Yankees. Following that failure, the remnants of Hood's army were thrown back to the south, some of them to Columbus, Mississippi. Dent was among the survivors who would go on to Mobile for the final defense of the city. Compared with the Atlanta campaign, the Virginia front in 1864 seemed more stable. But the Confederacy was losing there also, as in Georgia, and on neither front could the losses be replaced.

6

Virginia and the End: 1864–1865

After the battle of Gettysburg (July 1863), when General R. E. Lee retreated back into Virginia, the Union Army of the Potomac pulled down to the Rapidan River just north of Fredericksburg. Here, the Federals waited for months, resting and reorganizing, before unleashing the last major offensive of the war. In May 1864, General U. S. Grant would initiate a bulldozing campaign at the Wilderness, Spotsylvania, Cold Harbor, and Petersburg. While Grant prepared for this offensive, the Confederate Army of Northern Virginia under General Lee watched from their position south of the Rapidan.

This chapter touches on parts of the Virginia front in 1864 and then moves quickly to the last days of the Confederacy in 1865. Near the conclusion of the war, Chattahoocheans' letters become more scarce for obvious reasons. Several of the correspondents were dead. Survivors in the Southern armies were moving fast and fighting hard in a losing struggle to maintain a government that was crumbling before their eyes.

In the April period of quiet, just before the Federals crossed the Rapidan into the Wilderness, Thomas J. Barron wrote his sister from Orange Court House, Virginia. Here he communicated his "dreams" of being at home, his lack of Christianity, and the "auful sean" at the military execution of two Confederate deserters. Barron's and his comrades' concern for the next life was a natural result of their almost constant exposure to death.

Camp 14th Regt Ala Vols Near Court House, Virginia
April 23, 1864
Ada, Ever beloved Sister,

I dream very often being with you all I have had a dosen fourloughs if my dreams were true I love to dream of being with you there is so mouch pleasure for ones mind to wander back home blending with the famly circle while asleep on the pallet made from the [truth] your cheering letter was the base of one [thou] happy dreams last nigh...I love you for your parys given for in my behalf

Oh if I was a christen I would ever be happy but God has not given me the grace that I So often heard spoke of in the church...I witness an auful sean the other day the death of two deserters belong to the ninth Ala Regt the charg preferred a gaints them was for deserting their command trying to make their way to the Enemy carring their equipements with them They bouth were olde men ones hair was gray the proceedings of the court martials was read to them They [were] sentence to be shot to death with muskets They well knew the fate of deserters but they heeded not but this is dreadful to bring out a man in good health an in a moment plung his soul into ever lasting perdition Lieut Cumbe Commend their Souls to God then they was tied to stakes then the clicking of the trigers then the order aim fire an they were as no more on this earth Oh it was auful to the sight of human The oldest man I learn since had a hope in Christ he said so I heard that he was willing to die and The younger was Shot while praying a loud the last word I hear him say was God he prayed earnestly if ever I heard an earnest prayer Shirly his was one...

PS Excuse this sory writing for the wind blows so hard it pesters me an then it was done in a hurry

All of Richmond and the Confederacy anxiously awaited news of Grant's movements. Six days after Barron's letter, Preston Leroy Dodgen was in the Confederate capital, from which place he wrote his wife, Nancy. Dodgen, whose home was Hickory Flat in Chambers County, Alabama, was first sergeant in F Company of the Fifty-Ninth Alabama Infantry His regiment had served with Bragg in eastern Tennessee, Kentucky, at Chickamauga, and with General Longstreet at Knoxville and in northeastern Tennessee. Like Crowder (who was probably his relative), Dodgen was only recently arrived in Virginia from the west. While Crowder died at the Wilderness (5–6 May), Dodgen would survive until Spotsylvania, a short ten days later. Meantime, before Grant began the move that would within a month cost him 55,000 casualties and Lee 30,000, Dodgen wrote about impressment of food from civilians at home, that "Sis" not marry precipitously, and of hopes the war would end quickly. He had recently visited his family while on furlough.

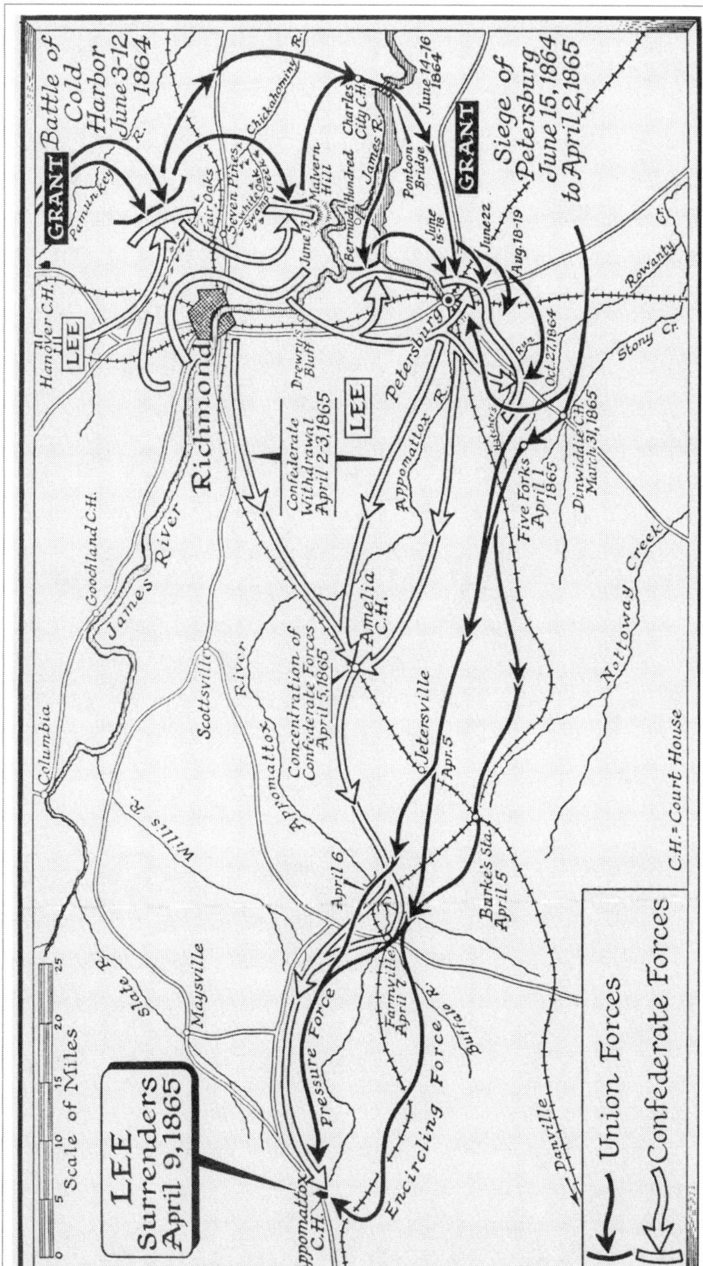

THE VICINITY OF RICHMOND, 1864-1865

Richmond, Virginia
April 29, 1864
Dear Wife and children,

I have not received a line from you sence I left home and I want to hear from you so bad I cant rest...Nancy we are hear at richmond we got hear today I cant tel how long we will stay hear we haint had nothing to eat in a day or so but they are drawing rations now I think we will fare better hear than we did in Tennessee...I hear so much bad news [from home] that I am nearly out of my sences. I hear that they are taken the tenth of the meat I want you to keep what little meat you have for you and the children to eat and I want you to wright to me how your [live]stock coms on and whether that one died or not that was down when I left home. Nancy I want you to plant as much sugar cane as you can and tobacco for they are both a great help tel Albert and the other boys to bee smart and make all they can and tel them to plant lots of watermelon sead for I think I will bee home in 3 months I believe the war will does before long. I wrote to you that I thought I would get to come home again but I mist it they told me that I could get a furloe by taken Bob Young back but it would not doo...

N. B. Sis I want you to bee a good girl and help your ma and bee good to the children take good care of Willie and Mary and dont fall in love with non of the boys tel the war breaks I tel you this for I want you to doo well...

On 4 May, Grant's army crossed the Rapidan in force. Lee's outnumbered but brave Confederates deterred the Federals at every turn, inflicting heavier losses than they sustained at the Wilderness (5–7 May), Spotsylvania (8–21 May), Cold Harbor (1–3 June), and Petersburg (15–18 June). When Grant could not take Richmond from the north, he cut south to attack the city's line of supply through Petersburg, laying an extended siege to that place.

The Confederates in Virginia sustained another significant loss in May 1864 when General Jeb Stuart, cavalryman, the "eyes and ears" of Lee's army, was killed at Yellow Tavern near Richmond. Without this flamboyant and sometimes brilliant leader, the Confederate cavalry nevertheless continued to ride, harassing the Federals and supplying Lee whatever intelligence they could gather.

One of these mounted Confederates, who was temporarily out of sorts, was William H. Bray. As a planter from Eufaula, Alabama, and member of C Company, Alabama Battalion of Cavalry (probably the Fourth), Bray had assisted in the recent successful defense of Richmond and hoped that place was now permanently secure. Not yet recovered from a stomach disorder that hospitalized him, he was anxious to return to the field. Having attended church at Richmond, he saw President Jefferson Davis and left an interesting description of him. Bray's company was a hard-riding, fast-moving group, but he wanted some gold for advantageous use in case he was captured by the numerous Federal troops in Virginia. Recently, Confederate General Jubal Early had drawn some Union forces back to Washington by his obvious demonstration against that city.

Officers Hospital Richmond
July 15, 1864
My Dear Wife,

I have been Suffering fom Diarhea and Dysentary for the last week & have hardly been out of my room Since Sunday I am much better to day & if I do not get any Sett back Shall leave for the field in 3 or 4 days as Soon as I Can gain a little Strength I am very thin—never was more So in my life. I am very anxious to get back to the Co—had much rather be with them than here I Cannot bear Confinement & inactivity...I have thought a great deal of my wheat crop & hope Mr J managed to Save the most of it in good order I hope you will write me all about the Crops I attended church at St Pauls on Sunday & had a good look at the President. He was dressed in a brown linen Suit with a Straw Hat—which was made I think & lined with black silk He looks much better than his pictures make Him...All think here that Grant Has nearly played out & our fears are excited for Atlanta It is reported & I hope true that Genl Longstreet is going with His Corps to help out Johnston [at Atlanta]. [Confederate General Jubal] Early Seems to be playing the Wilds in Md & I trust He may be successfull & have a Safe return It is acertained that Grant is sending a part of his forces to Washington & if So one of the objects of the [Early] expedition will be accomplished I hope the Hardest part of the Campaign is over in Va & then there will be Some rest hereafter for Men & Horses The Cavalrymen had a hard time the Hardest they have ever had in the Same length of time Our Co is now about 15 miles below Petersburgh on the W[eldon] R.R. but...we may [be] 100 miles from here in a week from now I am now Coveting some of the good things you are having now Such as potatoes Tomatoes green Corn & melons which I Suppose you are having in great abundance We get none here—or next to none they are So high—for instance Irish potatoes $4.00 per quart Tomatoes

1.00 Do [ditto] Butter 12.00 per lb., Sugar Do Bread 1.00 pr loaf as big as your fist Milk 3.00pr quart &. I have bought me Some Cloth for a winter Suit I got it at goverment price 15.00 per yd Dble fold...I wish you would tell Nate to send me $10 in Gold & 2 or 3 dollars in Silver & He Can take out as much if He Chooses or make a memo of it as I hardly think I Shall use it I might get taken prisoner in which Case it would be useful Send it by Roberts or Some other Safe Hands Capt McKenzie of Louisville [Alabama] will be Coming before long Tell Nate to write me the Condition of our affairs. I am very anxious to have our N Y Debts paid & if He Has not paid them I would Sell enough Cotton if I Could not get the money otherwise & pay them up...

Despite Grant's massive assaults on Petersburg in June 1864, the city held out through a long siege until April 1865. A month after the siege began, J. Walter Perry wrote from a military hospital in Petersburg to his father in Blakely, Georgia. This young man from the Chattahoochee Valley in southwestern Georgia made minimal complaint, despite his dread of the harsh treatment of "bleeding." Only a fragment of Perry's letter remains.

July 20th

A Friend has promised to take this for me to Augusta tomorrow and it will thus reach you sooner than by mail clear through. Since I closed this other sheet my old blood disease has been annoying me very much and this morning I feel it ready to break out all over my face and arms and body. I am going to be bled. There seems no other help for it. Although I am very weak still I will have to be bled. If I were at home I could cure it otherwise but not here. I am cross, peevish, feverish, and fretful. Think I would come all right in about four hours if the General was to take me with him. Hope that he may do it in double-quick time. I had a Georgia peach yesterday—oh! how good it tasted. Did you send me one? This day is going to be a scorcher and you can well imagine what I will have to suffer. Please write me often and send it [by] hand as far as you can every time to Petersburg if possible...

Although yet unwell, Lieutenant William H. Bray rejoined his company in the field. His cavalry unit was scouting and harassing the Union lines south of Petersburg. Bray's concern for matters at home, especially financial solvency in the last stages of a losing war, did not necessarily reduce his efficiency as a soldier.

Camp near Reams Station

Aug. 1, 1864

My Dear Wife,

I left the Hospital the 20th [July]...There is a fatality attending my letters Somehow but Keep Writing at least twice a week for you have no idea how Eagerly I look for them & perhaps they will get to Coming right Soon (Aug 2d)...Just as I had written the Above the Bugle Sounded "Saddle Up" & We had to leave for a new Camping place near Stoney Creek Station farther down toward Weldon. Where We now are...I have realy been too unwell to do any thing but my duties & when they were through I would lie down in the nearest resting place...I have been troubled Since my return to duty With a return of Diarhea & Dysentery. I feel much better to day & hope I Shall now get entirely Well if I do not I Shall go to the Hospital again for I Cant Stand it much longer in the field I Shall begin to feel uneasy if my Bowels do not get right before Many days I Will write oftener from now out as our mail facilities are much improved in the field Every Brigade Has a Carrier that goes every day I hope Capt R[oberts?] had none of my money I think however you might have Sent that gold I ordered by Him & if So I Suppose it is lost. Capt R is truly unfortunate—I am looking for him now daily & Shall be glad enough to be releived of the Responsibility & Care of the Command. This acting Captain & being 2d Lieut I am tired enough of & Dont intend to Stand it much longer What I Say about these Matters you must not repeat...I want all the other Cane made up into Sugar that Can be Spared & leave enough for Seed I hope to have at least 10 or 15 bbls Syrup to Sell this year as I must pay for the Mill out of the Syrup & have an abundance for Myself. I wrote you to Send me the exact amount of the Wheat...We have a box for our mess I hope you got a finger in the [pie]. He had to leave the Boxes in Petersburgh We have Sent for themd [I] am expecting a heap of good things I want you to tell Nate to Write me all about my affairs All our Stock Dividends & Everyting...

W. H. Bray's health improved enough for him to remain in the field. His next letter was from the Richmond area, far to the north of Reams and Stoney Creek where he had recently been. Bray's view of "ungrateful" Confederates was perhaps realistic, at least from his upper-class point of view. Bray could have been a part of Lee's reinforcement of Jubal Early in the Shenandoah Valley, where Phil Sheridan was preparing a large Federal strike.

Near Richmond

Aug. 13, 1864

My Dear Wife,

We are about 3 miles North of Richmond for two hours or So to get dinner & & Suppose When We Start We Shall have to travel All night We are going to Culpepper C H & if We do not encounter the Enemy We Shall go on to the [Shenandoah] valey probably...I want to Caution you on a Subject of Doing too much for Soldiers. Mr K & I was talking about it to day They are the most ungratefull Sett in the world & lots of them after receiving your Hospitality Will turn right round & Steal from [you] We See these things every day & have been very much disgusted with them there is another thing. Mr K & I have Concluded that We are doing enough to be in field ourselves & that it is as little as those at home Can do to attend to this part of the War another reason with us both is that we fear that you will not have enough left for yourselves Therefore I say be Cautious The Horn blows & We have to Leave good bye Will write again the 1st opportunity.

We poor Soldiers have not a moment We Can Call our own With Much Love...

William Bray next described the throes of man and beast during the hard cavalry movements in the late summer of 1864. Given the difficulties of the situation, the real miracle was that Lee's army managed to hold out until April 1865. Meantime, Bray's group was turned back from Shenandoah because Sheridan had withdrawn from an impending attack on Early and because Grant had launched a new effort against Lee. This latter move resulted in the Federal capture of the Weldon Railroad on 18 August.

In the Saddle

Aug. 15, 1864

My Dear Wife,

When I Wrote you last We were 3 miles north of Richmond Enroute (as I thought) to Culpepper C H & thence to the Valey Well we march[ed] by forced marches for two days and got as far as "Beaver Dam" Station on the [Virginia] Central R R & were then ordered back to Richmond We Were hurried off at 3.O.C. this morning After getting Wet through to the Skin & being up nearly all night in Consequence—Of Course men & Horses are completely Jaded & ourselves & Every thing—Blankets over coats & all wringing Wet. But our poor

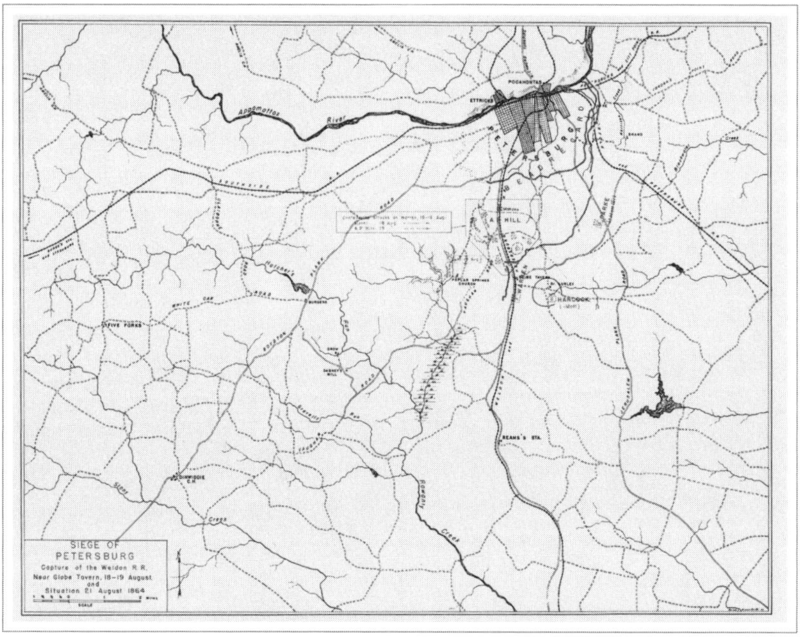

SIEGE OF PETERSBURG, 1864-1865

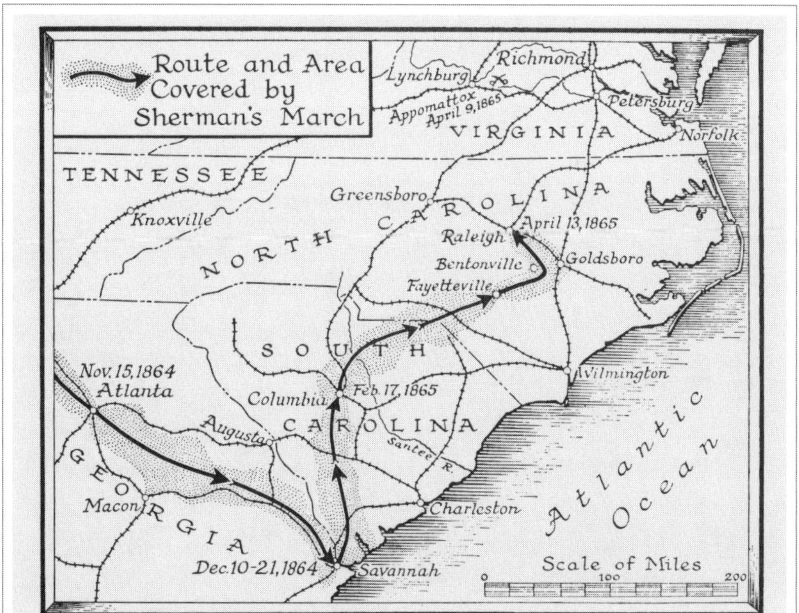

SHERMAN'S MARCH THROUGH GEORGIA AND THE CAROLINAS, 1864-1865

Horses Suffer most in these Hard marches frequently getting nothing to eat for two or three days & their Backs all raw. But Such is War Men nor horses are not regarded...at all but everything Has to give Way to the Military necessities...of the moment We suppose We are going back the other Side of Petersburgh & that the reason of Turning back is that the Yankees are Crossing over a large Cavalry force the South Side of the James & trying to Steal the march on the P & W [Weldon & Petersburgh] RR...I write as the Column [rests] for a Moment but must Stop now for We move on...

While R. E. Lee continued to field a force to protect Richmond, General John B. Hood, as previously noted, had all but lost his Army of Tennessee at Franklin (30 November) and at Nashville (15–16 December). The retreat from Nashville was orderly, but only about 15,000 Confederates found their way back into northern Mississippi. Hood voluntarily resigned in January 1865 to be replaced by General Richard Taylor as the principal Confederate commander in the lower states. Escaping death and capture in this ill-fated campaign, S. H. Dent wrote his wife in January 1865, probably from northern Mississippi. In the fragment of this letter that remains, Dent spoke of fighting Sherman in Georgia and of uniting western troops with Lee's in Virginia. But such was mere rumor, as subsequent events would show. State-rights particularism and Confederate military policy never allowed the South to concentrate its numerous but scattered forces into a few large armies that could compete more effectively with Federals in strategic places such as Virginia, Mississippi, or Tennessee. Dent exaggerated the size of Kirby Smith's army.

[Northern Mississippi, January, 1865]

[Rumor says] that we are going to Geo. But still nothing here indicates it. Sherman seems to be having every thing his own way in Georgia and unless we can keep open our communications with Richmond Lee [may] be compelled to evac[uate]— we ought to bring 30[000] men over from the [trans] Miss Dept. Kirby Smith has sixty-five thousand men over there doing nothing—as many if not more troops than Lee & Hood have both together...if I thought we would remain here any time I would try and get some place for you to stay and get you to come up & see me—but Genl E [Lee?] says we are only here temporarily. The men need clothing very badly—are exposed to all weather having no shelter. Genl [S. D.] Lee is here wounded slightly in the foot—he is to be married [in] a short time...

When Captain Dent next wrote from Columbus, Mississippi, on 1 February, he was awaiting transportation to Mobile for the final, futile defense of that city. As Dent and others proceeded south, some regiments of Hood's former army were sent east into North Carolina to assist General Joseph Johnston's last effort to stop Sherman's force. By now, Sherman was proceeding from Savannah into South Carolina from whence he would eventually enter the Tar Heel State. On his way to Mobile, Dent expected little from the rumored peace negotiations. In fact, he still hoped Jefferson Davis was "not whipped." The Hampton Roads Conference occurred on 3 February without Franklin Pierce. The peace talks amounted to nothing, and war continued.

Near Columbus
Feb. 1, 1865
My Darling,

We are still in Columbus. Expecting to leave every day—but no boat has arrived to take us off yet. It is now said that we will leave tomorrow. The [Tombigbee] river is falling very rapidly and I think boats will soon find navigation difficult unless we have more rain...Darling write your next to Mobile Ala—Dents Battery—nothing more and I think I will get them...Is there much talk of peace about Eufaula? I was astonished to hear so much said about it up here. For my own part I have very little confidence in the ability of our Commissioners to make peace—so if it comes I will only be the more rejoiced because it will be totally unexpected. I do not know what we are to do in Mobile—but the rumor now is that we will be fitted up for field service again in the Spring. This I think doubtful—for I do not think we can procure the stock necessary to fit out so many batteries. I am suffering with a rising in my left ear. It pains me a good deal this evening. I have them frequently of late—and am afraid it will injure my hearing. I have no news here at all. I have not seen a newspaper for more than a week and am entirely behind in current events. Maj Courtney left us a few days ago for Macon Geo where he was ordered to take command of Hotchkiss' Battalion. There is not a single major here to go to Mobile with us. Capt Doug[las] has left for Texas on a ninety days furlough. Garrity is presently Commanding the Battalion. We have two other companies attached to our Battalion now—Barry's and Tarrants Batteries. We have five companies in all. Ziegler has just returned from Columbus—says there is no boat yet—but one is expected every hour. I am afraid the river will get so low that we will be compelled to march some distance to meet the boat. Nothing else new. I am about to start for Columbus myself and therefore must hurry up this letter so I can mail it—oh yes! Ziegler did bring another piece of news which was that the U S Government had appointed Commissioners to confer with ours and that Ex Pres Pierce was among the numbers. This looks like something might be done...I do not think I would know what to do with myself if peace should be made—but I do not look for it and I am afraid these negotiations will do us much harm. Every one will be looking for them for great results when I am afraid nothing will be done. I hope Mr Davis is not whipped. I have heard some such expressions but I do not believe them...

From Mobile, Dent criticized the city's weak defenses. Morale was also low. He attributed much of the trouble to numerous "liquor shops." As a prohibitionist, Dent took some comfort in General Franklin Gardner's court-martial for drunkenness. Mobile held off the Federals until 12 April, three days after Appomattox.

Mobile Alabama
Feb. 10, 1865

I am about to get settled at last. Garrity's Battery and mine have been assigned to Battery 'M' and a redoubt near it. We are about a half a mile from the Bay and about two miles from the central part of the city. We succeeded in moving at last but after a long struggle...We are to have muskets and charge of a Battery of heavy Guns—drill about four times a day and work the remainder of the time. We will be pretty busy—but I am glad of it. We are promised that as soon as horses and artillery equipments can be obtained that we will be sent back in the field at Light arty. This promise I expect is made as a sort of inducement to do well now and not murmer at the duties imposed now. There seems to be a good deal of discipline here on paper and very little elsewhere. I do not wonder at the success of the Yankees in taking our cities if the defences of all others were like those about Mobile. Gov [Thomas H.] Watts has closed up the liquor shops here—but plenty of whiskey is still afloat in the city. Maj Genl Gardner is being tried by Court-Martial for drunkenness when the Yankees made their raid on the Mobile and Ohio Rail Road some time ago. From what I hear I expect he will be acquitted—and yet I am pretty sure he was drunk. He is a fine officer— but no man in the habit of getting drunk is fit for any position of responsibility—our cause has suffered a great deal already from this cause. Genl

Gardner promised Genl Bragg when he recommended him for Brigadiership that he would not drink and I believe he kept that promise so long as he was in Bragg's army. But I suppose the temptations around here were stronger than his resolutions. I am here without my horses and consequently will not go about much. I am invited out to dine on Sunday at Mr Robert H. Smith's one of the nicest gentleman in Mobile. If I can I shall attend church and then go there. I have met with a good many acquaintances since I arrived here most of whom are located around here. We can see the Yankee ships from the bay—five were in sight yesterday. If the expedition now in preparation at New Orleans is coming to Mobile we will have something to do here before long—but if as reported it is going to Galveston we will have a lazy time of it. I want to see if we cant go to houseKeeping while I am down here—but we will talk this over when I get home which I hope to do by the first of March or very soon thereafter. Capt Fenner [?] is Commanding our Regt now in the absence of Lt. Col Hoxton who remained in Columbus [Mississippi] to stand up with Genl [S. D.] Lee who was to be married last night...

When Mobile fell to the Federals, S. H. Dent was among those Confederates who retreated into Mississippi, where they finally surrendered, along with General Richard Taylor, near Meridian in early May. Meanwhile, one of the Stanford brothers, either Monroe or William, wrote the other about his experience in eastern North Carolina. The Thirty-Ninth Alabama Regiment, to which the Stanfords belonged, had, like Dent's Battery, been at Dalton, Atlanta, and Nashville. But when Dent went to Mobile, the remnant of the Thirty-Ninth proceeded east to Joseph Johnston's army in North Carolina. The Yankees used New Bern as the point of naval supply for Sherman's 60,000 footsore veterans who had just crossed the Carolinas.

Kenansville NC
March 15, 1865
Dear Brother,

I have just returned from [Swansboro, N.C.] It took me two days to go I spent three days there and then two to come It is a lovely out of the way looking place but I spent the time pleasantly there I went over on the banks of the Atlantic & gathered a good many curiosities Killed Some fish Some Gulls and other Seafowls. It is a beautiful scene there are some high rocks over which the ocean rolls with a tremendous roar that can be heard for many miles...we had a meeting of our Company to day, there are about 60 able bodied men 15 of the old Company as good men as ever I Saw we are ordered to leave next Wednesday for Raleigh & from there I dont Know where the Yankees are near Newbern in 6 miles 15,000 strong and all day Thursday I heard the guns & I fear that the City is taken over...Sunday 16th the Yankees have taken Newbern and a good many of our men are killed & taken, the Yankees landed 50,000 men, they it is thought will now march on Goldsboro & Raleigh as they have cars & the Rail Road that I think out of the question our people will surely not let them get possession of our roads this is Sunday though I am going out recruiting. I am tired half to death from anxiety of mind Setting up and hard work but I will Continue to work to get our company in Camp As it is necessary that we should get arms as soon as possible. Some people are badly frightened & ready to give up—but I am not. Newbern is of no great value. It is dividing the Yankee forces as well as ours I believe though if our authorities dont concentrate our forces and make a bold stand all will be lost from the fact that our people are losing confidence. We have just been badly whipped in Missouri and the Union feeling is beginning to show its self strongly in this state...I start for Goldsboro...

At the battle of Bentonville, North Carolina (19–21 March), Sherman's force repulsed General Johnston's attack. Then, while Sherman waited at Goldsboro to see whether Grant needed his army to defeat Lee in Virginia, Thacker Howard Owens wrote his sister from Smithfield, North Carolina. Here, Owens was as critical of the dismal countryside as he was over-hopeful of the Confederates' ability to beat Sherman. Despite Owens' hope, after Lee surrendered to Grant at Appomattox Court House, Virginia, on 9 April, Sherman marched on Raleigh, North Carolina, forcing Johnston to surrender on 18 April. Owens' Thirty-Fourth Alabama Regiment, like Stanford's Thirty-Ninth, had come to eastern North Carolina from Nashville.

Camps Near Smithfield, N.C.
March 31, 1865
Dear Sister,

I thought I would...let you know that I am still in the world but it is a sorry portion of it. It is the poorest country I ever saw in my life for forage. We cant get anything to eat but what we draw and that is not much about half enough but we have to make out on it. I have got my fill of this state. I have been in one General engagement and one picked charge since I have been in the state and also marched in mud up to my knees. We have been in camps now about a week but I dont know how long we will remain here. Sherman is at Goldsboro he is at a standstill so they say. I hope he will not make another move soon. I expect he will try to go to Richmond the next move he makes. Some of the soldiers seem to think that Gen Lee will have to pull back from there but I hope not. I think we gave old Sherman a flogging the 19th of this month and that is the reason he is staying still so long. He has got cars running to Goldsboro. I am farther from home than I ever was in my life I think...I dont know what I will do for clean clothes to wear. I cant wash and even if I could it would be impossible for me to carry them...

It is perhaps appropriate that this collection should end with a death notice. This one was written by George Newman of the Sixth Alabama Cavalry Regiment. Newman's home was at Abbeville in Henry County, Alabama. He wrote from Evergreen, Alabama, and described the movement of Union troops against the city of Mobile, which at this time had not yet fallen to the Federals. The Confederates at Blakely, Alabama, held out against Federal attackers from 21 March until 9 April.

Camp 6 Ala Cav near Evergreen Ala
April 1, 1865
Mr. Howerton,

Dear Sir it becomes my Painfull duty to inform you that your Son James was wounded last Saturday the 25th of March & fell in The Hands of the Enamy & lived untill the next tusday morning that is What I learn from Mr Bloodworth who Saw him dy I would a Telegraff to you only it was imposuble for his body to be go[t] write away he is 7 miles below Pollerd.

Your Son Tom is all write. Our Regiment was Cut All to Smatt[ers] thar was 25 priseners from our compny in cluding Capt McRae & Lt Coe. We Under Stand the Enemy is Moving in the dire[c]tion of Blakelly near Mobile...

Letters like the one from George Newman were both painful and comforting to receive. The end of the war was at hand. On the same day Newman wrote of James Howerton's death, General R. E. Lee's lines were penetrated at Petersburg. This was prelude to the Confederate retreat from Richmond and official surrender eight days later at Appomattox. Of course, some fighting continued for a time in outlying areas.

But the cause was lost. And Confederates from the Chattahoochee Valley were saddened by their obvious defeat.

But as they remembered their war experiences, they also had a reason to be proud. These letters show they were honorable men. They had their weaknesses, of course, but shortcomings were more than offset by virtues. They were strongly attached to homes and families. They were generous in relations with comrades. They were proud of their heritage. They bore enormous hardships with minimum complaint. Their admirable support of a cause in which they sincerely believed reflected credit on them and on the region from which they came.

Appendix A

Roster of Confederate Correspondents Included in the Text
with Bibliographical Note and Acknowledgement of Contributors

Andrews, W. W. (in Crowder Papers)
Thirteenth Alabama.
Residence: Milltown, Chambers County, Alabama.
Contributors: Jean Crowder Williams, Langdale, Alabama (owner), and Ruth Crump, Lanett, Alabama.

Aycock, Joel
Private and corporal in Company C, Third Georgia Reserves.
Contributor: Dick D. Grube, curator, National Infantry Museum, Fort Benning, Georgia.

Barron, Greenberry Clay (father of T. J. Barron)
Corporal, Company D, Fourteenth Alabama.
Residence: Milltown, Chambers County, Alabama.
Contributors: Gladys Phillips, Lanett, Alabama (owner), and Ruth Crump, Lanett, Alabama.

Barron, Thomas Jefferson (son of G. C. Barron)
Company D, Fourteenth Alabama.
Residence: Milltown, Chambers County, Alabama.
Contributors: Gladys Phillips, Lanett, Alabama (owner), and Ruth Crump, Lanett, Alabama.

Bigbie, L. W. (brother of Thomas T. Bigbie)
Company G, Thirty-Third Alabama.
Residence: Pondtown, then Dale now Geneva County, Alabama.
Contributor: Allen Jones, archivist, Auburn University, Alabama.

Bigbie, Thomas T. (brother of L. W. Bigbie)
Company G, Thirty-Third Alabama.

Residence: Pondtown, then Dale, now Geneva County, Alabama.
Contributor: Allen Jones, archivist, Auburn University, Alabama.

Bray, William H.
First sergeant, Company C, Alabama Battalion, Phillips' Legion, Young's Brigade of Cavalry.
Residence: Eufaula, Alabama.
Contributor: Bertha Merrill, Eufaula, Alabama.

Burton, A. J.
Residence: Lafayette, Chambers County, Alabama.
Contributor: Ruth B. Herren.

Bush, G. D. (in Bigbie Papers)
Company G, Thirty-Third Alabama.
Contributor: Allen Jones, archivist, Auburn University, Alabama.

Byron, L. R.
Company D, Thirty-Ninth Alabama.
Residence: Barbour County.
Contributor: J. Fletcher Jones, Andalusia, Alabama.

Cantey, James
Colonel (later general), Fifteenth Alabama.
Residence: Russell County, Alabama.
Contributor: Charles Tigner, who published the letters in the Phenix Citizen, January–March 1978, Phenix City, Alabama.

Clark, Furney
Sergeant and Lieutenant, Company A, Fifty-Fourth Alabama.
Residence: Dale County, Alabama.
Contributors: Lillian V. King, Montgomery, Alabama, and Frank E. Bradley, Jr., New York City.

Crowder, James P.
Company I, Forty-Seventh Alabama.

Residence: Milltown, Chambers County, Alabama.
Contributors: Jean Crowder Williams, Langdale, Alabama (owner), and Ruth Crump, Lanett, Alabama. Mrs. Williams made excellent copies of the near illegible Crowder letters.

Denny, D. M.
Company B, Thirty-Seventh Alabama.
Residence: Randolph County (?), Alabama.
Contributor: Allen Jones, archivist, Auburn University, Alabama.

Dent, Stouten Hubert
Adjutant and lieutenant, Company B, First Alabama; lieutenant and captain in Artillery.
Residence: Eufaula, Alabama.
Contributors: Mary H. McCullohs, Eufaula, Alabama, and Allen Jones, archivist, Auburn University, Alabama.

Dodgen, Preston Leroy (in Crowder letters)
First Sergeant, Company F, Fifty-Ninth Alabama; also Company A, Second Battalion, Hilliard's Legion.
Residence: Hickory Flat, Chambers County, Alabama.
Contributors: Jean Crowder Williams, Langdale, Alabama (owner), and Ruth Crump, Lanett, Alabama.

Garner, Andrew Jackson
Residence: Either Dale or Barbour County, Alabama.
Contributor: Mrs. C. E. Hutchins, Eufaula, Alabama.

Lewis, J. Cook
Major, Third Alabama.
Residence: Russell County, Alabama.
Contributor: Eufaula Heritage Association, Eufaula, Alabama.

Lewis, J. H.
Private, Company E, Third Georgia Cavalry.
Residence: Stewart County, Georgia.

Contributor: Jamie G. Espy, Eufaula, Alabama.

Lewis, William (in Bigbie Papers)
Company G, Thirty-Third Alabama.
Contributor: Allen Jones, archivist, Auburn University, Alabama.

Merrill, Allen Hunter
Private, Eufaula Light Artillery.
Residence: Eufaula, Alabama.
Contributor: Bertha Merrill, Eufaula, Alabama.

Moore, Thomas Josephus (in Barron letters)
Private, Thirty-Eighth Tennessee Volunteers.
Residence: Probably Chambers County, Alabama.
Contributors: Gladys Phillips, Lanett, Alabama (owner), and Ruth Crump, Lanett, Alabama.

Newman, George
James McRae's Company, Sixth Alabama Cavalry.
Residence: Henry County, Alabama.
Contributor: Mrs. C. C. Murphy, Abbeville, Alabama.

Owens, Thacker Howard
Private, Companies I, S, and G of Thirty-Fourth Alabama.
Residence: Loflin, Russell County, Alabama.
Contributor: Clara Owens Mihalko, Fort Mitchell, Alabama.

Perry, J. Walter
Private (later lieutenant) in Company K, Third Georgia Volunteers.
Residence: Blakely, Georgia.
Contributor: Analene Felder Nelson, Blakely, Georgia.

Pouncey, William T.
Private, Company E, Fifteenth Alabama.
Residence: Daleville, Dale County, Alabama.
Contributor: Mrs. Ibbie Jones, Daleville, Alabama.

Prather, Israel Wade
Residence: Marcoot, Chambers County, Alabama.
Contributor: Nell Orr, Lafayette, Alabama.

Shealy, George Washington
Lieutenant, Company G, Thirty-Seventh Alabama.
Residence: Chambers County, Alabama.
Contributors: John T. Higginbothem, Jr., West Point, Georgia (owner); Margaret P. Milford and Ruth Crump, Lanett, Alabama.

Stanford, Monore or William (brother of T. Q. Stanford)
Private, Company G, Thirty-Ninth Alabama.
Residence: Bush Community on Barbour-Henry County line, Alabama.
Contributor: John Q. Stanford, Winter Haven, Florida, and Eufaula Heritage Association, Eufaula, Alabama.

Stanford, T. Q.
Captain, Company G, Thirty-Ninth Alabama.
Residence: Bush Community on Barbour-Henry County line, Alabama.
Contributor: John Q. Stanford, Winter Haven, Florida, and Eufaula Heritage Association, Eufaula, Alabama.

Wellborn, R. A.
Private, Kolbs Battery of Light Artillery.
Residence: Barbour County, Alabama.
Contributor: J. Fletcher Jones, Andalusia, Alabama.

Appendix B

List of Sources Not Included because of
Previous Publication, Residence of Correspondent, or Content

Abernathy, David H. B.
A diary kept during the War Between the States. He was in Company I, Forty-Seventh Alabama.
Owner: Mrs. W. R. Sharman, Lafayette, Alabama.

Allen, Brenda Heath
Several Confederate letters and poems by Isham Cumings, Benjamin H. Milam, A. B. Stewart, Burrell Orr, David Ellison, Jr., and others not identified.
Contributors: Brenda Heath Allen, Huguley, Alabama (owner), and Ruth Crump, Lanett, Alabama. Mrs. Crump made copies of near illegible letters.

Barrow, James H. and Family
Several Confederate letters, published in *Word from Camp Pollard, C.S.A.*, edited by William H. Davidson (West Point, GA: Davidson, 1978). Barrow was a private in Company F, Sixty-First Alabama Volunteers. Residence: Providence Church, Chambers County, Alabama.

Chambers, Joseph Sanders
Three Confederate letters, published in J. V. Chambers and Mrs. J. V. Chambers, *Reminiscences of Judge Joseph Vernon Chambers, A Lifetime Residence of the Chattahoochee River Valley* (Tuscaloosa, AL: N.P. 1969).
Contributors: Judge and Mrs. J. V. Chambers, Lafayette, Alabama, and Ruth Crump, Lanett, Alabama.

Chappell, Absolom H.
Letter: Absolom H. Chappell to wife, 16 December 1860, on eve of secession. Chappell served in Company D, Fourth Georgia Volunteers. Residence: Columbus, Georgia.
Contributor: John L. Lupoid, Columbus College, Columbus, Georgia.

Cody, Barnett Hardeman and Family
Numerous Confederate letters: "Letters of Barnett Hardeman Cody and Others, 1861–1864." Edited by Edmund Cody Burnett. *Georgia Historical Quarterly.* 23/3–4 (September and December 1939) 265–318.
Contributor: William Nordan of Henry County Historical Society, Abbeville, Alabama.

Davidson, William H. and Others
"War Was the Place: A Centennial Collection of Confederate Soldier Letters." *Chattahoochee Valley Historical Society* (Bulletin 5, Chambers County, AL, 1961). Includes numerous letters from the following correspondents of the Chattachoochee Valley: Thomas J. Atkinson, James H. Barrow,* John C. Curtwright, Thomas L. M. Davidson, Jesse C. Dorman, Elijah Ford, George Tip Hodnett, H. H. Hodnett, John M. Hodnett, John W. Hodnett, Samuel G. Hodnett, Thomas Jefferson Hodnett, William H. H. Hodnett, John D. Johnson,* James H. Jones, James Leggett Lovelace,* Lucius Todd Cicero Lovelace,* Louis Merz, John W. Miller, Nicholas W. Miller, William Anderson Stephens, Ansel Sterne, John Calhoun Tillery, George Augustus White, Alfred Flournoy Zachry.
*These have letters in other collections named in Appendix B.

Hopkins, John C.
A letter from Hamilton County, Tennessee, 24 August 1862. His residence was Camp Hill, Tallapoosa County, Alabama.
Contributor: O. G. Harris, Opelika, Alabama.

Jackson, Benjamin Franklin and Family
Several Confederate letters published in *So Mourns the Dove: Letters of a Confederate Infantryman and His Family.* Edited by Alto Loftin Jackson. New York: Exposition Press, 1965. B. F. Jackson was in Company B, Thirty-Third Alabama. Residence: Dale County, Alabama.
Contributor: Alto Loftin Jackson, Clio, Alabama.

Johnson, John David

A letter from Tennessee, 8 March 1863, also published in "War Was the Place: A Centennial Collection of Confederate Soldier Letters." *Chattahoochee Valley Historical Society* (Bulletin 5, Chambers County, AL, 1961). Johnson was in Company D, Third Georgia Cavalry and in S. H. Dent's Battery of Artillery. Residence: Harris County, Georgia.
Contributor: Margaret Milford, Lanett, Alabama.

Loachapoka Homecoming Association and Nunn Family
Editors, *Yesterdays* (Loachapoka, AL: Loachapoka Homecoming Association, 1968), contains numerous lists of Confederates from the area and several wartime letters by T. Otho Culbreath, Thomas Hill, John J. McKendree, Henry Marian Rowel, J. H. Christian, G. W. Ross,* J. M. Ross, John W. Ross.
*Has letters in another collection named in Appendix B.

Locke, William H.
Letters Written by William H. Locke During the Civil War, 1861–1865 (Dawson, GA). Locke was in the Confederate Cavalry in Virginia under Wade Hampton (1864). Residence: Eufaula, Alabama.
Contributor: Frances Parker Tyler, Montgomery, Alabama.

Lovelace, James L., John T., Lucius T. C., and Samuel L.
Confederate letters also published in "War Was the Place: A Centennial Collection of Confederate Soldier Letters." *Chattahoochee Valley Historical Society* (Bulletin 5, Chambers County, Alabama, 1961). The first three brothers were in Company D, Fourth Georgia Volunteers. The last brother, Samuel, was in Company E, Forty-First Georgia. Residence: West Point, Troup County, Georgia. Compiled by Janie Lovelace Heard, West Point, Troup County, Georgia.
Contributor: Margaret Milford, Lanett, Alabama.

McFarland, L. B.
An eleven-page letter, dated 1 April 1915, to Mrs. W. B. Higginbothem, president, Fort Tyler Chapter, U.D.C. The letter describes Confederate defense of Fort Tyler at West Point, Georgia, against Union General James H. Wilson on 16 April 1865, apparently published as "Confederate Records, Volume 5,

Reminiscences, Chapter History, Fort Tyler Chapter, 1914–1915," by Imogene Griggs Smith, historian.
Contributors: Mrs. R. S. Heard (owner) and Ruth Crump, Lanett, Alabama.

Mallett, C. N.
Two letters from northern Virginia. Mallett was in the Fifteenth Alabama. Residence: Pike County, Alabama.
Contributor: Agnes D. Phipps, Columbus, Georgia.

Morris, E. H. C.
Letter.
Contributor: Virginia Brannon Smith, Langdale, Chambers County, Alabama, and Ruth Crump, Lanett, Alabama.

Owens, John Smith (brother of T. H. Owens) and Reverend J. N. Owens (father)
Two Confederate letters. Residence: Loflin, Alabama.
Contributor: Clara Owens Mihalko, Fort Mitchell, Alabama.

Patterson, A. J.
Three letters, July 1862 (with Burton letter). Patterson was in Company A, First Battalion of Hilliard's Legion. Residence: Tallassee, Elmore, Tallapoosa Counties, Alabama.
Contributor: Ruth B. Herren.

Register, Elias and John (brothers)
Four letters. Also published in Fred S. Watson, *Hub of The Wiregrass*, Anniston, Alabama: Higginbotham, Inc., 1912. Elias was a private in companies A and B, Sixth Alabama; and in Company C, Twenty-Sixth Alabama. Residence: Dale County, Alabama.
Contributor: Larry C. Register, Dothan, Alabama.

Ross, G. W. and Family
Letters. Ross's nine letters are also published in Loachapoka Homecoming Association, *Yesterdays* (1968). He was in the Loachapoka Rifles, Sixth Alabama. Residence: probably Macon County, Alabama.

Contributor: Allen Jones, archivist, Auburn University, Alabama.

Shelly, Mark P.
Letter. Company E, Sixtieth Alabama. Residence: probably Henry County.
Contributor: Dewey Shelley, Headland, Alabama (owner), and W. W. Nordan of Henry County Historical Society, Abbeville, Alabama.

Snuggs, R. G. and Family
Letters during and after the war. Residence: North Carolina.
Contributors: Jean Crowder Williams, Langdale, Alabama (owner), and Ruth Crump, Lanett, Alabama.

Tarleton, Robert
Several Confederate letters in "The Civil War Letters of Robert Tarleton," edited by William N. Still, Jr., in *Alabama Historical Quarterly* (Spring and Summer, 1970) 51-80. Residence: Talladega County, Alabama.
Contributor: Margaret S. Holman, Ozark, Alabama.

Unidentified Mother
Unidentified mother to her son at the Confederate front, 1 August 1864.
Contributors: Forest Ward, Shawmut, Alabama, and Ruth Crump, Lanett, Alabama.

Weedon, Hamilton M. and Mary E. C. Young, (Wife)
Letters: a valuable collection for the period after the war. Residence: Eufaula, Alabama.
Contributor: Emma Foy, Eufaula, Alabama.

Williams, Jefferson
Letter: Jefferson Williams to his sister Martha A. Barron (see Barron letters in the text). Residence: Randolph County, Alabama.
Contributors: Gladys Phillips, Lanett, Alabama (owner), and Ruth Crump, Lanett, Alabama.

Index